American Warsaw

American
WARSAW

The Rise, Fall, and Rebirth of Polish Chicago

Dominic A. Pacyga

The University of Chicago Press

Chicago and London

The University of Chicago Press, Chicago 60637
The University of Chicago Press, Ltd., London
© 2019 by The University of Chicago
All rights reserved. No part of this book may be used or reproduced in any manner whatsoever without written permission, except in the case of brief quotations in critical articles and reviews. For more information, contact the University of Chicago Press, 1427 E. 60th St., Chicago, IL 60637.
Published 2019
Paperback edition 2021
Printed in the United States of America

30 29 28 27 26 25 24 23 22 21   1 2 3 4 5

ISBN-13: 978-0-226-40661-9 (cloth)
ISBN-13: 978-0-226-81534-3 (paper)
ISBN-13: 978-0-226-40675-6 (e-book)
DOI: https://doi.org/10.7208/chicago/9780226406756.001.0001

Library of Congress Cataloging-in-Publication Data

Names: Pacyga, Dominic A., author.
Title: American Warsaw : the rise, fall, and rebirth of Polish Chicago / Dominic A. Pacyga.
Description: Chicago ; London : The University of Chicago Press, 2019. | Includes bibliographical references and index.
Identifiers: LCCN 2019001788 | ISBN 9780226406619 (cloth : alk. paper) | ISBN 9780226406756 (e- book)
Subjects: LCSH: Polish Americans—Illinois—Chicago—History. | Chicago (Ill.)—History.
Classification: LCC F548.9.P7 P329 2019 | DDC 977.3/11—dc23
LC record available at https://lccn.loc.gov/2019001788

For Beatrice,
whose sense of *Polskość* amazes me

CONTENTS

Polish Chicago

> History teaches us that nations do not die off so long as their *lud*
> (peasantry) continues to live, making it possible to revive the half-dead
> members of a nation and pour new life into it via the activities of its
> intellectual work.
> —DR. ANTONI KALINA, editor of *Lud*[1]

Writing any ethnic group's history in Chicago is a difficult task.
Especially challenging is trying to tell the story of as large and
influential an ethnic group as the Poles. The Chicago area has
long been a destination for Polish immigrants, and so the history
of Chicago's Polonia (i.e., people of Polish descent living outside
Poland) is one that straddles both the city and its suburbs. Scratch
a Chicagoan, and you may very well find a Polish connection.
Polish Americans are everywhere. The city often proclaims itself
as Poland's second city, with only Warsaw containing a larger
Polish population. And as mythical as this claim may be—and it
is a myth—there is some truth to it, as many Chicagoans know
the difference between kielbasa and pierogi and have a few other

Polish words in their vocabulary. Yet most real Poles will tell you that Chicago, with its vast ethnic and racial diversity and its capitalist mores, is hardly a Polish city. Nonetheless, there is something Polish about it because Polish immigrants and their descendants have left their mark on the city by the lake. More than fifty wholly Polish or Polish-dominated Catholic parishes, along with numerous Polish National Catholic churches, have dotted the landscape. In addition, Polish businesspeople, politicians, educators, and even mobsters have joined the ranks of Chicago's elite. Several Polish Catholic high schools educated the city's children across the North, South, and West Sides. Polish nuns taught generations of Chicago's children, not all of them Catholic or of Polish descent. Labor unions benefited from Polish membership and dues. Professional sports teams often went out of their way to include names such as Piet, Ostrowski, Kluzewski, Paciorek, Konerko, Pierzynski, Grabowski, and Ditka. The city's radio waves shook with the sound of polkas and with the religious preaching of *Father Justin's Rosary Hour*, as well as with the comedy of Bruno "Junior" Zieliński. Later television and radio programs hosted by Bob Lewandowski and others also shaped the local media. Polish could often be heard on the streets of the city—even if it was the mongrelized version known as *Po Chicagosku*. In the post-1945 era, Warsaw was the first of Chicago's many international sister cities.

Chicago has had a long and fruitful relationship with Poland and with what might be better called the Polish lands. Poles appeared in the frontier settlement of Chicago as early as the 1830s. The formative migration, however, began some twenty years later and culminated with the creation of St. Stanislaus Kostka Parish in 1867. Over the next sixty years, Chicago's Polonia expanded across the cityscape. Polish immigrants originally flocked to at least five distinct Chicago neighborhoods, which housed heavy industry, attracting the so-called new immigrants from southern and eastern Europe. Poles came in large numbers to work on factory, packinghouse, and steel mill floors during the huge economic migration they called *Za Chlebem*, or the migration for bread. This vast movement lasted from just before America's Civil War until the mid-1920s, when congressional fiat basically ended migration from the "Other" Europe. This, however, would not be the last movement of Poles to Chicago.

Afterward, at least three later migrations reshaped and invigorated Chicago's Polonia. The migration of displaced persons after World War Two, the small immigration during the Communist years, and the so-called Solidarity exodus all shaped the city. Polish Chicago has also long been marked by both a return migration to Poland and a movement to other places across the world, creating a web of information and economic ties. Indeed, since the year 2000, many Poles have returned to Poland or migrated to other parts of the European Union.

Polish immigration to Chicago and the United States is also a part of Polish history. While immigration has long played an important role in the history of the United States, Polish historians largely ignored or simply mentioned the great migrations of the nineteenth and twentieth centuries when writing the history of Poland. One of my arguments in this book is that Polish history cannot be fully understood without including the role of the emigration. Conversely, Polish Chicago and Polish America cannot be understood without understanding Polish history and, in particular, the history of the Polish peasantry and the forces that motivated them, especially after the 1860s.

In the nineteenth century, Poland struggled to regain its independence from the three powers—Germany, Russia, and Austria-Hungary—that had occupied Poland almost continuously since the end of the eighteenth century. The demise of the old Polish-Lithuanian Commonwealth, organized in the Middle Ages and once the largest state in Europe, obsessed Poles, and they constantly agitated for its reestablishment. The Polish quest to regain the country's independence haunted European politics for more than a century. While the three empires might compete with each other, they all agreed that Poland should not be reestablished. Major uprisings, led largely by the upper classes, broke

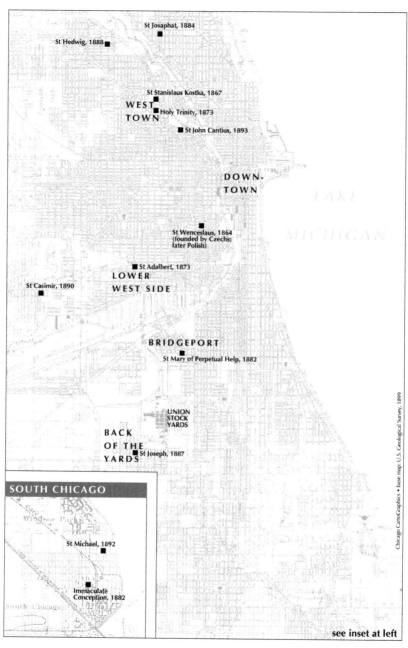

St Josaphat, 1884

St Hedwig, 1888

St Stanislaus Kostka, 1867

WEST
TOWN
Holy Trinity, 1873

St John Cantius, 1893

DOWN-
TOWN

LAKE

MICHIGAN

St Wenceslaus, 1864
(founded by Czechs;
later Polish)

St Adalbert, 1873

St Casimir, 1890

LOWER
WEST SIDE

BRIDGEPORT

St Mary of Perpetual Help, 1882

UNION
STOCK
YARDS

BACK
OF THE
YARDS
St Joseph, 1887

SOUTH CHICAGO

Windsor Park

St Michael, 1892

Immaculate
Conception, 1882

South Chicago

see inset at left

Chicago CartoGraphics • base map: U.S. Geological Survey, 1899

Map of the five original Polish neighborhoods in Chicago.
(Courtesy Chicago CartoGraphics.)

out in occupied Poland throughout the nineteenth century, and each ended in disastrous defeat. Peasants, for the most part, either ignored or opposed these rebellions, often seeing the occupying empires as their protectors or benefactors against the Polish nobility. Polish aristocrats and their brothers, the lower gentry, looked down on the peasantry whom they exploited and often did not consider to be true Poles. After the disastrous defeat of the 1863 insurrection against the Russian Empire, however, both Polish noblemen and intellectuals looked to the folk to help bring about the resurrection of the Polish state. The identification of the peasantry as the soul of the nation soon emerged.

This recognition occurred just as the huge economic flight from the Polish lands began in earnest. This peasant migration occurred as *uwłaszczenie*, the emancipation from serfdom, took place first in German Poland and later in both the Austrian and Russian Partitions.[2] This exodus haunted those who hoped for Poland's resurrection. Were those who had left lost to the nation? Would they disappear and melt into the receiving cultures, losing their sense of Polishness or *Polskość*? Alternatively, could they somehow help the independence movement? The mass of peasants heading for German and Dutch ports and sailing for the New World perplexed the Polish gentry and intelligentsia, as the concept of nationalism transformed Europe. The emigration and the rise of nationalism presented the question: Just who was a Pole?

Yet the development of national feeling among peasants proved to be a crucial factor in the rebirth of Poland both before and after World War One. Polish peasants, especially those who spoke Polish or at least a Polish dialect and practiced Catholicism, began to develop feelings of loyalty to the idea of Poland, despite its nonexistence on the political map of Europe. As Dr. Karol Lewakowski, a Polish patriot and minister of the Austrian government warned in 1895, "Without the Polish peasant Poland will not exist."[3] In Chicago and other immigrant centers, arguments over the definition of *Polskość* resulted in ideological, and sometimes violent, clashes as the concept tore the community apart. Could a

Pole be an Orthodox Christian, a Protestant, a Jew, or an atheist? Was a Pole anyone who believed in a free and independent Poland, even if their first language was Yiddish? Eventually a general agreement was reached, but how to grow and protect a sense of Polishness remained an issue, especially regarding the American-born generation.

The old Polish-Lithuanian Commonwealth, which disappeared at the end of the eighteenth century, contained a diverse population. Poles lived side by side with Jews, Lithuanians, Ruthenians (Ukrainians), Byelorussians, Germans, Czechs, Slovaks, Armenians, Tartars, and others. Most identified with the Polish king as his subjects. How did these groups fit in the definition of being Polish as the forces of nationalism, now unleashed by the French Revolution, altered Europe? Previously they and the Polish-speaking peasants were seen as sub-ethnic groups, but part of the Polish Commonwealth. By the end of the nineteenth century, however, these neighbors emerged as the "other." What this meant for the future resurrection of Poland posed a problem to Polish elites. In addition, the *sczlachta* (noble class), with its many privileges, often worked against each other and to the nation's disadvantage. The large and powerful aristocratic families at times made alliances with outside powers, especially Russia.

In the seventeenth and eighteenth centuries, large Polish estates provided much of the grain, wood, and other natural resources for urban development in western Europe and Poland witnessed an increase in serfdom. Throughout most of Polish history, the peasantry was seen as alien, whether they were Polish speaking or spoke one of the other tongues of the commonwealth such as Lithuanian, Belarusian, Ruthenian, Czech, or German. Of course, Jews made up the ultimate outsiders in Poland, as they did throughout Europe. The commonwealth encouraged Jewish migration to Poland in the Middle Ages, and the nobility used Jews as an economic bridge to the peasantry. Before the nineteenth-century rise of European nationalism and industrialization, this meant little to Polish unity. Afterward, who was a

Pole and who was not would mean a great deal. It also meant a great deal to the emigration from the Polish lands.

In Chicago, Poland's diverse population presented a different difficulty. While these various groups had often emerged as rivals in eastern and central Europe, in Chicago's communities, they became neighbors, and the relationship among them would be, for the most part, peaceful, though admittedly, at times it could be hostile here as well. In Chicago, they were all the "other," and urban politics, specifically Democratic Party politics, exploited various alliances based on Old World familiarities.[4]

Historians and sociologists have long pointed out that ethnicity is often a choice. It may not seem that way to someone born into a strong and vital ethnic community, but individuals decide where their loyalties lie.[5] One can choose to be a Pole, a Polish American, or simply an American. In cities like Chicago, ethnicity often revolved around music, food, and famous people, all of which acted as symbols of group unity. Chicago's Polonia used all of these to maintain group loyalty or at least a semblance of it. Of course, one can ignore one's ethnic background, and over time intermarriage certainly watered down ethnic identification, but a sense of *Polskość* has persisted over the generations in Chicago and in other Polonia centers. Sometimes this sense of Polish ethnicity runs deep in individuals, at other times it is only slight. Many of Chicago's Poles have maintained a vibrant sense of *Polskość*. To an extent, this is because of Chicago's special place in the worldwide Polish diaspora.

Through most of its history, Chicago has been the location of the largest "Polonia," a term depicting a Polish diasporic community. It housed and still houses the headquarters of all major Polish American institutions. Chicago's Polish-language newspapers had an impact well beyond the city's borders. In villages in Poland, Chicago seemed synonymous with the United States. The city's Polish leadership shaped much of the response of American Polonia to events in Europe. Here stood a Polish city, even if not a truly Polish city, that held the promise of the diaspora that it might come to the aid of a nation that had lost its independence and was dismembered, Chicago became Poland "elsewhere."

Austro-Hungarian Galicia grew to be a hotbed of Polish nationalism. Lwów, as the provincial capital and with its lively cultural and political life, provided a conduit for the revival of the Polish state. Beginning in 1867, Poles had largely controlled this outer province of the Hapsburg state. Led by the nobility and a growing intellectual elite based both in Kraków and Lwów, the province essentially developed as a semiautonomous entity. Lwów, in particular, played a very important role in the independence movement and as a link to the diaspora, especially in Chicago. The Polish communities in the two cities made an important connection before 1900. This was especially important in the 1890s, when the provincial assembly or *Sejm* sent an emissary, Professor Emil Habdank Dunikowski, to explore American Polonia and find out its relationship to the Polish lands. Dunikowski made two trips to the United States and convinced Chicago's Polish leadership to take part in the Lwów provincial fair of 1894. Intellectuals and politicians emphasized the fact that those who had emigrated were not lost to the Polish cause.

The long struggle for a free and sovereign state had been at the heart of Polish consciousness since the end of the eighteenth century. As a result of World War One, the three empires that had divided the Polish-Lithuanian Commonwealth collapsed and an independent Poland emerged. Within twenty years, self-rule came again under attack as Nazi Germany and Communist Russia partitioned Poland once again in 1939. Afterward, Poland fell under Soviet domination for more than forty years but then emerged as a leader in the fight against Communist tyranny that helped to bring about the demise of the USSR. Chicago's Polonia played a role in all of these battles, providing both blood and treasure during World War One, as well as financial and cultural support during World War Two, and serving as a center for the fight against the Communist regime during the Cold War. Poland has found itself at the center of much of the conflict of the twentieth century, and the

This view shows the buildings and rooftops located behind 1414 Emma Street (now Cortez Street) in 1914. The Polish district in the West Town community area, often called the Polish Downtown, was one of the most densely populated in the city. (Northwestern University Settlement Association Records Photographs, Series 41/6, Northwestern University Archives, Evanston, IL.)

bond between the homeland and Polonia always remained strong. Through all of these episodes, Chicago provided a strategic capital for the Polish diaspora.

That relationship with Poland would often be a difficult one, but one that remained close to the heart of the city's Polonia. If one truly celebrated *Polskość*, how could Poland not be a major concern? At times, the connection might seem distant or tenuous, as it did occasionally between the two world wars, but once Poland was in danger, that connection again jumped to the forefront. Poland under duress was always a major concern, even for those who did not have much of a direct link to the wider community. This may have been because of a feeling of communal solidarity with family, even distant relatives still in Poland, or perhaps just a romantic presentation of the history of a people long under a foreign yoke. Poland remained a powerful symbol for the emigration.

Chicago's Polish community extended its hand to those Poles who had to leave Poland and became displaced by the tragedy of war. Various waves of immigration caused tension in the community as the idea of what really constituted *Polskość* raised its head again and again and would often shatter the unity of the community.

Polish Chicago's unity has often been splintered, as the community fragmented over ideology, religion, or social class. This began early in the history of Chicago's Polonia, with the disagreement between the *Gmina Polska* (the Polish Commune) and the Resurrectionist priests of St. Stanislaus Kostka Parish. Here again the question was over the idea of Polishness. Who was a Pole? This evolved into the struggle between the Resurrectionist-backed Polish Roman Catholic Union of America and the Polish National Alliance supported by more secularist nationalists. It would eventually result in the independent church movement, and the schism that created the Polish National Catholic Church.

Such disagreements over who was a Pole has left a lasting mark on the community. That conflict shaped much of the institutional development of Polish America. Internal Polonia politics often mirrored political arguments in Poland. Even as Polish Chicago united in the struggle for Polish independence during World War One, Polonia split between those who supported the two major Polish factions in Europe: those who supported General Józef Piłsudski and those who favored Roman Dmowski's hopes for a resurrected Poland. Still, a sense of community prevailed even among warring factions.

The period between the close of World War One and the outbreak of World War Two brought more changes. Once Poland regained independence in 1918, the realities of life in the United States took center stage for Polonia, as Congress cut off immigration and the community faced the problems of poverty and prejudice, as well as of increased Americanization. Finally, in 1934, Chicago's Polonia, dealing with the Great Depression, increased pressure to assimilate, and attempting to hold onto the American-born generation, while maintaining a sense of *Polskość*, lead the

American diaspora in proclaiming its independence from Poland in the Conference of Poles from across the globe held in Warsaw that year. After World War Two the arrival of displaced persons brought both new blood to ethnic institutions and disagreement again over who was a real Pole. The later Solidarity immigration also resulted in conflict between the various generations of immigrants.

The divisions within Chicago's Polonia had a tremendous impact on the history of the ethnic group. While the conflict between the clerical and secular camps over who was a real Pole remained the most important, other cracks in unity appeared along various other political, economic, and even neighborhood lines. South Side Poles often did not trust North Side Poles, who they considered to be uppity and who controlled the leaderships of most of the fraternal organizations. Chicago's Polish socialists also ranted against both the clergy and the capitalist class. Gender, too, provided a division, as both the Polish National Alliance and the Polish Roman Catholic Union of America at first did not allow women to join on their own. This resulted in the creation of the Polish Women's Alliance in 1898, which championed both feminist and progressive issues and forced the opening of the other fraternal organizations to women. Polish Catholic sisterhoods also played a role in the increasing importance of women in the community. The very fact of emigration changed women's roles and liberated them from many Polish patriarchal traditions. Both industrialization and the creation of Polish American nuclear families, unbridled by long standing relationships with in-laws, basically transformed women's roles. A leading Polish feminist and long-time president of the Polish Women's Alliance, Emily Napieralska, played a crucial part in Chicago Polonia's response to the struggle for Polish independence.

The various divisions within Chicago's Polonia (mirrored in the national Polonia) shaped Polonia's politics. Chicago's Poles were never fully unified and had a difficult time reaching out to and compromising with other ethnic and racial groups in the city.

While they did form alliances with the Czechs and helped to create a citywide Democratic organization under the Chicago Czech leader Anton Cermak, they could not expand that role after his death. By 1930, Polish Chicagoans made up the largest white ethnic group in the city, but while Polonia had clout, it never effectively used it to take control of the Democratic Party in Chicago. This was also true for the city's labor movement. Again, Polish Chicagoans dominated certain industries, but time and time again they failed to attain leadership positions for any extended period. Their role in the city's Catholic hierarchy proved to be even more marginal, despite the fact that a Polish Chicagoan was named the first Polish bishop in the United States. The rise of important Polish American capitalists in the city also seemed stymied by a kind of ethnic provincialism, as many focused primarily on their own ethnic group and did not initially reach out beyond those cultural borders. In fact, they actively pursued a campaign against other ethnic businessmen, especially Czechs, Germans, and Jews.

That is not to say the Polish Chicagoans were unsuccessful in all of these matters; they played important roles in the political, religious, economic, cultural, labor, and neighborhood life of the city. But often the eyes of Polonia were more on the Polish struggle than on their place in Chicago or across the United States. The question of Polish independence was central to Polonia and its understanding of itself both in the diaspora and in relationship to the Polish lands. When World War One broke out, Polish Chicagoans spent both lives and money in defense of the homeland. World War Two brought a similar reaction. In 1939, Chicago's Polonia led the national diaspora in helping Poland by sending relief aid, both during and after the fighting. Its sons and daughters joined the American armed forces and toiled in the factories that made up the "Arsenal of Democracy." As home to the headquarters of the major Polish organizations, Chicago played a leading role in responding to events such as the Nazi and Soviet invasion of Poland in 1939, the Katyn massacre, the Warsaw uprising, the Yalta Conference, the tragedy of the displaced persons, and the long Cold War. As the twentieth century closed, Chicago's Poles rejoiced once a free and independent Poland was reestablished, joined the North Atlantic Treaty Organization, and became a member of the European Union. Chicago's Polonia has always kept an interest in the politics of the homeland.

Americans love a parade; this is especially true for Chicagoans. In Chicago, such public demonstrations quickly became a point of ethnic pride. Most major ethnic groups hold parades through the city's streets. They provide a sense not only of celebration but also of unity, as well as political and economic power. In Chicago parlance, a parade means "clout" or influence in a city that respects power more than it does education or culture. Since the beginning of the settlement, the city's residents have celebrated national and religious holidays, political events and rallies, and social class and ethnicity with public celebrations on its streets and in its public spaces. The St. Patrick's Day Parade is such an important Irish American tradition that the city holds two such events, one in the Loop and the other on the South Side. The city's Polonia has long understood the significance of the ethnic parade, especially since it has been internally divided in many ways during its long and tempestuous history. While Chicagoans love a parade, Polish Chicagoans *really* love a parade. From the first commemorations of historical events in the homeland to the dedication of buildings, monuments, and churches, Chicago's Polonia has proudly marched through the city's neighborhoods and downtown. Even today, Chicago's annual Polish Constitution Day Parade is billed as the largest Polish parade in the world. Along with all the excitement attached to such happenings, these celebrations traditionally played an important and dynamic role in the history of the American city.

The study of Chicago's Polonia is an important case study for historians and other researchers of both immigration and ethnicity. In this book, I have emphasized certain themes that highlight Polish Chicago's relationship both to its homeland and to the United States. These themes ran throughout Polonia's history and remain an important factor into the twenty-first century. The communal coping mechanisms employed by an essentially rural peasant people who found themselves in a massive urban industrial society are important for understanding larger issues in American history. The relationship between Polish Chicagoans and other ethnic and racial groups in the city also sheds light on the American urban experience. Above all, the connection between Poland and Polish Chicago ties the diaspora to even larger issues in American and Polish history as both those nations came to play such a central part in world events in the twentieth century. The idea of Polishness played a crucial role in this relationship and in the formation of Polish Chicago's response to the larger American society. Questions surrounding the Polish American role in politics, the economy, culture, and gender issues also are important and revealing as to the role of immigration in creating American society in the years after the Civil War. Polish Chicago provided much of the leadership for American Polonia. Women and men such as Piotr Kiołbassa, Rev. Vincent Barzyński, Josephine Dudzik, Władysław Dyniewicz, Bishop Paul Rhode, Emily Napieralska, Jan Smulski, Frank Świetlik, Charles and Wanda Rozmarek, and Aloysius Mazewski led Chicago's Polonia during good times as well as bad. Both America and Poland occupied their interests as they forged and maintained a sense of community. Finally, the reality of social mobility also shaped Polonia during its long tenure in the city. Polish Americans, especially after World War Two, increasingly joined the middle and upper-middle classes and moved to the suburbs. For many, this meant assimilation; for others it meant a renewed pride in *Polskość*.

Today, Chicago's Polonia is more suburban then urban, increasingly better educated, and has taken on middle-class American cultural values. While still transformed by immigration, it no longer is immersed in the so-called Polish question. Its postindustrial relationships with other ethnic and racial groups are now more American than Polish. The days of mass immigration from Poland seem to have passed; in fact, many Polish immigrants are leaving Chicago and returning to Europe. Yet we who were lucky enough to have been born into Chicago Polonia's vast and complicated history still love a parade and an argument over who is a real Pole.

This study owes much to those scholars who have illuminated various topics in Polish Chicago's history. W. I. Thomas and Florence Znaniecki's pathbreaking sociological study *The Polish Peasant in Europe and America* naturally deals in large part with Chicago. In 1975, Edward R. Kantowicz's *Polish-American Politics in Chicago, 1888–1940* set a high bar for the study of urban ethnic politics. That same year Victor Greene, published *For God and Country: The Rise of Polish and Lithuanian Ethnic Consciousness in America, 1860–1910*, which explored the rise of *Polskość* as a factor in Chicago and across the diaspora. Six years later, Joseph John Parot's *Polish Catholics in Chicago, 1850–1920* appeared and discussed in detail the emergence of the Polish American Church as an important factor in ethnic development. My own work on Polish workers in Chicago's steel and meatpacking industries explored working-class life and unionization. Mary Patrice Erdmans's *Opposite Poles: Immigrants and Ethnics in Polish Chicago, 1976–1990* looked at the Solidarity immigration and its impact on Chicago's Polish community. Other scholars, including Anna Jaroszyńska-Kirchmann, James Pula, John Bukowczyk, M. B. B. Biskupski, Joanna Wojdon, Dorota Praszałowicz, Adam Walaszek, and the late Ted Radzilowski, among others, while not looking solely at Chicago, have also contributed mightily to this study and are cited in this book.[6]

A note about word usage: in the Chicago ethnic tradition, I have often used "Polish" and "Polish American" interchangeably. This is still the practice of many Polish Chicagoans. The Chicago Polish community is of course made up of many generations, both immigrant and native born. Thus, the relationship between the terms "Polish" and "Polish American" is a complex one, given the various interacting generations and immigrant waves dealt with in this study. Obviously, I have used these interchangeably when talking about Polonia by referring to Chicagoans who identify as

Polish—whether of the immigrant or later generations—as "Chicago Poles" or simply "Polish." I will use the term "Polish American" in reference to organizations founded in the United States, including parishes, fraternal groups, political organizations, and so forth.

On a personal note, my family arrived from Podhale in Galicia (Austrian Partition) just prior to World War One. My grandparents settled in the Back of the Yards neighborhood adjacent to the Chicago Union Stock Yards. Our family stayed in that neighborhood for three generations, and a cousin still lives on South Winchester Street. While we were Americans, we also considered ourselves to be Poles. In that strange Chicago ethnic way, there was no real difference between the two. My family's home was a block or so away from my grandmother's apartment, and I grew up speaking that special patois we call *Po Chicagosku*. I attended a Felician Sister–run grade school, and most everyone I knew until I left for high school was Polish and pronounced my last name properly. As Chicago was, and is, a diverse and largely immigrant city, I knew there was a larger world beyond my immediate neighborhood filled with people who could not pronounce my name and who often considered me and my neighbors as foreign and, in many cases, inferior. This did not bother me, as I was secure in my American version of *Polskość*. My sense of security in my identity was in many ways a gift of the generations who had come before me. The question of why I maintained a sense of Polishness has often haunted me. While at a meeting of historians in Toronto in 1980, a Polish scholar told me that of course I was not Polish. This startled me and, in some way, his words still do. This study is an attempt to deal with that question of *Polskość*, but, like all historical projects, the research has led to many more inquiries. The themes in this book deal with ethnic identity, the relationship between Polish immigration and the Polish lands, the interaction between Polish Chicagoans and other ethnic and racial groups, the place of the diaspora in both Polish and American history, and the realities of upward mobility and assimilation.

Chapter 1 deals with Polish Chicago's participation in the Columbian Exposition (1893) and, later, in the Lwów Provincial Exposition (1894), as well as the campaign to erect a monument to Thaddeus Kosciuszko, a hero both in the United States—as a result of his Revolutionary War service—and in Poland, as a fighter for independence. These events, despite internal divisions among the participants, presented a united face to the rest of the city and to Poland. Chapter 1 illuminates many of the trends that will be explored in later chapters. The next chapter examines the origin of Chicago's first Polish neighborhoods and major institutions, detailing the ideological split that defined the early community, as well as important individuals who shaped both the Chicago and national Polonia. Chapter 3, in turn, details living and working conditions in Polish Chicago's various neighborhoods between 1880 and 1920 and sets the stage for much of the subsequent history. Chicago's Poles built institutions, fraternal organizations, labor unions, and political machines as they made their way through the ethnic maelstrom that was Chicago during the era before World War One. Chapter 4 looks at Chicago's role in the struggle for Polish independence during the Great War. The conflict proved to be a turning point for Polonia in several ways. Most importantly, Poland regained its independence and its place on the European map. For Polish Chicago, a liberated Poland meant the fulfillment of a long-held dream. As the city's Polish community looked forward to the postwar era, it also found itself immersed in an American society that had turned against immigration and demanded assimilation. Chapter 5 deals with the issues presented during the interwar period. Chicago's Polonia felt itself under siege and increasingly alienated from a newly independent Poland. Thus, the question of *Polskość* again presented itself, and the diaspora redefined it under new conditions. Still part of the American working class, Chicago's Polonia faced problems of juvenile delinquency and more serious crime. It struggled against what it saw as the unfair stereotyping of its members as slum dwellers, rallied itself politically, and joined grassroots organizations as well as Cermak's Democratic Party. During the 1930s, Poles again flocked to unions as the country struggled under the Great Depression and impending war. Chapter 6 deals with World War Two and its aftermath. The struggle led to the creation of a large umbrella organization, the Polish American Congress, in order to promote the idea yet again of a free and independent Poland. Chapter 7 details this ongoing struggle to both regain Polish independence from the USSR and to expand Polish culture in the United States, as well as to represent the postwar Polonia that was beginning to move away from its working-class roots. The election of John Paul II as pope and head of the Roman Catholic Church and the rise of the Solidarity movement in Poland brought new prestige to Polonia and its leadership. Chapter 8 depicts the Chicago Polonia's transition from impoverished immigrant group to suburbia.

In some 150 years, Chicago's Poles had made the leap from the peasantry to the working class and then finally the American middle class. In 1900, few would have predicted that by the dawn of the twenty-first century Polonia would have moved from the impoverished inner city to leafy suburbia. Today, as Chicago is slowly being eclipsed by other Polish immigrant centers, particularly New York and London, the city remains at the heart of the Polish American experience. Polish Chicago remains a vibrant and somewhat contentious community, now undergoing yet more change as it finds itself in a postindustrial global city.

1

Meet Me at the Fair

Poland's Fourth Partition

I was introduced to you as an American, but today I am a Pole, and
I am more a Pole than I ever was before. I grew up an admirer of
Poland, and some of my earliest lessons were those read of its dark
and tragic history. I learned as a boy to love it.
—MAYOR CARTER HARRISON, Polish Day, October 7, 1893, World's
Columbian Exposition[1]

On the morning of Saturday, October 7, 1893, thousands of Chicago's Polish residents gathered at Jackson Boulevard between
Wood and Paulina Streets to take part in a vast procession to the
site of the World's Columbian Exposition. Northwest Side participants first assembled on Noble Street in front of the rival parishes
of St. Stanislaus Kostka and Holy Trinity. Those coming from
Bridgeport, Town of Lake (Back of the Yards), South Chicago, as
well as St. Casimir's Parish in South Lawndale, met with those
from St. Adalbert's in front of both the church and nearby Pulaski
Hall on Seventeenth Street and Ashland Avenue. They marched
north toward Jackson Boulevard. By 9:00 a.m., brilliantly uni-

formed cavalrymen, carriages filled with Polish women, and a vast number of members of Polish fraternal societies and other community groups filled the boulevard. Promptly at 10:00 a.m., parade grand marshal Piotr Kiołbassa ordered the parade to proceed toward the Loop. Reportedly the largest crowd since the opening ceremonies of the fair saw them progress through the downtown. Bands, marching men, carriages and an array of floats advanced toward Michigan Avenue. Republicans and Democrats, Christians and Jews, socialists and anarchists, nationalists, Roman Catholics, and atheists, rich and poor all came together to celebrate Poland and their particular brand of *Polskość* or Polishness. Chicago's Polonia put itself on spectacular display before a city that had welcomed its members as poor, unskilled labor to work within its sweatshops, mills, packinghouses, factories, and tanneries.[2]

Chicago's Polish policemen, marching sixteen abreast, led the parade. Kiołbassa and Joseph Napieralski followed. Mayor Carter Harrison came next, riding in a carriage. The Polish Day Central Committee and many of the city's aldermen, led by Polish alderman Stanley Kunz, followed, as did various military societies and a float commemorating George Washington, Thaddeus Kosciuszko, and Casimir Pulaski. On and on went the parade, which included more than three thousand participants. As the first division crossed the river toward the Loop, the Jackson Boulevard Bridge swung open to allow a ship to pass, delaying the parade for some twenty minutes. Other interruptions occurred at both State Street and Wabash Avenue, where cable cars blocked the path. Once the parade got past these obstacles, it proceeded south down Michigan Avenue to the review stand at the Columbus Statue. The parade—with its sixteen floats costing more than $6,000 ($155,502 in 2017), its marching bands, its brightly dressed cavalrymen, and its society members—proudly proceeded to Twelfth Street (Roosevelt Road) and doubled back to Van Buren Street before proceeding by train to Jackson Park. A *Chicago Daily News* reporter, obviously bemused by the sight, described the parade as a sight never before seen on Michigan Avenue. He described the red caps, traditionally donned in Kraków, worn by many of the men in the parade as tent or barn shaped. A group of Polish girls marched in the procession wearing Krakovian folk costumes.

The parade floats depicted various historical events and allegorical scenes, all with the idea of convincing the city, and in turn, the world, of the righteousness of Poland's call for the restoration of its independence. These included a float offered by the Polish National Alliance illustrating the Polish Constitution of May 3, with King Stanislaus Poniatowski bestowing the charter to representatives of all social classes in Poland; another depicted "Poland in Chains." From Back of the Yards came a float portraying a Polish mother with a sword at her side, teaching her children to read. The Bridgeport Polish community's floats proved especially interesting. One portrayed Labor, with the Goddess of Prosperity carrying a horn of plenty and surrounded by Polish peasants busily at work, while young girls sat making floral wreaths. Two other Bridgeport floats included a Polish Jewish orchestra and a Krakovian wedding scene with participants again in colorful regional costumes. The final float came from St. Casimir's Parish. Titled "The Resurrection of Poland," it displayed a broken prison gate, from which emerged a female figure representing Poland with a number of dead Russian, Austrian, and Prussian soldiers lying about. The floats celebrated the peasant background of Polish Chicago and the independence movement and recalled Poland's martyrdom at the hands of its neighbors.

It was not until after 1:00 p.m. that the parade reached the gates of the Columbian Exposition. Marchers moved east to the lake, then circled the lagoon and the Hall of Commerce and proceeded to the Administration Building and from there to Festival Hall. The South Chicago Polish centenarian, Michael Adamski, with the aid of Judge Michael A. LaBuy, rang the new Liberty Bell three times. At Festival Hall, the orchestra played a rendition of the "Third of May Polonaise" and President S. Słomiński of the Polish Day Central Committee opened festivities with a short

Festival Hall, Columbian Exposition, 1893. (Photograph by C. D. Arnold. Chicago Public Library, Special Collections, WCE/CDA, vol. 3, plate 36.)

address that introduced Justice LaBuy, who proclaimed liberty as the common legacy of both Poland and the United States.

Mayor Harrison, who had virtually invented ethnic campaigning in Chicago, addressed the crowd of Polish Americans and their leaders:

> Until recently, we had but few Polish citizens, and these were poor people. But they arrived here full of energy, from a land where they had been oppressed. Today, we witnessed . . . a splendid spectacle. . . . Nothing of the kind would have been possible in your motherland, in your beloved Warsaw, where the Polish language is barred even from the schools. For a century, Poland has been struggling for liberty; for a century now, no Polish child has dared to sing a hymn of freedom. How long would the Czar remain on his throne, how long would he dare trample upon millions of people if it were otherwise, if the children of that country were permitted to learn and sing Polish national anthems?

Harrison claimed that it was great day when he saw Poles marching down the streets delaying what the mayor called the "the followers of the golden calf in their daily chase" without the aid of police, without violence, but with a quiet dignity. He proclaimed Poles good citizens and said that, if the United States was in danger, that at least twenty thousand Chicago Poles would fight for its defense. A musical program and a special fireworks display followed. Between eight and ten thousand people attended the ceremony at Festival Hall. Various reports claimed that twenty-five to fifty thousand Polish Americans attended the Columbian Exposition that day. The crowd at the Columbian Exposition on October 7, 1893, was one of the highest of the entire fair. This was a point of great pride for the community, even if the numbers were inflated because of out-of-town visitors arriving for the Chicago Day celebrations on Sunday.[3]

From the beginning, Poland, a nation that had disappeared from the map of Europe a century before, impacted the Columbian Exposition. As early as April 1893, Polish Chicagoans had met to discuss how to help visitors from Poland and decided to include a special information bureau and general headquarters for a reception committee, place bilingual guides on the exposition grounds, and organize a Polish Day for the fair. The major Polish American organizations, including the rival Polish Roman Catholic Union of America (PRCUA) and the Polish National Alliance (PNA), threw their support behind the venture. They hoped to raise the profile of American Polonia, but especially of Chicago's Polish community.[4]

On the second day of the World's Columbian Exposition, Tuesday, May 2, 1893, the renowned Polish pianist Ignacy Jan Paderewski performed with the Exposition Orchestra. Paderewski, at age thirty-two, was already the world's most famous musician. With his wild, voluminous red hair and artistic manner, he attracted crowds wherever he went. Young women apparently swooned during his concerts. At the end of April, Paderewski finished a series of Chicago concerts, and his friend, the orchestra leader

Theodore Thomas, asked him to stay and play at the fair. Paderewski agreed and also consented to not charge a fee. Fair officials demanded, however, that he play on an instrument provided by one of the companies that sponsored the fair. Paderewski, who favored Steinway pianos and had an exclusive contract with that company, refused, and the conflict made the city's newspapers. Daniel Burnham, the fair's lead designer, finally smuggled the maestro's piano into Music Hall, and the Pole, playing on his favorite instrument, thrilled the fair crowd. Later, Chicagoans lined up in the Loop to see the piano that had caused such a controversy.[5]

The Polish presence at the exposition was slight. Several Poles displayed their talents, but partitioned Poland had little impact on exhibits. On August 4, 1893, a lecture delivered by Polish Chicagoan Maximilian Drzemała, in the Palace of Fine Arts, presented an outline of Polish art, past and present. Many in the audience then proceeded to the inauguration of the Polish art section in the Palace of Fine Arts. The Chicago Polish leader and politician Piotr Kiołbassa opened the program with a speech that explained that political oppression in Poland had made the display difficult to arrange. Finally, he called attention to three paintings by Jacek Malczewski—*Death of an Exiled Woman*, symbolizing Polish martyrdom; *Jadwiga*, symbolizing the nation's spiritual strength; and *Wernyhora*, prophesying Poland's resurrection. After Kiołbassa's address, the gathering moved to the West Wing Gallery, where Drzemała spoke on the significance of this first exposition of Polish art in America. It contained a total of 122 paintings representing the work of fifty-nine artists. He remarked on the fact that these paintings constituted the only Polish representation at the fair and that they should remind people from all corners of the world of Poland's name. He thanked America for permitting Poland to take its place among the other nations at the fair.

Professor Emil Habdank Dunikowski, from Lwów University, spoke next, representing visitors from the Polish lands. "In view of our presence here and our efforts," he said, "Poland is not

Count Henry Lubienski incorporated the Polish Restaurant at the Columbian Exposition at a capital value of $25,000 ($647,924 in 2017). Lubienski put up $10,000 ($259,169 in 2017), while others purchased stock in the enterprise. (Chicago Public Library, Special Collections, WCE/SC, box 3, plate 71.)

lost—nor will it be lost!" Henry Nagiel proclaimed his joy at seeing the artists exhibited as Poles and not as Russians, Austrians, or Germans. Afterward, visitors attended a reception at the Polish restaurant on the fair grounds. The newspaper *Dziennik Chicagoski* pointed out that all factions of an often politically and ideologically divided Polish community attended the event.[6]

The Lwów Exposition

In 1892 and 1893, Dr. Dunikowski visited various Polish American communities across the country, including Chicago's. The Galician Sejm (regional assembly) had sent him on a twofold mission to evaluate if immigrants were lost to the Polish national cause and to convince Polonia leaders to participate in the projected 1894 Lwów Provincial Exposition. Lwów, the capital of Austrian Galicia, a province created from Hapsburg participation in the first partition of Poland in 1772, had long been a center of Polish nationalist feeling. In 1867, Vienna, under a program referred to as *Ausgleich*, gave Galicia semiautonomy and more or less gave the Poles a free hand in running the province. Two years later, Polish replaced German as the official language of the government and schools. Galicia exhibited many public expressions of Polish nationalism, while Russian and German authorities in the other two partitions frowned on such demonstrations. As a result of the relative freedom of these Poles to articulate their national feelings, Lwów became a center of nationalist agitation for Polish independence. In Lwów, the term "Fourth Partition," was coined to refer to all Poles overseas and, in particular, those in the United States. Dunikowski hoped to rally the capital of the Fourth Partition, Chicago, to the national cause and therefore to the exposition, which would highlight Polish culture as well as advances in industry, agriculture, and technology.[7]

In the nineteenth century, world's fairs were seen as a way of demonstrating the advances of industrial civilization. For Poland, partitioned and occupied by her neighbors, the Lwów exhibition provided a chance both to prove to the world that Polish culture still existed and even thrived and to make its case for independence. The proposed Lwów Exposition celebrated the Kosciuszko insurrection of 1794, which, while it ended in defeat and the Third Partition, temporarily rallied the peasantry to the Polish cause. At the end of the nineteenth century, Polish nationalists and intellectuals hoped to gain the peasantry's support for the independence movement. Traditionally the *szlachta*, or gentry, saw themselves as real Poles, while peasants were simply "the folk." At times, occupying powers used this to split the nation into two camps, and the Russians and Austrians especially portrayed themselves as protectors of the peasantry. This began to change slowly in the years after the January 1863 insurrection, and the Lwów Exposition hoped to further this movement and bring together all classes and regions of Polish society. Dunikowski knew that the immigration was largely a peasant migration, and he wanted to tie it to the nationalist cause. He wrote, "There seem to be enough of our people abroad then, to awaken us from the apathy with which we have looked upon emigration. We should interest ourselves in, and not underrate these Polish masses overseas, which in any case may give valuable contribution to our national cause."[8]

Earlier Polish visitors to the United States downplayed the importance of American Polonia. The writer Henryk Sienkiewicz, who won the Nobel Prize for Literature in 1905, came to Chicago in the 1870s and argued that the diaspora was basically lost to the homeland. He stated that when he arrived in the Polish neighborhood surrounding St. Stanislaus Kostka church he at first felt as if he were back in Poland, but watching and listening to Polish children gathering to enter the parochial school, he heard the influence of English on their speech. Sienkiewicz portrayed the knowledge of the Polish language in the small population as poor and quickly decaying under the influence of English. He complained of a separate Polish dialect being created in America with a mixture of English and Polish words that could scarcely be understood by other Poles. Sienkiewicz wrote, "In short the American Poles are not lacking in good intentions and in patriotism, but their speech, torn from the maternal stem, invariably deteriorates and decays, and loses its original spirit, and undergoes transformation like a plant transplanted to a strange soil." He pointed out that it was only a matter of time that denationalization would occur. While Dunikowski and others also complained about Polonia's language skills, he came to see whether that process was yet complete and whether Polonia held out any possible help for the future Polish national struggle.[9]

Officials of the Polish Roman Catholic Union of America greeted Dunikowski on September 2, 1892. A ten-carriage procession escorted him from the train station to the Northwest Side Polish neighborhood. Kiołbassa served as a guide for Dunikowski as he toured Chicago. Father Vincent Barzyński brought him to Władysław Smulski's home, where he stayed while in the city. On September 3, Rev. Barzyński hosted a banquet for Dunikowski in the church hall, where leaders of the PRCUA attended and toasted the professor. The famous Polish actress Helena Modrzejewska (known as Modjeska in the United States) was also in Chicago at that time, and Barzyński convinced her to play a role in an amateur production of Władysław Anczyc's play *Chłopi Arystokraci* (*Peasant Aristocrats*). The following week, Modrzejewska returned to star in a performance of *Jadwiga* by the immigrant playwright, Szczesny Zahajkiewicz. Some six thousand people packed the hall along with Dunikowski, as an overflow crowd gathered outside the entrance. Both the celebrity of Modrzejewska and the importance of Dunikowski's visit attracted the crowd.[10]

On Monday, September 26, 1892, the various societies of St. Stanislaus Kostka Parish held a farewell reception for Dr. Dunikowski after his return from a short visit to Wisconsin's Polish settlements. The festivities began at 1:00 p.m. and consisted of a banquet, a special program by schoolchildren, and a mass meeting in the evening. Long tables arranged with appetizers filled the hall decorated with banners and flowers. Dignitaries in attendance included Smulski, Rev. Barzyński, and Polish priests from Chicago and out of town, as well as prominent members of the Polish National Alliance. After the meal, Barzyński spoke, elaborating on the accomplishments of the Poles in America and expressing his hopes for the future. Dunikowski thanked the assembly for the cordiality shown to him and remarked that "the Poland along the Vistula, along the Warta, and along Lake Michigan is one and the same." Dunikowski marveled at the size of Polish Chicago and the number of young people who had come to pay homage to the idea of a free and independent Poland. Dunikowski made a toast expressing his hopes that the Polish National Alliance and the Polish Roman Catholic Union would make peace. Enthusiastic applause followed his address. Various other speeches followed, including the final toast by Zahajkiewicz, who asked the crowd to "love one another." He said, "I wish I could make this feeling of brotherly love permanent. There are different factions and different opinions among us, but in spite of all this there can be a common feeling in regard to general affairs. We can travel on various roads, but let these roads lead us to only one Rome—love for our fatherland. Love one another!"

Barzyński then addressed the crowd of six thousand, hitting on the themes of loyalty to Poland and unity in the community. He stated that a united Polish nation would be greater than any diplomatic or military force. He admonished Poles both in Poland and in the United States for their divisiveness, saying that nothing could be accomplished until they acted in unity. Dunikowski pointed out that "Polish life is growing everywhere" and urged those gathered to "work and the fatherland will rise once again." Dunikowski called for harmony as Polonia had long suffered from internal arguments, political and ideological divisions, hatreds, and even violence.[11]

After his return to Poland, the report that Dunikowski wrote was read with much interest in both Europe and the United States. The professor addressed Polish delegates to the Galician Assembly and the National Council on December 21, 1892, and outlined several proposals. Among these was a scheme to guide immigrants away from cities in order to avoid their proleterianization. Another hoped to create an organization to maintain contact with various Polish associations abroad in order to keep alive the Polish national spirit and raise the intellectual level of the diaspora. The *Dziennik Chicagoski* cautioned the Lwów Poles that American Polonia did not want to be dictated to by Polish leaders and intellectuals. This friction, to a degree, resulted from the diaspora's growing maturity but also from the class tensions that historically had marked the relationship between the Polish peasantry and the upper classes.[12]

On January 30, 1893, the directors of the Lwów Exposition sent a letter to Kiołbassa asking him to promote Polish American participation in the fair with the creation of a Polish American pavilion. The journal *Przegląd Emigracji*, addressed the Polish American press to ask for a closer relationship between them and their homeland and pointed out that, while the Polish American press sent copies of their newspapers to Poland, these failed to completely acquaint the Polish public with events in American Polonia. The journal encouraged the Polish press in the United States to participate in the Lwów Exposition. Furthermore, *Przegląd Emigracji* promised that the exhibit would include all the Polish, White Russian, and Lithuanian papers in the world, including all the Yiddish, German, and Russian papers published in Poland, thus making it representative of all the peoples of the Polish lands (those lost to the partitions and beyond). The *Dziennik Chicagoski* heartily supported the effort and its call for unity.[13]

Dunikowski's second visit to the states in August 1893 furthered the cause of Polish solidarity. He addressed the convention of the Polish Roman Catholic Union stating that "the anniversary which we are now observing is a sad one—it reminds us of Maciejowice [the 1794 battle in which Kosciuszko was defeated and taken prisoner by the Russian Army]—but are we to observe it in mourning? No! We mourn the dead, and Poland is not dead." Dunikowski again urged the Polish American community to take part in the Lwów fair the following year.[14]

Even before Polish Day at the Columbian Exposition, Dunikowski had called together a committee to organize Polonia's participation in the Galician Fair. He called the American Polonia "My brother Poles" and laid out the patriotic intentions of the exhibit. He stated that the fair was a way for Poles in all three partitions to become better acquainted with American Polonia. Dunikowski appointed the following Polish Chicago leaders to his committee: Rev. Vincent Barzyński, Piotr Kiołbassa, W. Smulski, S. Słomiński, Judge LaBuy, Dr. C. Nidowicz, W. Bardoński, Dr. Adam Szwajkart, M. Drzemała, L. Szopinski, and H. Nagiel.[15]

In September, Dr. Dunikowski appealed to the PRCUA's rival at the Tenth Convention of the Polish National Alliance held in Chicago. The first day of the convention opened at 9:00 a.m. at the PNA's central headquarters; from there, delegates proceeded to the nearby Holy Trinity Church for Mass. Holy Trinity's pastor, Rev. Casimir Sztuczko, preached the sermon and called on delegates to devote themselves to work for Poland and not to seek personal fame, proclaiming "he who seeks fame, works for himself, not for Poland." The priest went on to speak of Poland's sad plight and its need for aid in the struggle to regain independence. He adjured the delegates to keep in mind throughout the discussion the general welfare of both the Polish National Alliance and Poland. Sztuczko warned that Polish American youth were losing their sense of Polishness and were ashamed to speak the Polish language. He admonished the delegates to increase their efforts to counter this trend. When Mass ended, the delegates marched from the Northwest Side church to Pulaski Hall.

Dr. Dunikowski addressed the convention on the third day. He spoke of several matters and concluded with a description of the upcoming Lwów Exposition. After several delegates spoke in favor of participation, a delegate named Machek criticized Dr. Dunikowski, saying that he consorted with the rival PRCUA and, as the representative of the Polish magnates, promised much but accomplished little. Another delegate asked if Dr. Dunikowski had produced his credentials as a delegate. Others answered that his credentials were in order and that his name alone gave him the right to speak. Dunikowski took the floor to answer the charges, saying that he did not come to America simply to address the PNA, but to visit Polish communities in general. The president of the convention asked that the delegates honor Dr. Dunikowski by rising. All, except the handful who shared their resentment against Polish elites like Dunikowski, rose to their feet. Several delegates then spoke to the importance of the Lwów Exposition for the national cause. The convention passed a resolution that $500 ($12,958 in 2017) be appropriated toward the erection of a Polish American pavilion at the exposition. In addition, delegates donated $65.65 ($1,727) for the proposed exhibit.[16]

Polish American participation in the Lwów Exposition soon

became a major concern for the various Polonia organizations. The participation of American Polonia was often couched in terms of its obligation to the memory of the Polish and American hero Thaddeus Kosciuszko. The *Dziennik Chicagoski* newspaper reminded its readers that General Kosciuszko had donned a peasant coat and united all Polish classes in the national struggle. Kosciuszko was seen as a bridge both between America and Poland and between the gentry and peasantry. The Lwów fair organizers obviously hoped to make this connection with American Polonia and to draw its members to the Polish cause. The fair's goal was to show Polish cultural and economic advances so that the world would not forget Poland's plight. Such an outright proclamation of the importance of Polish culture, and even economic development, would have been impossible in the other partitions. For this reason alone, the Lwów Exposition attracted support from Polish American organizations, especially those situated in Chicago.[17]

A central committee to erect the pavilion was formed in Chicago, with local committees in New York City and Baltimore. The first task was to raise funds for the enterprise. The PRCUA voted $300 ($7,775 in 2017) and along with the PNA's $500 ($12,958), funding the project began. Other Polish organizations in the United States also pledged to help. The central committee determined that the cost of the pavilion would not exceed $2,000 ($51,834) and that a Polish American architect should design it in a style popular in the United States. Dr. Dunikowski was to direct construction of the pavilion. While $800 ($20,734) had been promised by the two major Polish organizations, another $1,200 ($31,100) needed to be raised before construction. It remained for other organizations and the public to get behind the project. Despite the national economic depression, Chicago's Polonia took the lead in working for the pavilion. Chicago's Polish-language newspapers recognized that it wouldn't be easy for wage earners to contribute during the difficult times, but they claimed that the hundreds of Polish organizations nationwide should be able to raise the funds needed. They also pointed out that Polonia was not bereft of wealth and that many well-to-do people could and should come forward with donations.

The committee recommended an exhibit dealing with various aspects of the American diaspora. The *Dziennik Chicagoski* suggested the exhibit cover Polish American religious life, its school system, its press, and its social life, especially the creation of the various fraternal groups and institutions. The Catholic Church would of course be prominent, given the more than 170 Polish Catholic parishes in the United States and given its importance both in Poland and in the diaspora. Visitors to the pavilion would get a clear picture of the religious life of Polish America and of Polish parochial schools in America. In addition to the information on Catholic schools, organizers planned a discussion of Polish reading rooms and libraries. The exhibit would not ignore the Polish American press, as the publishing of books, pamphlets, and newspapers was an important part of Polish community life. Polish American leaders wanted to express that, despite their peasant backgrounds and their situation in the American working class, they provided for the education of their children and the future of the Polish community.

Organizers felt that the most extensive section of the Polish American exhibit would be that which dealt with social activities, fraternal organizations, and the theater, but they admitted that some of these, particularly Polonia's various semi-military organizations, did not fit into the original proposal request, which emphasized economic and cultural accomplishments. Nevertheless, Polonia leaders felt these groups and the Polish Falcons in the United States (Polskie Towarzystwo Gimnastyczne "Sokół"), a semi-military gymnastic organization, should participate. Organizers called for them to submit their constitutions, emblems, institutional records, and building and convention photographs, as well as their histories, to the central committee. They also called for the various welfare and immigrant aid societies to provide information. Organizers further hoped that the records and regulations of Polish building and loan associations, of which there were now about twenty in the United States, would be featured in the exhibit. The Polish American theater promised to take a prominent position at the exposition. Photographs of plays, samples of tickets, playbills, and copies of plays written by Polish Americans found a place in the showcase. In addition, a call went out to display items representing Polish American efforts in industry, handicrafts, and agriculture. Small shops harbored craftspeople across the major Polish American communities. Also, a large number of Polish farmers worked the land in Wisconsin and Michigan. Polish American industrialists and architects also planned to take part in the fair. All of this was to show European Polish society the gains that had been made by the diaspora and to emphasize its possible contribution to Polish independence.[18]

By November 1893, the Polish American committee showed considerable progress, and as the month began, leaders reported that industrialist Erasmus Jerzmanowski of New York had sent a check for $500 to the committee. He had previously sent $200 (a total of $700 or $18,142 in 2017) to help cover expenses. The committee proclaimed that the construction of the Polish American building in Lwów was now a certainty. At the Thursday, November 2, meeting the architect, Theodore Lewandowski, presented a sketch of his proposed structure for the Lwów exhibit and the committee approved it unanimously. It also supported a proposal that Polish women in the United States contribute to the fair. On Thanksgiving Day, St. Stanislaus Kostka Parish held a bazaar to raise funds for the pavilion. An orchestra provided entertainment until almost midnight, as beer flowed freely and cigar smoke filled the hall. Prizes tempted participants to try their luck. The fair resulted in $215 ($6,182 in 2017) for the exhibit committee. The steel mill community in South Chicago also sent donations, as almost the entire Polonia responded to the call for participation in the fair.[19]

Construction of the pavilion began in March 1894 at a location between the Fine Arts Building and the pavilion of the city of Lwów. Donations had come from across American Polonia, but the

Lewandowski's rendition of the Polish American Pavilion at the Lwów Fair, 1894
(From Stanisław Osadę, *Historia Związku Nardówego Polskiego*, vol. 1, *1880–1905*
[Chicago, 1957].)

committee was still short about $1,500 ($38,875 in 2017). Donated
exhibits had to be packed and shipped before April. Shipping costs
were estimated to run from $250 to $300 ($6,479 and $7,775).[20]

The fair opened on June 5, 1894, the largest exposition held
in the lands that once made up the Polish-Lithuanian Commonwealth. The undertaking had sixty-three pavilions, including
thirty-seven private ones and more than one hundred and thirty
buildings situated in the Stryski Hills district of Lwów. It marked
a great patriotic celebration, as Count Adam Sapieha welcomed
participants from all three partitions and opened this celebration
of *Polskość*, calling it a Polish exhibit and not simply a Galician
event. It featured the *Racławice Panorama*, a 360-degree visual presentation, situated in a neo-renaissance stucco building, detailing
the famous battle led by Kosciuszko against the Russians. The

multipanel cycloramic painting drew hundreds of thousands of visitors. Well over one million people visited Lwów during the four and one-half months of the exhibition.

Numerous exhibits emphasized technological progress, but this did not take away from the celebration of ethnography at the fair. Exhibits portrayed Galicia through its varied folk cultures. In many ways, this was the height of what historian Larry Wolf has called *chłopomania* (peasant mania) in Poland during the 1890s. Unlike the Columbian Exposition, which featured ethnic exhibits from around the world, the Lwów Exposition only displayed Galicia's folk cultures. An ethnographic catalog by Włodzimierz Szuchiewicz (the Polish translation of the Ukrainian writer Volodymyr Shukhevych) portrayed Galicia in terms of its diversity and insisted on a division between highlanders (Polish Gorale and Ruthenian Hutsuls) and lowlanders. The ethnographic pavilion attempted to avoid the growing national and religious tensions in Galicia, but to the vexation of Ruthenians (Ukrainians), Jews, and others, the fair assumed that Poles were the leading civilizing force in the province. Other exhibits, such as the Bride's Room arranged by Countess Anna Potocka, encouraged Polish folk crafts. Potocka proudly proclaimed that there was no need to look to the rest of Europe when the Galician peasantry produced such beautiful objects with which to adorn one's home. The visit to the provincial fair by Emperor Franz Josef, his only state visit to Galicia, emphasized the importance of the exhibition for the Austro-Hungarian Empire and especially for his Polish subjects.[21]

The Polish American Committee named the industrialist Erasmus Jerzmanowski honorary president, and along with Adam Szwajkart, as manager of the Polish-American Pavilion, he represented the committee in Lwów. The large wooden Queen Anne-style structure opened on June 24, 1894. Prince Sapieha thanked American Polonia and said that the hearts of European Poles would always be with them. After his talk, fair officials invited Polish Americans to an American buffet as an African American orchestra entertained them. At a breakfast meeting the next day between the Polish American contingent and the leadership of the Lwów Exposition, Szwajkart stated that American Polonia, the Fourth Polish Partition, wanted close connections to Poland and he emphasized that they remained Polish. Polonia's participation in the fair was a huge success. The exhibits were unanimously awarded an honorary diploma, the highest award of the exposition. For Polonia, this event raised its status and solidified the idea of a Fourth Partition that would come to the aid of Poland in its struggle to regain independence.[22]

The Kosciuszko Monument

Along with international expositions, the building of monuments to mark important historical figures or events became more and more popular as the nineteenth century progressed. On February 5, 1892, Chicago's Polish leaders incorporated the Kosciuszko Monument Association, naming John F. Smulski as secretary. The organization, established in 1886, had been trying for years to get the West Park Board of the Chicago Park District to grant it the right to erect a monument in Humboldt Park on the city's Northwest Side. The board finally acquiesced, and the association began a drive to collect $25,000 ($647,925 in 2017), with the unrealistic goal of presenting the completed statue during the Columbian Exposition. Later, it was decided to have a panel of Polish artists in Lwów decide the final design, and the monument association announced a contest for a model of the proposed memorial. Dunikowski was put in charge of the competition to be held in Lwów.

Donations flowed into the committee's coffers and demonstrated optimism that the project would be accomplished quickly. By April 1892, over nine hundred persons contributed over $1000 ($26,917 in 2017). Even small organizations such as the St. Casimir Society donated $15.00 ($389). Polish parishes and organizations sent money for the monument. At a commemoration of the November 1830 uprising against Russia held on December 11 in Back of the Yards, local Poles collected $26.00 ($674) for the fund.

In April 1893, the Polish Policemen's Club sponsored a ball to raise money for the endeavor. Several thousand people attended the event at Schoenhofen's Hall and collected an estimated $1,500 ($38,876). Of course, the project was not without its critics. Some called for support of other undertakings, such as the Immigrant Home in New York City or a Polish hospital in Chicago that would bear Kosciuszko's name, as a more appropriate response. The criticism arose out of need for such institutions in Chicago and across the United States. Nevertheless, the movement to build a monument proceeded.[23]

By January 1893, the United Association of Fine Arts in Lwów announced the competition and encouraged Polish sculptors to enter the contest, which would close on May 15, 1893, with a winner to be announced two weeks later. Ironically, the Chicago committee eventually chose a different artist to complete the project. The committee had raised roughly $4,000 ($103,667 in 2017) by this time but needed to raise perhaps $30,000 ($777,510) more to build the monument.[24]

Chicago's memorial to Kosciuszko reflected a flurry of monument building in the Polish partitions. The Polish-Lithuanian Commonwealth did not have a tradition of building such structures. In fact, Poles argued over the erection and placement of a statue of Adam Mickiewicz, the renowned poet laureate of Poland, in Kraków, which did not finally occur until 1898. By this time, the importance of the construction of monuments became more and more apparent as a reminder of Poland's past, in order to inspire the masses for the restoration of the country. For Chicago's Polonia, a statue honoring Kosciuszko erected in an important park spoke to the prestige and growing political power of the Polish community and was a way of expressing national life and prestige on both sides of the Atlantic.[25]

With continued tough economic times in the United States, it became difficult to raise cash for the Kosciuszko monument. By 1895, many in Polonia complained about the Kosciuszko Monument Association, which continually asked for funds. For a time, the association abandoned efforts to collect more money. It loaned $5,000 ($137,856 in 2017) to Holy Trinity Parish at 5 percent for one year to enable it to build a new school. The following year, the committee reported that $8,468 ($233,474 in 2017) had been raised and asked for more funds. After expenses related to the Lwów contest, only $7,390 ($203,752) remained, a sum far too low to build a monument. At one point, the committee even appealed to the poor, asking for penny contributions. The committee eventually chose the Kraków artist Kazimierz Chodziński to cast the model for the monument for $18,000 ($507,072). It was to be twenty-five feet high, and the base would measure twenty-nine feet by twenty-nine feet. Kosciuszko and the horse would be one and a half times their natural size.[26]

The *Zgoda*, the official publication of the Polish National Alliance, asked how long the monument committee would keep Polonia in suspense and charged that money had ended up in the pockets of one of the organizers. The paper displayed annoyance with the lack of progress and asserted that the public would like the PNA to take over the project and complete it. The committee denied the accusations. *Zgoda* countered that the commission should have been giving regular reports to the public. As for the signing of the contract with Chodziński, the paper claimed that if the process had been more open, thousands of dollars might have been saved. The journal demanded that committee members should be replaced and that a new sense of urgency would then appear in the movement to create the monument.[27]

The collection of funds continued, and in June 1904, twelve years after the incorporation of the committee, the monument committee sent out an invitation to all Polish societies to attend the unveiling of the memorial. Fund-raising continued as the committee sold badges for twenty-five cents in order to help pay for the installation. On Sunday, September 11, Chicago's Polonia gathered for the long-awaited unveiling. At about noon, Chicago's

Northwest Side became a hub of activity as parade marshals gave orders and brought floats into place for the grand parade. Meanwhile about three hundred Polish societies from various parts of the city and the country took their places, amid the sound of band music, the beating of drums, and cheers from the sidewalks crowded with people. At about one o'clock as it began to rain, the massive procession of perhaps ten thousand Polish Americans headed by the event's grand marshal Anthony Lisztewnik began. Intermittent showers did not dampen the mood. The monument draped in Polish and American flags awaited the throng as it made its way to the site. Thousands filled Humboldt Park. On the lawn to the right of the monument, a chorus of seven hundred men and women gathered, while the members of the monument committee as well as members of the clergy, dignitaries, and representatives of the press sat on the rostrum. After the orchestra played the opening hymn, Judge LaBuy spoke in English about the life of Kosciuszko. City Attorney John F. Smulski, vice president of the committee, then presented the monument to West Park Commissioners. He read a telegram from President Theodore Roosevelt, congratulating Chicago's Poles on their accomplishment. Maria Szopinski, robed in an American flag and aided by four young girls dressed in Polish folk costumes, pulled the cord that unveiled the monument. Whistling, tooting horns, clapping of hands, and the cheers of an estimated nearly hundred thousand people broke out. Adam Szwajkart, now a West Park Board commissioner, accepted the monument. After his speech, the standard-bearers of the various groups posted their colors around the monument, and all the different societies and military organizations began tendering their salutes to Thaddeus Kosciuszko. Senator Albert Hopkins gave the keynote address, and the day concluded with an address in Polish by M. B. Stenczynski, president of the Polish National Alliance. Of course, even this ceremony was marked in part by acrimony. Chicago's Lithuanians protested that Kosciuszko was a Lithuanian, and they had not been invited to the unveiling.[28]

Celebrations and Chicago's Polonia

In Poland, religious processions were a normal form of public piety as well as communal unity. They were common experiences shared by all. In the latter half of the nineteenth century, secular public demonstrations became more common there. In the United States, a more secular society in general, parades often demonstrated political and cultural concerns. As the European population became more diverse, parades and celebrations served the purpose of communal unity. Eventually such parades also took on a political character. By the end of the nineteenth and the beginning of the twentieth century, these trends of accord and politics often merged.[29]

Chicago's Polish community was no stranger to celebration. As early as January 22, 1865, Chicago's Poles marked the anniversary of the 1863 insurrection against the Russians. Czechs, Moravians, and South Slavs joined them in a show of Pan-Slavic unity. On January 22, 1873, the community celebrated the tenth anniversary of the insurrection at the Czech hall, Lipa Slovenska, on Canal and Taylor Streets. Chicago's Polish leadership attended the festivity, held under the auspices of the Gmina Polska, an antecedent of the Polish National Alliance. In 1879, Polish Chicagoans celebrated the fiftieth anniversary of the start of poet Józef Ignacy Kraszewski's literary career at the Aurora Turner Hall on Milwaukee Avenue. On September 12, 1883, Chicago's Polish neighborhoods celebrated the two hundredth anniversary of King John Sobieski's victory over the Turks at Vienna. Large numbers attended masses at both St. Adalbert's and St. Stanislaus Kostka Churches. Over five thousand men and boys marched from the churches to the Central Music Hall on State and Randolph, where a crowd of at least three thousand greeted them. The procession was so large that it interfered with horse streetcar and cable car traffic. Three years later, Chicago's Poles celebrated the fifty-sixth anniversary of the 1833 Polish revolt against the czar in the Russian partition, again at the Aurora Turner Hall on Milwaukee Avenue. Even as

Polish Chicagoans took part in the Lwów fair, they planned more celebrations and demonstrations in the city.[30]

The three events—Polish Day, the Lwów Exposition, and the creation of the Kosciuszko monument—were important for Polonia as it attempted to define itself in regard to both Poland and America. The struggle to unify the city's Polish population shed light on the various fissures within the group. These large and expensive affairs strained the economic resources of a community made up mostly of unskilled workers, with a thin cadre of businessmen, clergy, and intelligentsia in leadership roles. During the celebrations at the Columbian Exposition and the Lwów Exposition, Polish workers suffered under the impact of a nationwide depression in the United States and the Pullman strike, which hurt both the Stock Yard District and the Pullman neighborhood. While Polonia celebrated the unveiling of the Kosciuszko statue, the Poles of Back of the Yards were again involved in a massive packinghouse strike. Nevertheless, the community struggled to make these events happen because it mattered on so many levels.

The lack of unity, though, proved to be a constant theme. The rivalry between the Polish Roman Catholic Union and the Polish National Alliance provided only the most obvious rift in the American diaspora. Poles split along American political lines, supporting both the Democratic and Republican parties, while others were socialists, and even anarchists. Some called for a church independent of Rome, and some were atheists. Different visions of what a resurrected Poland might look like also divided the group. The older Polish Roman Catholic Union provided a home for those who defined Poles first and foremost as Catholics. These tended to mobilize around Chicago's first Polish Roman Catholic parish, St. Stanislaus Kostka. Nationalists gathered around Holy Trinity Parish, the Gmina Polska, and eventually the Polish National Alliance. Their definition of Polishness included non-Catholics, Jews, and others. The two parishes stood just blocks apart from each other on Noble Street in the West Town neighborhood.[31] In addition, what might be called parish civil wars often broke out in Polish neighborhoods, including street violence. Eventually, the argument between nationalists and Catholics resulted in the creation of the Polish National Catholic Church.

Beyond religion and politics, regionalism also divided the community. One of the first questions a Polish immigrant might ask of another was: *Skąd jesteś?* (Where are you from?) Polish peasants often did not trust or relate to those from different regions. Class differences also mattered, as peasants were often not considered Poles before the late nineteenth century. Of course, the partitions increased such tendencies. Immigration and ethnic historians have written about peasants overcoming old-country regionalism in the United States. Thus, Calabrians and Neapolitans became Italian in America. But the same process was occurring in Europe. In Poland in the nineteenth century, peasants from various regions began to recognize their Polishness as well as their regional identification as important. The upper classes pushed the idea of national identification as seen in the Lwów Exposition, as well through other commemorations and celebrations. Education, of course, also played a major role in the nationalization of the peasantry. This also occurred in other European countries, as the countryside became more connected to urban centers. The national culture began to subsume local cultures.[32]

The emergence of nationalism in Poland was a slow development that picked up speed in the nineteenth century. The spread of literacy and the emergence of dominant national languages played a central role in the process. Print languages laid the basis for national consciousness. Speakers of the various Polish dialects, or even the other Slavic and non-Slavic tongues in the old Polish-Lithuanian Commonwealth, might be brought together by a common printed language. This is why the struggle both for and against the Polish language in the partitions proved so important, and why Galicia became central to the national cause. A people rapidly coalescing around a common language could honor artists and intellectuals. The painter Jan Matejko, the composer Frédéric Chopin, the poet Adam Mickiewicz, the historian

Joachim Lelewel, and the writer Józef Ignacy Kraszewski, all became symbols of the national struggle. Chicago's Polonia celebrated these heroes and commemorated historic events. Immigrants, who had been part of the national awakening in the Polish partitions, could not help but be affected by these movements and events in the home country and to bring these with themselves to the United States. In Galicia, the argument over language proved very intensive. While German did not supersede Latin as the official language of the Hapsburg Empire until the nineteenth century, both Hungarian and Polish speakers quickly pushed back against the decision to adopt the vernacular. The compromises of the 1860s resulted in a tripartite elevation of national languages in the empire. For a partitioned Poland, this meant the creation of a larger imagined community that rooted itself in the historical experience. For Polonia, a sense of Polishness aroused a great deal of national feeling and shaped the Polish American response to both the homeland and the receiving country. Poland's struggle became a source not only of national pride but also of ethnic identification and self-esteem in the diaspora.[33]

Chicago's Polish community had largely peasant roots, and the relationship between the peasantry and the gentry—as well as with the larger idea of Poland—proved crucial to any sense of *Polskość* in the new setting. This was especially true in Galicia, where a peasant jacquerie occurred in 1846 in response to a gentry revolt against Hapsburg rule. The peasants, who sided with the Hapsburgs, slaughtered over eleven hundred nobles. Forty years later, however, the peasantry aligned itself with the national undertaking. During the two hundredth anniversary of King Jan Sobieski's victory at Vienna, Polish peasants came to Kraków to celebrate the event. In 1894, the "folk" celebrated the Kosciuszko-led battle for Polish independence and cheered the Polish cause. They flocked to Lwów to see the exhibition and, in particular, the *Racławice Panorama*, which celebrated Kosciuszko's peasant-born scythe men and portrayed him in a traditional peasant coat. The peasantry now embodied the Polish spirit.[34]

Nevertheless, even the image of Kosciuszko was a contested one. Peasants saw him as their liberator, vowing to abolish serfdom, while the gentry saw the hero as a representative of the old noble commonwealth. After emancipation (1848), Galician peasants began to enter the public sphere, not only taking part in politics but also being actively involved in clubs, reading circles, and fraternal organizations. Immigrants carried these new traditions with them to Chicago and established an institutional base that supported churches, schools, fraternal organizations, libraries, and a very active ethnic press. As Keely Stauter-Halsted has pointed out, emancipation altered the power relationship between *szlachta* and peasant creating the possibility of alliances across class lines. Villagers became the focus of Polonization efforts by the upper classes, who wanted their support for the national liberation movement. This is of course what brought Dunikowski to the shores of Lake Michigan. Still, peasant identities remained strong as did regionalisms, whether in Poland or in the diaspora. The acquisition of land, learning a trade, or even moving either to a Polish city or across the ocean to America did not change those basic relationships. A *rodak*, someone from the same village or region, always remained a *rodak*. Others did not fit that category or warrant that special bond.[35]

Importantly, the question of the relationships among Polish-speaking ethnics, Polish Jews, Lithuanians, Belarusians, and Ruthenians (later called Ukrainians) also divided the community. All these groups had been part of the pre-partitioned Polish-Lithuanian Commonwealth. All were also going through the process of developing a national consciousness. What was their relationship in Europe as well as in Chicago? How did they all fit or not fit into the concept of a resurrected Poland? What role would nationalism play? Polish American participation in Polish Day, the Lwów Exposition, and the building of the Kosciuszko monument all tried to answer these questions. Involvement in these events spoke to the larger problem of exactly what was the role of the Polish diaspora in regards to Poland and the emerging independence movement. The diaspora attempted to resolve these issues, in part, through the medium of public demonstrations. The institutional life of the Polish community in Chicago was roughly thirty years old by the 1890s. Some 120,000 Polish speakers lived in the city, and they emerged as a potentially powerful economic force, as well as a political force. The more distant past, but also the events of the late nineteenth century, had a tremendous impact on the future of Chicago's Polish community.

Settling In

Creating Polonia's Capital

But we Poles want to preserve our national identity, which after God, is most dear to us. So dear Reverend Father, have pity on us and send us a Polish priest. . . .

—PIOTR KIOŁBASSA, in a letter to Fr. Hieronim Kajsiewicz, Superior General of the Congregation of the Resurrection in Rome[1]

While Chicago's Polish community might seem unified to out-siders, it rarely was. Polonia was riven by differences in social class, ideology, and politics from the very beginning. Four men would come to symbolize the many fissures within the commu-nity: Antoni Schermann, an early entrepreneur and community activist; Piotr Kiołbassa, a Civil War cavalry officer, politician, and community organizer; Rev. Vincent Barzyński, Polonia's great brick-and-mortar priest (i.e., a builder of churches) and defender of the Catholic faith; and Władysław Dyniewicz, journalist, pub-lisher, and Polish patriot. Together they set the tone for struggling over the idea of just how to be a Pole in America. What was *Polskość* or Polishness? What did the diaspora mean for the homeland? How were Poles to acclimate to Chicago, to America—or should they not?

Doesn't every ethnic immigrant group face these questions? Yes, but these questions were all the sharper for Poles for two reasons: the rigidity of their traditional class and ethnic structures and their lack of a politically independent homeland. Eventually, arguments over what it meant to be Polish in Chicago would tear the community apart and lead to violence in the streets. Rival fraternal groups claimed and built new public spaces, Polish parishes fought and split, and new organizations, including a feminist nationalist one, took shape in the emerging Polish American milieu of the late nineteenth and early twentieth centuries. Differences aren't always destructive; they can lead to growth. Disputes over what it meant to be a Pole in America helped make Chicago the capital of the Polish diaspora.

The roots of this division lay in the historical social structure of the multiethnic Polish-Lithuanian Commonwealth, but the partitions exacerbated the situation. Poland and its many ethnic groups could not fully take part in the modernization and nationalization processes that transformed Europe after the French Revolution. As a result, Polish lands remained behind the times until late in the nineteenth century. The emigration of hundreds of thousands, and then millions, of Poles further transformed the Polish countryside. As Poland changed, so did the emerging Chicago Polonia, which was defined first by immigrants from the Prussian partition and then by those from the Austrian and Russian sectors. Poles came to Chicago from many different Polands. No wonder they often argued.

Pioneers, Chaos, and Conflict

As early as the 1830s, refugees from the Polish-Russian War (1831–33) looked to settle in Illinois. While this colony never came to fruition, some Poles did make their way to the Prairie State and Chicago. Captain John Napieralski, a veteran of the war, is gener-

Anton Schermann's Polish Agency. Schermann operated this immigration bureau and was credited with bringing many Poles to Chicago. He was in many ways a transitional character who provided a bridge between the first wave of European immigrants to Chicago, such as the Germans and Czechs, and the second wave Poles. By the end of his life in 1900, Schermann was definitely identified as a pioneer in the quickly growing Polish community and became one of the wealthiest men in the Polish diaspora. (From the collection of the Polish Museum of America, x2007.001.004.)

ally believed to have been the first Pole to arrive in the city. Little is known of these early settlers, and they developed no sense of a larger community. Some twenty years later, in 1851, Antoni Schermann (sometimes referred to as Sherman, Smagorzewski, or Smarzewski), born about fifty miles outside of Poznań in Prussian Poland in 1818, arrived in the West Town neighborhood with his wife and three children. The neighborhood housed a small and largely German population, and the young ambitious Pole spoke their language. Schermann, a transitional character, maintained ties to that community throughout his lifetime, as his German-language family bible, now in the possession of the Polish Museum in Chicago, shows. A shrewd businessman, he worked with all groups in the area.

At first Schermann was a laborer for the Chicago & Alton Railroad, but in 1867 he opened a tavern and grocery store on Noble Street. The next year, Schermann added a Polish immigration agency to the store. When he first arrived in Chicago, the Northwest Side neighborhood where he settled was rural. A flat plain bordered by the North Branch of the Chicago River with a small woodland, it must have reminded the immigrants of their homeland. About thirty Polish families joined Schermann in Chicago during the early 1860s. This was the beginning of the neighborhood that would emerge as the capital of Polonia.

The small Polish colony to the northwest of Chicago's growing downtown faced a critical problem. The peasant Catholic group could neither go to confession nor celebrate traditional Polish holy days because of a lack of a Polish-speaking priest. So, Schermann hoped to organize a Polish Roman Catholic parish but had difficulty until the arrival of a handsome, charismatic character, Piotr (Peter) Kiołbassa. Kiołbassa, like Schermann, was born in Prussian Poland in 1837. He had come with his parents as part of the Polish migration to Panna Maria, Texas, the first permanent Polish settlement in the United States. At the beginning of the American Civil War, Kiołbassa joined the Texas Cavalry, was captured, and was brought to Illinois, where he then joined the Union Army. He served in the Sixteenth Illinois Cavalry and then as a captain in the Sixth U.S. Colored Cavalry, an African American unit. As a cavalry officer, he cut a dashing figure and fit into the traditional Polish military mystique of the cavalryman.

Schermann and Kiołbassa, who was on leave in Chicago during the winter of 1863–64, organized the St. Stanislaus Kostka Society as the first step in establishing a Polish parish. Kiołbassa contacted his former pastor in Panna Maria, Rev. Leopold Moczygemba, and suggested he quit his Texas mission and come to Chicago. Moczygemba accepted the invitation, albeit on a temporary basis, and arrived during Easter season of that year. Meanwhile, the cavalry officer returned to the front, and Schermann's business affairs diverted him from parish building until Kiołbassa's return in 1866. In that year, a newly reconstituted St. Stanislaus Kostka Society worked toward the establishment of a parish. Most of these early Polish settlers originated from the German or

Piotr Kiołbassa, Polonia pioneer and organizer of St. Stanislaus Kostka Parish. Kiołbassa also initiated Polish participation in the city's political culture. (From the collection of the Polish Museum of America, x2005.001.0406.)

Prussian Partition, understood German, and also felt close ties to their fellow Slavs, the Czechs. Father Francis Molitor, the pastor of the West Side's Czech St. Wenceslaus Parish, offered Mass and preached in Polish at St. Joseph's German Catholic Church. So at that time, Poles often attended German-speaking Catholic parishes, but they wanted a place of their own in which to worship.[2]

Kiołbassa emerged as an important figure in the establishment not only of the parish but also of the growing community. He joined the Chicago police force in 1866 and rose to the rank of sergeant the following year. For years, Kiołbassa ran a notary office in the St. Stanislaus Kostka Parish neighborhood, often referred to in Polish as Stanisławowo. The office, often a gathering place for immigrants looking for help in understanding the ways of the city and the United States, operated as a social service agency, legal aid bureau, and a kind of secular community center for Polonia. He frequently acted as a go-between for newly arrived Polish immigrants and helped them to cope with Chicago and America.

In 1869, Kiołbassa wrote the superior general of the Resurrectionist order, Rev. Jerome Kajsiewicz, asking for a Polish priest to be sent to Chicago. The Congregation of the Resurrection of Our Lord Jesus Christ, which served the small Texas immigrant community from which Kiołbassa had come, was founded in 1836 in Paris by Poles who had left Poland as a result of Poland's defeat in the 1831–33 Russian-Polish War. Kiołbassa received a favorable reply before returning temporarily to Texas. In September 1869, construction began on the new wooden frame church at a cost of $6,885 ($118,959 in 2017). Kiołbassa wrote to Kajsiewicz that the community was made up largely of Poles from Upper Silesia, the Duchy of Poznania, and Kashubia, all in the German Partition. He complained of another group of Poles who had formed the Gmina Polska, a more secular band, in 1866. Władysław Dyniewicz emerged as a leader of this nationalist group dedicated to the resurrection of the Polish state.

When the Resurrectionist Rev. Jan Wołłowski arrived on November 1, 1869, the parish already had a new pastor, much to his disappointment. At first, the administrator of the Chicago Diocese, Rev. John Halligan, appointed Rev. Joseph Juszkiewicz as pastor of the embryonic parish in October. The Resurrectionists did not give up hope in establishing themselves in Chicago, however, and the next year saw a series of moves on the part of the order and their supporters to take control of St. Stanislaus Kostka Parish.

In 1870, the Resurrectionist priest Rev. Adolph Bakanowski arrived from Panna Maria and took up residence with the Stasch family, parishioners of St. Stanislaus Kostka. Kajsiewicz had ordered him to return to Rome, but using the Franco-Prussian War as an excuse, Bakanowski stayed in the United States and made his way to Chicago, where he became involved in the increasingly divided Polish community. Some parishioners wanted Bakanowski to take over the pastorate of St. Stanislaus Kostka. At one point, masked men attacked and beat Rev. Juszkiewicz. Meanwhile Superior General Kajsiewicz once more called Bakanowski to Rome, but the priest again ignored the order. At this time, Kajsiewicz was of the opinion that American Polonia was doomed and that it would soon be assimilated into American society and saw little reason to send priests to serve the community except perhaps to cater to the aged. Bakanowski, however, saw a great opportunity for the Resurrectionists in Chicago. Father Juszkiewicz soon left the parish. He would not be the last Polish pastor to be threatened with violence when various factions in the neighborhood attempted to take control. Finally, Bishop Thomas P. Foley appointed Bakanowski as temporary pastor and invited the Resurrectionists to take over the fledgling parish and attend to Chicago's growing Polonia. The Irish bishop must have hoped to wash his hands of the confusing and constantly warring Poles. Kajsiewicz's visit to the city in July 1871 changed his mind about American Polonia, and he decided to allow Bakanowski to stay and serve the community.

Superior General Kajsiewicz's opinions concerning the Polish diaspora in America shifted dramatically. In fact he had always felt that the Resurrectionists could not abandon the thousands of Poles who lived beyond the borders of partitioned Poland. Kajsiewicz and Bishop Foley successfully negotiated a pact giving the order the right to administer to all non-diocesan Polish parishes in Chicago for ninety-nine years. Earlier, the Gmina Polska leader, Dyniewicz, and his allies insisted on wording the deed to the church so that only Poles could use it. The bishop disagreed and refused to consecrate the church. The Resurrectionists, however, agreed to the bishop's demands and carried the day by handing the parish deed to Foley. This pact proved to be a great victory for Schermann, Kiołbassa, and the Resurrectionists as opposed to the Gmina Polska. The local Catholic diocese in America, not parishioners or some benefactor, held title to parish property. The Gmina Polska faction wanted the community to own the property and thus have total control over the parish.[3]

The argument between the Gmina Polska and the Resurrectionists grew and again threatened violence in the neighborhood. The confusing ideological split between the two parties centered on the idea of Polishness or *Polskość*. Was a Pole first and foremost a Roman Catholic or was he or she a nationalist dedicated to the reestablishment of Poland? Could a Pole be a non-Catholic or even an atheist? Around these competing ideas emerged one of the most fearsome intra-ethnic disputes in American history. Certainly, both groups agreed on the preservation of a Polish identity in the United States, but the clerical group saw being Catholic as most important. Also, many in the Gmina Polska saw emigration to the United States as only temporary. They felt that all Poles would return to Poland once the occupying powers had been vanquished.

The conflict was based on historical experience. The Polish-Lithuanian Commonwealth, which had been partitioned by its neighbors at the end of the eighteenth century, contained many ethnic groups, including Poles, Lithuanians, Ruthenians (Ukrainians), White Russians, Germans, Czechs, Slovaks, Armenians, Jews, and others. Traditionally, these were all subjects of the Polish state. Increasingly, though, as the nineteenth century progressed, a more modern idea of nationality arose in the Polish lands, which identified Polish-language speakers as true Poles. The simultaneous and parallel budding nationalism of Lithuanians and Ukrainians furthered this definition, and these two groups began to speak of their own nations. The rise of Zionism also entered the picture, as the Polish lands included the world's largest population of Jews. For the Gmina Polska, a simple definition sufficed. If one believed in the resurrection of the Polish state, then one was a Pole. For the emerging clerical party, a true Pole spoke Polish and was a Roman Catholic.[4]

The Foley-Kajsiewicz agreement further alienated the nationalist faction, especially Dyniewicz. Shortly thereafter, Kiołbassa returned to Chicago from Texas. Dyniewicz claimed that the Resurrectionists and their adherents, the St. Stanislaus Kostka Society, had become involved in a conspiracy with Chicago's Irish hierarchy to exploit the Poles and to have them assimilated into American society. Dyniewicz then encouraged Gmina Polska members to establish themselves in various parish societies, especially the newly organized St. Joseph Society.

About fifteen hundred families belonged to the young parish in 1871, and Fr. Bakanowski soon found himself overwhelmed by his responsibilities. The Great Chicago Fire of that year had created a need for labor in the city, and more Poles flocked to Stanisławowo. The parish facilities quickly proved inadequate for the rapidly growing Polish population, and rumors of a new parish spread through the neighborhood. Given the past agitation by the Gmina Polska, it was obvious that such a move would again cause conflict. Meanwhile, the Gmina Polska–dominated St. Joseph Society agitated for a new parish and raised $10,000 ($193,101 in 2017) to purchase a tract of land just three blocks south of St. Stanislaus Kostka. This caused an eruption between the two factions, as the Resurrectionists saw it as a major provocation.[5]

Meanwhile, in Union, Missouri, far from Stanisławowo, a newspaper called *Pielgrzym* (The pilgrim) appeared, edited by the Rev. Alexander Matuszek, a Jesuit priest, and John Barzyński, the brother of a Resurrectionist priest, Fr. Vincent Barzyński. The paper seemed to signal an alliance between the two orders. Dyniewicz felt that *Pielgrzym* favored a policy of assimilation and feared an Irish-Resurrectionist-Jesuit plot to control American Polonia. John Barzyński stated openly his feelings about American Polonia and editorialized in *Pielgrzym* that the newspaper would always work on behalf of the Polish community, but any Pole born in the United States could never be a European Pole. Here appeared a major split in the diaspora: Barzyński wanted all Poles in the United States to preserve their Catholic faith, learn the language and history of Poland, and at the same time become good Americans. For the youthful editor, Catholicism stood at the center of his idea of what it meant to be Polish. Father Vincent Barzyński not only agreed with his brother's editorial policy but also used *Pielgrzym* to attack the Gmina Polska and like organizations, which the clerical party often referred to as Masonic and socialistic in nature. The priest called for a Resurrectionist-Jesuit alliance to save souls in the diaspora. This policy of assimilation won over many adherents who felt the emigration was more or less permanent and that a Polish national liberation and the subsequent return of immigrants seemed far-fetched.

Meanwhile, back in Chicago, Fr. Bakanowski became emboldened and moved against the St. Joseph Society and their efforts to create a competing parish. The priest received various anonymous letters advising him to stop his attacks. Bakanowski ignored these and then received death threats. Of course, the pastor remembered what had happened to his predecessor, Fr. Juszkiewicz, and began carrying a revolver. The St. Joseph Society then seceded from St. Stanislaus Kostka Parish and founded another parish, Holy Trinity, just three blocks south, creating the parish village of Trójcowo. Thus, began a twenty-year struggle that tore Chicago's Polonia apart. The Gmina Polska arranged to have the new parish's deed to the property made out in the name of the St. Joseph Society. The trustees of the new church, built in 1873, refused to sign the title of the property over to the diocese. Bishop Foley declined to consecrate the new church and insisted on Resurrectionist control. In 1880, Fr. Albert Mielcuszny became pastor without being recognized by the bishop and Foley immediately excommunicated him.

Bakanowski, worn out by the constant conflict and possibly afraid for his life, resigned his post and returned to Texas. The Resurrectionists sent Fr. Felix Zwiardowski to be pastor of St. Stanislaus Kostka Parish. He offered to retain Holy Trinity, but only as a mission of St. Stanislaus Kostka Parish. The organizers of Holy Trinity responded by creating a Committee of Public Safety to keep the Resurrectionist order out of their church. Zwiardowski soon also returned to Texas. Reverend Symon Wieczorek replaced him, but lasted only eight weeks before also retreating to the Lone Star State. In five years, four pastors had tried to serve the turbulent community. It seemed as if the Resurrectionists would give up the parish. In the autumn of 1874, the thirty-six-year-old Fr. Vincent Barzyński made his way to Chicago in hope of calming the waters and holding onto the Resurrectionist beachhead in Chicago.[6]

Barzyński's arrival proved to be fortuitous for the Resurrectionist cause. It heralded an era of unprecedented institutional growth for both his religious order and Chicago's Polonia. The young, energetic priest took control of St. Stanislaus Kostka Parish and placed it on a firm footing. He was born in the Austrian Partition in 1838 and ordained in 1861; he participated in the January 1863 uprising in the Russian partition. Two years later, he became a member of the Resurrectionist Order and was sent to Texas in 1866 to serve the Polish immigrant community there. After coming to Chicago, Barzyński saw the need for Polish institutional development tied to the Catholic Church. He channeled his energy into the creation of churches, schools, religious societies, fraternal organizations, welfare agencies, orphanages, and hospitals across Chicago's Polonia. The growth of various parish organizations is testament to Barzyński's methods and the organizational ability of his parishioners. No other Polish Catholic priest came close to his accomplishments as a brick-and-mortar priest, defined as one who built the physical infrastructure of institutions. Many Poles ostracized those who disagreed with Barzyński's hierarchical approach. The pastor saw socialism, masonry, and anarchy as the most powerful enemies of his flock and was not reluctant to accuse those who opposed his methods with these "sins." An uncompromising leader, he and his brothers, Rev. Joseph Barzyński, a priest but not a Resurrectionist, and John, a devoted Catholic journalist, moved against the Gmina Polska and the secular nationalists.

In October 1873, John Barzyński proposed a national organiza-

The Barzyński Brothers with their father. The three Barzyński brothers had a tremendous impact on the development of Chicago's Polonia. *From left to right,* Father Joseph Barzyński Jr., Father Vincent Barzyński, CR, Joseph Barzynski Sr., and John Barzyński. (Photo: W. M. Rozanski, Washington Photo Studio. From the collection of the Polish Museum of America, x2005.001.0046.)

tion to unite all Poles in America. Several months earlier, Fr. Theodore Gieryk had also called for a national organization. He made contact with Resurrectionists in Chicago in an attempt to promote his project. In December 1873, after talking to John Barzyński, Gieryk organized a meeting in Detroit. The meeting almost broke up over an argument between nationalists and those who favored a more Catholic organization. Nevertheless, a new organization appeared and the participants agreed to meet again the following October in Chicago. St. Stanislaus Kostka Parish hosted the gathering a month after Vincent Barzyński's installation as pastor in the divided parish.

The second convention in 1874 established the organizations goals, which mirrored those of the Resurrectionist order. The association vowed to preserve the Catholic faith and the Polish culture of the immigrants. Its objectives included the creation of Polish parishes, parochial schools, libraries, hospitals, convents, and a teachers' college. John Barzyński moved his newspaper to Detroit that same year and renamed it *Gazeta Polska Katolicka*. Members also adopted the official title of the Polish Roman Catholic Union of America (PRCUA) as the first national society of Poles in the United States.

The PRCUA held its convention in Milwaukee the following year. That meeting proved more contentious, as the issue of *Polskość* came up yet again. This time, Fr. Gieryk and Fr. Dominik Majer proposed that non-Catholics be allowed to join the organization. The Catholic Barzyński group defeated the nationalists, and Gieryk left the PRCUA. Majer stayed on initially but left in 1880 to join the new Polish National Alliance (PNA). Father Vincent Barzyński now controlled the PRCUA and shifted its focus to the needs of the Polish immigrant community rather than on the quest for Polish independence as the nationalists, both secular and clerical, had hoped the organization would.

In May 1875, Władysław Dynniewicz reacted to the creation of the PRCUA by calling for the formation of a rival organization based on nationalist principles and open to all who believed in Polish independence, regardless of their religious beliefs. The appeal, however, failed. Three years later, Henryk Kałussowski, a longtime Polish patriot and activist, wrote to his comrade from the 1863 rebellion, Agaton Giller, in Rapperswil, Switzerland, calling for the establishment of a patriotic organization among Polish immigrants in the United States. Giller responded to this appeal by publishing a long letter in the Lwów press, which also appeared in Polish American newspapers under the title "The Organization of Poles in America." Giller urged Polish immigrants to join mainstream American society and saw the proposed organization as one dedicated to the idea of Polish independence. His appeal proved very effective, as it united the material goals of the immigrants for a better life and the patriotic aspirations of the secular leadership. When a famine struck Polish Silesia in 1879, American Poles raised money to help those affected. This crisis provided a foundational moment for what became known as the Polish National Alliance. Its organizers held a meeting in Philadelphia in February 1880. Giller praised it for its potential to unite Poles and Lithuanians in America for the Polish cause. On June 3, 1880, Dyniewicz's *Gazeta Polska* published the Philadelphia call for creating the PNA. The following month, at a meeting held in Michał Majewski's tavern, a favorite meeting place of the Gmina Polska, organizers requested for the first PNA convention to be held in Chicago.

The first PNA convention opened in Chicago on September 20, 1880, with a religious service at St. Wenceslaus Church, a Czech parish on the West Side. The church provided a neutral, but Catholic, place for the group sparring with the Barzyński brothers. After the Mass, delegates and nonvoting members went to the Palmer House, then Chicago's most prestigious hotel, to conduct the first *Sejm* (congress). Gmina Polska members dominated the meeting. The constitution of the newborn PNA promised support for Polish independence, something the PRCUA did not do, and also the establishment of an insurance fund for immigrants. The aims of the organization, however, remained a continuing subject of debate, and the relationship with the Catholic Church constantly provided a point of conflict. Many of the founders were anticlerical to say the least. They resented the power of the clergy and their involvement in political and nonreligious affairs.

The PNA established its headquarters at 338 South Clark Street in Chicago's Loop. Later, it rented office space in the heart of the

Polish neighborhood on the Northwest Side. Both the PNA and PRCUA recognized Chicago as the obvious capital of American Polonia. Also, Polish Chicagoans controlled many of the important offices of both organizations and wielded power. While religious issues remained a bone of contention, the real difference between the two organizations was how they defined *Polskość*. What did it mean to be Polish? This was a question both in Poland and across the diaspora. Nationalists claimed that Jews, Protestants, Orthodox Christians, and even nonbelievers of every possible stripe could be Polish as long as they yearned and worked for a free and independent Poland. It was not that the Resurrectionists and the PRCUA did not also hope for Polish independence, but they saw Catholicism as the defining aspect of identity in the lives of Poles in both Poland and abroad. Members of the PNA, for the most part devout Catholics, denied the authority of priests to influence their political goals. They refused to be told who could and who could not be members of their organization, and they made Polish independence their first objective. This might seem like a strange ideological disagreement for modern ears, but it stood at the heart of the conflict.

Giller and the other Rapperswil Poles, in exile in the West after the failed 1863 insurrection, advised the American Poles not to break with the Roman Catholic Church but to embrace it as an ally. This became a very difficult thing to do at times, given the intransigence of Barzyński and the Resurrectionists about Roman Catholic identity. Many PNA members also embraced the romantic ideals of the Polish insurrectionists, while the PRCUA leadership took a different approach, calling for "organic" work to rebuild the Polish nation. The two groups also differed on their attitude toward the diaspora. The PNA originally saw it as temporary and believed that once Poland regained its independence immigrants would return to the homeland. The PRCUA recognized that the immigration was more or less permanent.[7]

Nowhere did this breach become more intense than in the struggle over Holy Trinity Parish. In 1893, the Vatican, troubled by the ethnic conflict that seemed to threaten the American Church, sent a Papal Ablegate (Delegate), Archbishop Francis Satolli, to the United States to address the issue. The Papal Ablegate ended the conflict over Holy Trinity by siding with the nationalist faction and installing the Holy Cross Fathers in the parish rather than handing it over to Barzyński and the Resurrectionists.

On Monday, June 5, 1893, Holy Trinity reopened as a parish of the Archdiocese of Chicago. Archbishop Satolli arrived at 7:00 a.m. to offer a devotion in the church. Many attended, despite the fact that the time and day of the week made it difficult for the working-class men and women of the neighborhood to join in the celebration. Members of the PNA and the various parish societies gathered and stood in military fashion and then marched from Milwaukee Avenue to the doors of the place of worship. The appointment of Rev. Casimir Sztuczko, a member of the Holy Cross Fathers, as pastor proved to be important not only for the parish but also for the nationalist movement. Holy Trinity now became a bastion for the PNA and guaranteed at least the tacit approval of the organization by the Vatican. The PNA, however, maintained its insistence on the separation between the church and secular matters even as it retained the blessing of the church in the public's eye.[8]

Satolli's verdict did not end the dispute, and the Papal Ablegate did not give in on the matter of the ownership of the parish property, which the American Catholic Church recognized as its special privilege. Among the more ardent nationalists, the issue continued to fester and resulted in more conflict. This struggle led to increased violence across American Polonia and to the eventual creation of the Polish National Catholic Church in schism with Rome. While the Satolli settlement brought a cautious calm to the neighborhood, it did little to alleviate the ever-sharpening debate over *Polskość* and the place of Poles in the American Catholic Church.

Reverend Vincent Barzyński called for an organization to bring together the various factions in Polonia to stem the surge of independent Catholic parishes resulting from this conflict. He proposed an umbrella organization, Liga Polska (Polish League), that would stand above all factions. Organizers held the first convention in May 1894, but nationalists soon saw Barzyński's hand behind an effort to seize the organization for the clerical party and walked out. In turn, Piotr Kiołbassa and the St. Stanislaus Kostka group captured most of the elected offices. While the more conservative faction of the PNA stayed in the league, many nationalists joined the independent church movement. The magnetic cause of Polish independence shaped the responses of the fraternal organizations, especially the PNA. The ideological divide now threatened the relationship between the Polish nation and the Roman Catholic Church.[9]

Meanwhile, Kiołbassa continued in leadership positions both within Polonia and in the city's political sphere. In 1878, he ran as a Republican for the Illinois State Legislature and was the first Pole to be elected to that body. After losing to August J. Kowalski, another Republican, in the Sixteenth Ward Aldermanic race in 1888, he bolted to the Democratic Party and was the first Polish Chicagoan to win citywide office as city treasurer in 1891. He earned the nickname Honest Pete because he returned interest earned on city funds to the public rather than pocketing it himself as had been tradition. Kiołbassa's election marked the beginning of the so-called Polish Block in the city's Democratic Party. Finally, in 1896, Kiołbassa captured the position of alderman of the Sixteenth Ward and later served as Chicago's commissioner of public works from 1902 to 1904 before he died in 1905.[10]

Polish Women

Both religious and secular female-centered institutions sprang up in Chicago. Catholic sisterhoods played a crucial role in the development of Polonia, including the Felician Sisters, Sisters of the Holy Family of Nazareth, the Franciscan Sisters of Chicago, and the Sisters of the Resurrection. Polish nuns became more influential in America than in Europe, where German and Russian authorities frequently banned them for nationalist activity. In the Austro-Hungarian Empire, they had more freedom because of Catholic Hapsburg society. When the Russian government barred the Felicians in 1864 as a result of the Polish insurrection, the order reestablished itself in Kraków in Galicia. Polish women created other sisterhoods abroad, and these often turned toward serving the Polish diaspora.

Polish nuns played a crucial role in maintaining a sense of *Polskość* and later as a bridge to the wider American Catholic community. In 1874, Fr. Józef Dąbrowski invited the Felician Sisters to come to the United States. They soon operated schools in Chicago and were followed in 1885 by the Sisters of the Holy Family of Nazareth. In 1900, the Resurrection Sisters arrived in the city. They established schools throughout Chicago and the United States. By 1909, the Felician sisters alone were teaching thirty-six thousand children in ninety-eight schools across the United States. The Felicians helped to socialize immigrants into a confusing urban industrial world. The order grew rapidly in the United States, and its success in Chicago and other Polonia centers resulted from the recruitment of a generation of American-born women. In Poland, the order drew its membership largely from the upper classes, but in the United States, most Felician sisters came from the immigrant working class. Becoming a nun provided upward mobility for these young women and afforded a socially acceptable and relatively inexpensive way to gain an education and leave the world of the factory behind. Early on, these schools came under attack by both religious and lay critics. Young girls, who had little education, often filled the ranks of these orders. Overcrowded classrooms and poorly written textbooks plagued the schools, and some observers claimed that these young nuns were able to make neither good Poles nor good Catholics out of their students.

In 1881, Josephine Dudzik arrived in the United States, along with her parents, to join three of her sisters who had immigrated to Chicago earlier. She had been born in Płocicz in Prussian-occupied Poland in 1860. At an early age, service to the poor and elderly drew Dudzik. On her arrival in the city at the age of twenty-one, she joined the Third Order of St. Francis, a religious society. When her father died in 1889, she continued to take care of her mother but opened her small apartment to poor women, allowing them to stay in her family's small living quarters. After a while, Dudzik decided to rent or purchase a home in St. Stan-islaus Kostka Parish as a shelter for the poor and elderly. She and her Third Order colleagues approached Rev. Barzyński with the idea. The pastor encouraged the project but insisted that the young women organize as a religious congregation. They became known as the Franciscan Sisters of Blessed Kunegunda in 1894, and Dudzik took the name of Sister Mary Theresa. The new order opened the St. Joseph Home for the Aged and Crippled in 1897 in the Avondale neighborhood. They later launched the St. Vin-cent Orphan Asylum and the Guardian Angel Home for Working Women and Day Care Center in the Back of the Yards neighbor-hood in order to better serve the poor of the Polish community.[11]

Secular Polish immigrant women in Chicago formed the Pol-ish Women's Alliance (PWA) in 1898 as a response to the refusal of the PNA and the PRCUA to accept women members or allow women to buy life insurance except through their husbands. Many young single Polish immigrant women arrived in the city, and while they often married shortly after their arrival, they could not purchase death benefits. As the new institution solved that problem, it also turned to other matters. The PWA appeared as the Progressive movement became a major social, political, and cultural force in society, and its members embraced many of the same goals as the reformers concerning women and children. In particular, the PWA espoused the aims of the movement's feminist leadership, especially Jane Addams. The organization vigorously supported women's rights and the education and protection of children. It campaigned against abusive husbands and played an important role in the emerging Polish independence movement. Its newspaper, *Głos Polek* (The voice of Polish women), combined nationalism, ethnic solidarity, and the emancipation of women to form its focus. The PWA also supported the labor movement and campaigned against the abuse of alcohol in the community. In 1900, largely in response to the Polish Women's Alliance, the PNA finally allowed women to join their ranks, but the PWA still grew into the third largest fraternal organization in Polonia.[12]

The Polish Church Wars in Chicago

By the late 1870s, Poles had spread across the city into neighborhoods beyond the confines of the city's first Polish parish. Again, any Polish community was largely defined by the organizing of a Polish Catholic parish. In 1874, Poles founded St. Adalbert's (in Polish, *Sw. Wojciecha*) in Pilsen on Chicago's Lower West Side.[13] The Resurrectionists gave Rev. John Klimecki the task of organizing the new parish. By late 1874, construction began on a brick church on Seventeenth and Paulina Streets. Only the substructure of the church had been built by 1884, but in June of that year, Archbishop Patrick A. Feehan dedicated an imposing red brick church, the first such structure for Pilsen's Poles, who called their neighborhood Wojciechowo, after the parish.[14]

Residents of Wojciechowo often found jobs in the garment industry along Halsted Street, the lumberyards along the South Branch of the Chicago River, the West Side railroad yards, and at the McCormick Reaper Works on Blue Island Avenue to the southwest, all of which were within walking distance or an easy streetcar ride from the neighborhood. Defined as unskilled labor, they eventually made their way into nearby Bridgeport and Back of the Yards, where they worked in the Union Steel Rolling Mill at Archer and Ashland and in meatpacking plants. Like the older Northwest Side settlement, Wojciechowo quickly developed institutionally. Labor strife immediately affected the Lower West Side community. In 1876, Pilsen's Poles joined their Czech coworkers in a walkout in the nation's largest lumberyards. "Communistic" agitators supposedly led the strikers. The following year, the Great

Railroad Strike rocked the country, and police with the help of the military put down the strike. They fought the lumber shovers (men who unload lumber to or from boats, storage, or mills), railroad workers, and a large group of rolling mill and packinghouse men in the so-called Battle of the Viaduct. Poles and Czechs made up many of the dead and wounded. The next year, the *Tribune* again pointed to Polish and Czech support for the city's socialists. By 1881, observers wrote that the two Slavic groups dominated the lumber industry in Pilsen and the Lower West Side.[15]

Along with this rise in class consciousness, Wojciechowo saw an upsurge in Polish nationalism that paralleled the clashes that had occurred on the Northwest Side. The Gmina Polska always had a presence in St. Adalbert's, but the nationalist hold on parishioners increased as the nineteenth century progressed. In 1887, St. Adalbert's priests refused to mark the death of the great Polish writer Józef Ignacy Kraszewski. Divisions in Chicago mirrored those back in Galicia. Eight years previously, Kraków's bishop Albin Dunajewski showed little support for the 1879 celebration of Kraszewski's work. The writer had refused to go to confession and receive the Eucharist before that celebration began. Saint Adalbert's parishioners organized a march to the predominantly Irish Jesuit-run parish, Holy Family Church, on Twelfth Street (Roosevelt Road) to celebrate a High Mass for the deceased poet. Eighteen societies, made up of some three thousand men marched from Seventeenth and Paulina Streets to Holy Family. After the Mass, the group processed to the Twelfth Street German Turner Hall and held literary readings. The poet Teofila Samolińska read a letter she had received from Kraszewski. Her reading was followed by various speeches and the reading of telegrams sent by priests who belonged to the Polish National Alliance stating their regret that they could not attend to celebrate the "greatest poet of the nineteenth century." The celebration ended with the singing of the traditional Polish hymn "Boże Coś Polskę" (God Bless Poland).[16]

This would not be the final clash between parishioners and

their clergy. In 1888, the pastor of St. Adalbert's, Rev. John Radziejewski, attempted to take control of the Towarzystwo Świetego Imienia Pana Jezusa (the Brotherhood of the Holy Name of Jesus), a lay parish organization. This resulted in a rebellion of roughly two thousand parishioners. Radziejewski refused confession to some 150 members of the congregation. The group's original constitution listed no provision to place the society under the control of either the parish or the archdiocese. In January 1888, the pastor moved to take control by introducing several amendments to the bylaws to give him power to attend all meetings, veto any proceedings, and make decisions about who could be a new member. According to one of the proposed bylaws, members who had failed to attend either of two celebrations held by the society during the year had to make confession in order to be approved by the pastor at the next meeting. After a vote in August 1888 defeated the proposed amendments, Radziejewski again denied confession to his opposition. Further, the priest forbade the use of church property by the society and withdrew church membership from his opponents. The membership claimed in vain that this was a matter outside of the Catholic Church's jurisdiction. On September 8, the priest's supporters met and approved the amendments and elected a new leadership. The next day the majority of members met and nullified the September 8 election, electing their own slate. The minority refused to recognize the second election and appropriated the charter. By January 1890, the quarrel came before Cook County Illinois Circuit Court Judge Richard Tuthill. He ruled that the September 8 meeting had been illegal and declared the September 9 election valid. The court further held that the society was for the benefit of widows and children, not a religious institution, and ruled that Radziejewski had no right to interfere in the society's proceedings or dictate to the membership.[17]

While Polonia would always remain largely loyal to the Church of Rome, laypeople often did not welcome what it considered the "tyranny" of the priesthood. This resulted in the independent church movement and eventually led to the creation of the Polish National Catholic Church in schism with Rome.[18] In April 1895, after a long drawn-out battle between many of the parishioners of St. Hedwig's Parish and the pastor, a group of Northwest Side Poles decided to create an independent parish. They dedicated a temporary chapel on June 12, the Feast of Corpus Christi. The action was a result of a disagreement over parish finances with Fr. Joseph Barzyński, the pastor of St. Hedwig Parish and brother of Rev. Vincent Barzyński. Several riots occurred, and a group of parishioners left St. Hedwig's. By August, they laid the cornerstone of a permanent church building at Lubeck and Robey Streets (now Dickens and Damen Avenue). One hundred police gathered at the local police station, fearing rioting between those supporting the former assistant pastor at St. Hedwig's, who now served as the new pastor of the breakaway parish, Rev. Anthony Kozłowski, and those favoring Barzyński.

On November 10, 1895, parishioners dedicated a permanent edifice for All Saints Church, built at a cost of $35,000 ($964,994 in 2017). The parish of some 1,750 families also purchased twenty-eight acres for a cemetery, as the now excommunicated parishioners could not be buried in a Roman Catholic graveyard. A parade of Polish civic and military societies preceded the dedication of All Saints. Military organizations opened a path through the immense crowd to allow some three hundred schoolchildren to proceed from the temporary chapel to the new church. Clergymen followed and the overflow crowd filled the church and street. While this parish initially remained loyal to Catholic doctrine and theology, it refused to acknowledge the authority of the Chicago Archdiocese.

In the summer of 1897, the Parish of All Saints, together with other local independent Polish parishes, elected Kozłowski as bishop. On November 21, he was consecrated in the schismatic Old Catholic Cathedral of Bern, Switzerland, by the Rt. Rev. Edward Herzog, bishop of Switzerland. Three bishops of the Old Catholic Church assisted in the ceremony. Accordingly, the Parish of All

Saints became a Polish Parish of the Old Catholic Church. Bishop Kozłowski died in 1907, and two years later, All Saints Parish joined the newly formed Polish National Catholic Church.[19] The Polish church wars rocked Polonia and the American Catholic Church. The conflict largely ensued over what some considered the loyalty of Polish priests to the Irish-dominated Catholic hierarchy and the authoritarianism and arrogance of the Resurrectionist order. Rebellions against pastors broke out across Chicago's Polonia including St. Joseph's in Back of the Yards and St. Josephat's on the Northwest Side.[20]

The conflict also resulted from the refusal of the American Catholic hierarchy to consecrate a Polish bishop. The peculiar reality of the Catholic Church in the United States proved to be problematic not only because of the Irish-dominated hierarchy but also because of the increasingly Catholic immigrant groups arriving in the United States after 1890. The issue of Americanization divided Church leadership. Conservatives encouraged the preservation of ethnic cultures. Progressive bishops hoped to make the Catholic Church an American institution and frowned on the growth of parishes organized by individual national groups such as the Poles, Germans, or Czechs. They especially opposed the appointment of specifically ethnic bishops and maintained that all bishops should serve all Catholics. In part, this resulted from the fact that the dominant Protestant culture in America remained largely hostile to the Church of Rome. The Irish understood this and did not see the language preservation of new immigrants as an important concern but, instead, worried about the survival of Catholicism in America. Liberals also pointed out that the goal of converting Protestants would be hurt if the Church remained a foreign institution and was seen as a menace by native-born Americans.

The hierarchy saw integration and assimilation of the immigrant communities as its ultimate goal. To the contrary, Polonia's clerical party hoped to maintain Polish culture in the United States while integrating immigrants into the larger social structure. Nationalists, led by the Polish National Alliance, rejected any talk of assimilation. Polish clerics felt that, without the preservation of immigrant cultures, they might lose many to the independent church movement and saw the appointment of a Polish bishop as a way to give the Polish community more of a voice in the American Church.[21]

Father Vincent Barzyński had proven to be the leading pastor of Chicago's Poles. He fought the nationalists on all fronts, and his anger toward the independent church movement knew no bounds. The priest organized the Polish Roman Catholic Union and several national congresses to deal with the problem. Barzyński died from pneumonia on May 2, 1899, at the age of sixty-one. This was a great shock to Polonia in general and to the clerical party in particular. None would match the accomplishments of Barzyński, who defined the future growth of Polonia for several generations by establishing Polish Catholic parishes across the city and leading a congregation of nearly fifty thousand St. Stanislaus Kostka parishioners, perhaps the largest Catholic congregation in the world at the time.[22]

A Polish American Bishop

The various conflicts in Polonia eventually resulted in the ordination of Bishop Paul Rhode in 1908. Rhode was born in 1871 in Wejherowo (Neustadt) in the Kashubia region, near Gdańsk, in German Poland. He became a priest on June 16, 1894, and joined St. Adalbert's Parish as an assistant to Rev. Radziejewski. The Poles of the McKinley Park neighborhood petitioned for a parish, and Radziejewski championed his assistant for the position of pastor. Within a year's time, Archbishop Patrick A. Feehan asked the newly minted priest to organize a parish in the neighborhood just northwest of the Union Stock Yard. The young priest took on the job and helped to establish a church on Thirty-Sixth and Charlton Streets (now Justine Street) in what would later be the Central Manufacturing District. He celebrated the first Mass on December 22, 1895, and held regular services from that point on. The consecration of the parish church was planned for 1896. Polish Catholics from St. Adalbert's and from nearby Back of the Yards and Bridgeport took part in a celebration and the blessing of the church bell. A Polish patriot, Rhode often spoke at events marking important events in Polish history. A young, smart, energetic priest, he later took charge of St. Michael's in the Bush neighborhood adjacent to the giant Illinois Steel Company's plant (U.S. Steel's South Works). Under his leadership, the parish grew from five hundred families to twelve hundred. In 1907, he announced the construction of a new large church building to be constructed at Eighty-Third Street and Bond Avenue (South Shore Drive). During the erection of the huge neo-Gothic cathedral-like structure, his fellow Polish priests nominated Rhode as the first Polish bishop in the United States.[23]

Polish priests in the United States had a poor reputation in Rome. Even Mieczysław Cardinal Ledóchowski, the highest-ranking Polish prelate in the Vatican, questioned the quality of Polonia's priests. The many conflicts and riots and the independent church movement did not reflect well on the clergy. Polish American efforts for *równouprawnienie*, or equality in the Church, hardly seemed likely to succeed. Though Barzyński had often been recognized as the de facto bishop of Polonia, his one attempt to become a bishop in 1890 failed and he instead pursued accommodation with the local archbishop. With Barzyński's death, however, the call for a Polish American bishop increased. Soon two priests began to emerge as candidates. Neither was a Resurrectionist and both proved to be more open to nationalists. The priest, journalist, and historian Wacław Kruszka of Milwaukee, himself often a controversial figure, and the Rev. Casimir Sztuczko took up the mantle of leadership of Polonia's clergy. Kruszka, the most prolific spokesperson for the Polish community in the early twentieth century, called for ecclesiastical equality for Poles. He created a propaganda campaign aimed at forcing the Irish hierarchy in America to appoint a Polish bishop and proposed that bishops must be multilingual in the diverse dioceses of the United States.

In 1901, the Second Polish Catholic Congress elected Rev. Sztuczko as national secretary of the Executive Committee. Stopping the independent church movement provided the main order of business. Accordingly, representatives introduced the concept of ecclesiastical equity to the congress, which in turn authorized Kruszka and Rev. Jan Pitass of Buffalo to take Polonia's case to the American archbishops and eventually the Vatican. A memorial dated November 10, 1901, called for the appointment of auxiliary Polish bishops in those dioceses with large Polish immigrant populations. They did not call for a national bishop for all the Poles in the country or a separate ethnic diocese but argued that the appointment of numerous bishops throughout the country would stop the movement toward schism. American archbishops, who took a strictly legalistic stance, refused and stated that it was not up to them to appoint auxiliary bishops.

This denial led to Kruszka embarking on a policy of intrigue. He convinced the German American archbishop Fredrick Katzer of Milwaukee to forward a petition to the Vatican that called for Polish ordinaries or auxiliary bishops in twelve diocese including Chicago and Milwaukee. Katzer and Ledóchowski met, but the aging Ledóchowski died suddenly afterward. Katzer returned home, and the following summer he died as well. In 1903, Polish American clerics authorized both Kruszka and Pitass to represent them at the Vatican. On July 1, 1903, Franciszek Albin Cardinal Symon, himself a Pole and the personal representative of Pope Leo XIII, granted Kruszka an audience. After the pope's death and the election of Pope Pius X, Kruszka resumed his campaign and finally received an interview with the pontiff on April 15, 1904. The pope told Kruszka that the matter would somehow be resolved. Meanwhile, in Scranton, Pennsylvania, Rev. Francis Hodur formulated a national appeal for the creation of the Polish National Catholic Church, and the feared schism became a reality.

Finally, in 1905, the Vatican sent Cardinal Symon on a tour

of American Polonia. In Chicago, he extolled the Resurrectionists, praising their accomplishments and service to the Church and Polonia, but made no announcement about a Polish bishop. On returning to Rome, Symon presented a report that called for the appointment of Polish auxiliary bishops in several American cities. The Office of the Propaganda of the Faith accepted the recommendation and instructed Archbishop James Quigley of Chicago to call for an election by the Polish pastors of Chicago of a Polish priest to become a bishop. Quigley proved to be a champion of the Polish cause and had earlier spoke out in favor of *równouprawnienie*. He scheduled the election for August 16, 1907, at the parish hall of Holy Name Cathedral and reminded the pastors that the newly elected bishop would serve the entire diocese and not just Poles. Quigley also enforced a one-man, one-vote rule and did not allow the largest parishes to dominate the proceedings. Twenty-six of the thirty-two Polish pastors voted for Paul Rhode of St. Michael's Parish.[24]

On July 28, 1908, Rhode left his parish for Holy Name Cathedral accompanied by his mother, Mrs. Christine Rhode. After arriving at the rectory, a platoon of mounted police and seven hundred priests and bishops, as well as members of the major Polish American organizations, escorted him to the cathedral. Archbishop Quigley presided over the ceremony and Archdiocesan Chancellor E. M. Dunne of Chicago read the papal elevation of Rhode to bishop proclaiming him titular bishop of Barca and auxiliary bishop of the Archdiocese of Chicago. A Pontifical High Mass followed, and at the close of the Mass the procession exited the cathedral as the choir sang "Boże Coś Polskę." People wept as the song ended the ancient ritual. A banquet for the attending clergy followed the Mass. Father Francis Wojtalewicz, of Immaculate Conception, BVM, Parish in South Chicago, served as toastmaster. He commented that the eyes of eight million Poles living in the United States were all on Chicago.

After the banquet, Bishop Rhode returned to South Chicago,

where his parishioners erected triumphal arches and crowds filled the streets. As the new bishop appeared, the bands blared out, the people cheered, the church bells pealed, and even the mighty whistles of the nearby South Works shrieked out to welcome and congratulate the prelate. After the benediction of the Blessed Sacrament and the blessing of the crowd, Rhode hurried to nearby Immaculate Conception Parish to repeat the ceremony. From there he rushed to the Polish Northwest Side for the evening festivities.

That evening's events began with another parade, as some twenty thousand men in uniform made their way through the streets of Chicago to mark Rhode's ordination. Nearly two hundred thousand people celebrated throughout the Northwest Side's Sixteenth and Seventeenth Wards. Residents decorated thousands of houses along the parade route and throughout the neighborhood with bunting, flags, and flowers. Bands played, and fireworks thrilled the crowds as the joyous fete played its way through the night. Many wore buttons with Rhode's image and a red and white streamer attached. At St. Stanislaus Kostka Parish, the newly anointed bishop addressed some ten thousand people in the schoolyard. Then thirteen hundred people attended a banquet that lasted to well past midnight.[25]

Although for some it was not enough recognition for Polonia, the importance of these events cannot be underestimated. Still, the feeling that Poles had been dismissed by the Catholic Church's Irish and German leadership did not disappear. On July 15, 1915, Bishop Rhode left Chicago to become bishop of Green Bay, Wisconsin. In Chicago the appointment of Archbishop George Mundelein later that year further muddied the waters for Polish Americans, as the German American archbishop and later cardinal refused to have a Polish auxiliary bishop and openly fought with the leadership of the Polish priests in the city. The battle for Polish equity in the American church would continue well into the twentieth century.[26]

Public Space and a Public Sphere

While the battle between the nationalist and clerical parties divided Polonia, it also led to the creation of public or social space and a viable ethnic public sphere. Public space in the American city has been contested and led to clashes throughout history. The conflict at Holy Trinity, St. Hedwig's, St. Adalbert's, and other Polish parishes was largely over the use of social space. Who regulated church structure? Who could hold meetings and air issues? Did parishioners make these decisions or the clergy? What role would public space play in deciding various ideological battles? Would Barzyński and the Resurrectionists determine who could speak in the community and control information and public opinion?

In the late nineteenth and early twentieth centuries, social space was always at a premium and hotly debated in American cities like Chicago. Public space included parks, boulevards, and other such places. Privately owned and controlled space included churches, picnic groves, and saloons, which, while open to the public, were owned by religious, fraternal, and ethnic institutions or by private individuals. These presented various options to urbanites and might more correctly be called social space. Chicago developed a rich network of such social and public spaces, and various groups contested those who used them.[27]

These issues played out on the streets of Polonia and in the Polish press, which maintained a large and avid readership. While the nationalist faction attempted to create Holy Trinity Parish, it soon found itself locked out of the traditional meeting places controlled by the Resurrectionists at St. Stanislaus Kostka Parish. Two non-Polish urban spaces—Walsh's Hall and Schoenhoffen Hall—provided access to meeting facilities for Polish organizations. These "rented" places proved crucial for those who could not or did not want to gather in church halls. Poles often used German-, Czech-, and Irish-controlled spaces until they could build their own, and even then, such places provided much needed additional space in crowded urban neighborhoods. Most of these, however, could not compete with church buildings. The St. Stanislaus Kostka complex included a huge hall and a five thousand–seat theater with a fully equipped stage and a balcony running along threes sides of the auditorium. When the pastor of St. Adalbert's denied access to the church's facilities by rebel members of the Brotherhood of the Holy Name of Jesus, he threatened their very existence as a fraternal organization.[28]

Although the vast majority of St. Adalbert's parishioners remained in communion with the Catholic Church, Wojciechowo persisted as a hotbed of nationalist feeling, and demands for a secular meeting place emerged. By 1889, residents of the neighborhood organized the Pulaski Hall Society with the intention of constructing a secular meeting place for the Polish community. Four years later, sixteen Polish societies dedicated Pulaski Hall on the 1700 block of South Ashland Avenue in Wojciechowo. About two thousand people attended the ceremony. Judge Tuthill, who had decided against the pastor of St. Adalbert's in the Brotherhood of the Holy Name of Jesus Case, addressed the crowd, congratulating the men who built Pulaski Hall, saying that it would stand many years as a testament to the Polish devotion to liberty and freedom. It quickly became a major meeting space for Polish nationalist organizations. On January 21, 1893, South and West Side Poles held a remembrance for the 1863 January Uprising against czarist Russia at Pulaski Hall, while North Side Poles held their celebration in the German Schoenhofen Hall on Milwaukee Avenue.[29]

While Pulaski Hall was the most prominent of the non-church-controlled halls, others also provided public spaces in Polonia to promote nationalist efforts. Columbia Hall (Słowacki Hall) in Back of the Yards, Mickiewicz Hall in Bridgeport, Stanczyk's Hall in Pullman, and many saloon halls provided public gathering places across Chicago's Polish neighborhoods, though Polish Roman Catholic Union groups had more access to church-controlled space as the argument over *Polskość* continued throughout American Polonia, but especially on the streets of Chicago.

The brick structure, with an ornamental terra-cotta front, cost about $50,000 ($1,295,850 in 2017) to complete. It stood three stories high, seventy-five feet wide and 125 feet deep. Pulaski Hall contained an assembly hall for public gatherings and balls, eleven meeting rooms for various Polish societies, a library, and a gymnasium. (Photograph by Jan Zawilinski. From the collection of the Polish Museum of America.)

Social space allowed Polonia's residents the opportunity to meet and to discuss issues of importance to them and to celebrate and organize. The Polish National Alliance erected a new building on Milwaukee Avenue in 1896 to house its organization and to provide meeting space for its various activities. On July 12, Polish Chicagoans gathered at Division and Noble Streets to witness the laying of the cornerstone of the new Polish National Alliance home. The PNA censor did the laying of the cornerstone and placed a box in it that included copies of the *Chicago Tribune*, *Zgoda*, and three copies of Chicago's *Gazeta Polska*. The box also included coins, society badges, the PNA constitution, and other documents. After the laying of the cornerstone, celebrations continued throughout the Polish neighborhoods of the city. The Polish National Alliance dedicated the building on November 22, 1896. Some three hun-

The dedication of the Polish National Alliance Headquarters (*third from the right*) on Division Street on November 22, 1896. While the building housed the headquarters of the PNA, a museum and library were also included in the four-story building, which was to serve as a cultural and educational center for Polonia. The structure also housed the editorial offices and printing facilities of the PNA newspaper *Zgoda*. (Courtesy of *Zgoda*.)

dred PNA organizations from across the United States planned to take part in the festivities.[30]

The idea of a public sphere has been defined as a largely middle-class notion, rising, on one hand, out of the print revolution and, on the other, as a result of the rise in the consciousness of the middle class as an important force in society at the time of the Enlightenment and the French Revolution. The public sphere became crucially tied to the rise of capitalism and the spread of newspapers, journals, coffeehouses, and public spaces outside of the control of the government. This new reality allowed for the creation of democratic public discourse, which led to political and social action. Chicago's immigrant communities often fashioned working-class public spheres.

Newspapers played an important part in the process that created a public sphere for Polish Chicago. Dyniewicz's *Gazeta Polska* and John Barzyński's *Gazeta Polska Katolicka* discussed issues central to the clerical-nationalist debate. The Resurrectionist Order controlled *Wiara I Ojczyzna* (Faith and fatherland, 1887–99), *Kropidlo* (Holy water sprinkler, 1887–88), and the *Dziennik Chicagoski* (The Chicago daily, 1890–1971), as well as the later daily, *Dziennik Zjednoczenia* (The daily union, 1921–40). The publication of *Zgoda* (Harmony) by the PNA beginning in 1880 as well as the *Dziennik Związkowy* (The daily alliance, 1908–present) provided an outlet for the rival secular and nationalist camp. All Polish American newspapers presented news, entertainment, and a conduit for competing views and ideologies. Editorials often attacked each other in a battle of words that defined much of Chicago's Polonia.[31]

Chicago's Polonia held a conversation over a wide range of political and ideological issues. Polonia, like other immigrant/ethnic communities in the United States, contained a wide range of classes that were sometimes invisible to outside observers. When Władyslaw Dyniewicz created *Gazeta Polska*, he aimed his editorials at the entire community, as did his adversaries at *Gazeta Polska Katolicka*.[32] The published word proved crucial for the development of a uniquely Polish American public sphere, whether from a Catholic or secular point of view. Newspapers provided only a part of the printed word for Chicago's Polonia. As in other parts of the diaspora, there was a great demand for fiction and nonfiction books, theatrical plays, music, religious publications, and textbooks for Polish parochial schools. Books imported from Europe proved to be too expensive for the majority of immigrants. Dyniewicz published locally printed books along with the *Gazeta Polska* and later the *Tygodnik Lietracko-Naukowy* (The literary educational weekly). He also distributed a wide range of fables, folktales, short stories, historical novels, dictionaries, and educational works, as well as joke books, songbooks, lives of the saints, and other items that appealed to a wide audience.

Władysław Smulski, a relative of the Barzyński brothers, organized with them the Smulski Publishing Company to continue publication of the *Gazeta Katolicka* as well as a children's publication, *Dzień Święty* (The holy day). Smulski specialized in republishing Polish textbooks and readers for Polish schools in the United States. These proved so popular that two binderies catered exclusively to Smulski's press. Eventually, in 1920, Smulski's Polish American Publishing Company merged with Dyniewicz's company. Its chief rival, the Polish Publishing Company, printed the daily newspaper *Dziennik Chicagoski*, along with textbooks, prayer books, and other Polish-language publications. The two presses issued hundreds of thousands of books yearly before the Great Depression.[33]

The Polish press, with Chicago at its center, played a crucial role both in tying the community together and in dividing it. Newspapers provided a source of information not only of the diaspora but of Poland as well. They explained the larger social, economic, and political context in which the immigrant community found itself and called on the diaspora to work for Polish independence and to send relief whenever disaster struck. The *Zgoda* and other newspapers routinely reported news from the three partitions. Polish and Polish American journalists kept in contact with each other and maintained a two-way exchange of news, especially in the era before World War One.

The Polish American press ran the gamut of political views in Polonia and in the United States more generally. The Polish section of the American Socialist Party published the *Dziennik Ludowy* (The people's daily) in Chicago from 1907 to 1924. The Polish Socialist Alliance put out the short lived *Robotnik* (The worker) in Chicago from their offices on Milwaukee Avenue. Many of these provided outlets for the various religious, fraternal, or political organizations, but others were independent. Readers became involved in the lively exchange of ideas and points of view.[34]

The reality of ethnic private and semi-public space also had an impact on the creation of public discourse. Pulaski Hall, church halls, saloon halls, beer gardens, and ethnic-owned private parks as well as public spaces such as the small Chicago Progressive Era parks provided spaces to discuss political, economic, social, ideological, and religious issues. Chicago's Polonia held a lively exchange of viewpoints from its very origin. These often led to divisions in the community, and an image of chaos to outside observers, but also allowed unity to emerge whenever the community sensed danger from the outside or when the interests of the homeland presented themselves to the diaspora.

3

Living in Polish Chicago, 1880–1920

Eating, sleeping, giving birth to children, the nursing and rearing of children, the care of the sick and the care of the dying are all managed after some painful fashion in these cramped quarters. As anyone who will measure this space off on the floor will agree that it is inhumane and hardly credible.

—ROBERT HUNTER, *Report of the Investigating Committee of the City Homes Association* (1901)

Chicago's Polish community spread quickly across the city. While the oldest settlement located to the northwest of the city's downtown expanded up Milwaukee Avenue and remained the city's largest and most prestigious Polish colony, others developed in various sections of the city including Pilsen, Bridgeport, Back of the Yards, and South Chicago. Later, Hegewisch had a large Polish population as the steel and other industries continued to expand across the Southeast Side. From these original neighborhoods, Poles moved up and down principal streets to create yet more Polish districts, such as Brighton Park, McKinley Park, Avondale, and Jefferson Park, and industrial suburbs such as Calumet City, Harvey, Chicago Heights, and Cicero. They also followed the steel industry into northwest Indiana, including Gary, Hammond, East Chicago, and Whiting.

All of these places had one thing in common: an industrial base that required cheap unskilled labor. Chicago's industrialists drew on a diverse ethnic population to replenish their industrial workforce. Poles, many of whom had experienced some ethnic diversity in the Polish lands, now found themselves enmeshed in the ethnic hodgepodge that was Chicago at the turn of the twentieth century. Here, they mixed with many of the peoples of the world as Chicago's voracious appetite for labor mingled ethnic and racial groups together on factory floors.

Originally, Polish immigration to the United States, and in particular to Chicago, came in three waves. The first settlers arrived mainly from the German Partition. Western capitalism first transformed Poznania and Silesia. Railroads and industrialization rapidly altered these areas. Bismarck's Kulturkampf, aimed largely at eradicating Polish culture and the influence of the Catholic Church, further affected the local population, as did various colonization attempts to replace the Polish population in this part of the German Empire. Immigration from the German Partition lessened after 1890 as employment opportunities widened in Germany, especially in the Ruhr Valley. After 1890, migrations to the United States occurred largely from the Austrian- and Russian-occupied Polish lands.[1] In addition, Poles from all three partitions took part in seasonal labor migrations in order to build capital. Between 1870 and 1914, over two million Poles left the country in both a continental and overseas migration. In the decade prior to the outbreak of World War One, over eight hundred thousand Poles worked annually in Germany.

Before 1885, American labor agents regularly traveled to Europe to recruit workers. Afterward, the U.S. government outlawed labor contracting, and steamship agents from Bremen, Hamburg, and Antwerp spread the word that America and other locations, such as Brazil, desired immigrants. Of those Poles that came to the United States, three-quarters worked in the coal, steel, metal, and meatpacking industries. Chicago, with its vast industrial base, became a magnet for many of these job seekers. During the 1880s about 100,000 Poles arrived in America. Annual totals grew from roughly 30,000 in 1890 to 50,000 ten years later. In 1910, 130,000 arrived in the United States, and three years later 175,000 came. All told, between 1880 and 1914, roughly 7–8 percent of the rural population of the Polish lands left for America. Many eventually returned to Poland, and some also made several trips back and forth across the Atlantic in search of higher wages.

The migration of Poles to cities like Chicago was part of a global capitalist system of interrelated parts. Technological change made this vast movement possible. Once Poland became incorporated into the modern industrial capitalist system, the mass introduction of railroads changed ancient employment patterns and brought transformation to the countryside. Railroads opened the European East as they did the American West. Migration from eastern Europe became a routine matter as steamships made the Atlantic crossing reasonably cheap and comfortable. Simply put, wages were higher in western Europe and the United States—and much of what was earned abroad went back to the Polish countryside to help families. Taken as a whole, immigrants sent a huge amount of money to the Polish countryside during the era of mass migration. From 1902 to 1906, money orders from the United States to Russia and Austria-Hungary amounted to $70,000,000 ($1,814,189,518 in 2017). In 1902 alone, Polish immigrants sent $3,500,000 ($96,499,442) in money orders to Austrian Galicia, not counting cash in small bills mailed by immigrants to friends and family. In addition, return migrants brought $4,000,000 ($110,285,077) to Galicia. This internationalization of labor generated the transmission of wage-derived capital. As a result, a growing proportion of Polish rural households became dependent on migration incomes.[2]

Poland "Elsewhere"

Polish settlers, like others who arrived in Chicago from different countries, attempted to create a sense of community based on traditional values, culture, and relationships. They established a multilayered community with its own cultural, social, and business institutions to serve residents and preserve *Polskość*. This communal response hoped to re-create the Poland they had left behind and establish a sense of Poland "elsewhere." While never totally successful, the communal response provided a buffer between immigrants and an at-times hostile receiving society. The founding of a church provided the most important step in creating this sense of community. Other institutions soon followed, especially a Polish parochial school. Immigrants opened small businesses such as taverns, groceries, bookstores, music stores, pharmacies, and funeral parlors. These, combined with fraternal organizations and social clubs, formed a social web. In the spirit of taking care of members "from cradle to grave," the Polish community, often in cooperation with their Czech neighbors, founded cemeteries. Eventually, larger business enterprises, high schools, seminaries, orphanages, hospitals, welfare agencies, and even a college came into being to serve Polonia. In the end, Poland could not be re-created elsewhere, but a Chicago Polish American community was established.[3]

Before 1871, about a thousand Poles lived in Chicago; fifteen years later, nearly forty thousand lived in the city, and many worked in its factories, tanneries, packinghouses, lumberyards, sawmills, and wood-working facilities. Noble Street just north and south of Division Street developed as the major business and cultural street of Polonia. Many Polish businesses opened on the street, as did two Catholic parishes, St. Stanislaus Kostka and Holy Trinity. Subsequently, Polish and Polish/East European Jewish businesses spilled up and down Milwaukee and Ashland Avenues as well as along Division Street in the area later called the Polish Downtown.[4]

Poverty haunted the area, and an especially rundown part of the neighborhood existed just west of St. Stanislaus Kostka Church. Housing on Cleaver, Holt, and Dickenson Streets was the worst in the district. Local residents called it the Black Spot, a section where poorly maintained wood frame houses not connected to either city sewers or the water system prevailed. Water hydrants, covered with a brick vault to avoid freezing during Chicago's winters, stood in the street. Poles largely rented these homes, and the owner of most of the properties refused to make improvements. Renters avoided paying for renovations on their own as they might be evicted and lose their investment. It seemed that the legal system protected the owner, despite the fact that the city charged him several times with breaking the law.

The nearby North Branch of the Chicago River attracted industry such as tanneries, lumberyards, and other manufacturing plants that provided employment. Polish women tended not to like domestic work so they often labored in the garment industry, located on the city's West Side, especially along Halsted Street near the river. Both boys and girls found work in cigar factories and other industrial enterprises. The goal of all this work was the purchase of a family home. Polish Chicagoans often acquired additional real estate. Already in 1886, several Poles had substantial holdings. The Polish community maintained several building and loan associations. Four Polish newspapers served Chicago. There were at least five Polish doctors, seven druggists, an artist, and several people with literary abilities in the various Polish neighborhoods. In addition, Polish grocery stores, meat markets, shoe stores, restaurants, a bookstore, and saloons appeared up and down the streets.

Polish Chicago had a very active social life. Balls, picnics, and other such festivities filled the calendar and raised money for various community and Polish patriotic purposes. Young Polish women, dressed in brightly collared shawls, filled the streets, while older women almost always wore dark scarves. Men and women tended to marry at a young age and have large families.

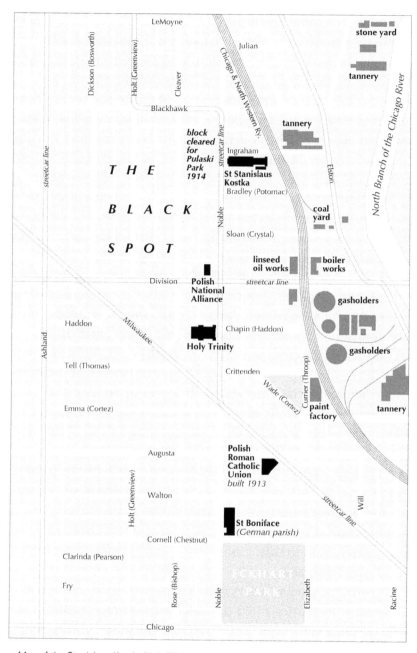

Map of the Stanislaus Kostka/Holy Trinity neighborhood, including the Black Spot in 1900. Also marked is the eventual location of Pulaski Park opened in 1912. The construction of the park removed much crowded housing in the area. Notice the proximity of the district to the industrial corridor along the North Branch of the Chicago River, on Halsted Street, and near Clybourn Avenue. (Courtesy of Chicago CartoGraphics.)

Sadly, as in other working-class wards, the infant death rate remained high.

Polish patriotism permeated the neighborhood, and Poles largely remained loyal to the Catholic Church, which had pre-served the Polish language despite attempts to erase it by the Russian- and German-occupying powers. Generally, immigrants held priests in high esteem and parents sent their children to parochial schools. Over two thousand children attended St. Stanislaus Kostka Parish School in the 1880s. This important attempt to maintain *Polskość* proved to be an essential factor in maintaining community in the diaspora. Polish American parochial schools were a social product of the immigration. They helped to unite the community and provided an institutional bond between the various generations. Eighteen Sisters of Notre Dame taught the students at St. Stanislaus Kostka School. The entire school day was not held in Polish, as Irish nuns also taught English to students. In 1886, Fr. Mahoney gave English lessons and ran military drills for older boys including the use of firearms and bayonets with the idea that they might someday return to Poland and fight for its independence. Parochial schools taught children at least until the child had received first communion when they either left school to work or attended public schools.[5]

By 1895, the *Chicago Tribune* reported, Chicago's Polish population had reached more than a hundred thousand; most lived on the Northwest Side. The great majority came from peasant backgrounds. Children seemed to be everywhere in the crowded district. A policeman remarked that he did not arrest many Poles but said that those from Galicia would "stick a knife into a man as quick as an Italian." He claimed that Poles were a loud group but said when he heard "Jezus Maria!" he knew the Galicians were fighting. He explained that a Pole always yelled when he fought, and the louder he yelled, the harder he fought. Still he claimed that as a whole the Poles were a moral group. Those who strayed usually headed off to other neighborhoods and took up with others like themselves in places like the Levee red-light district.

Observers pointed to Poles as industrious and frugal, which many times led to overcrowding in the small homes of Stanisławowo. Polish immigrants spent little on clothes but saved ferociously to buy a house, and even the poorest home or apartment had a lace curtain in the front window. On a warm day, it was not unusual to see a dozen men, women, and children sitting on the front steps of a house, passing around a growler can of beer and a loaf of brown bread. On neighborhood streets, small groups of Polish women gathered in animated conversation. The average Polish family included seven people.

Weddings provided a significant event in the neighborhood. A bridal procession began at the bride's house and included a band that accompanied the priest, the couple, and their retinue to the church. After the ceremony and a Mass, the procession returned to the bride's home for festivities, which included plenty to eat and drink. While some attempted to maintain the peasant country tradition of a three-day celebration, generally this could not be done in industrial Chicago, where the factory whistle called men and women to work each day. Most Poles married within their nationality, and large families were the norm, as alluded to earlier. Wakes and funerals were also major events. Visitors arrived at the home, and in later years, the funeral parlor, to mourn the dead for three days before the burial. These, too, were communal events that involved many members of the neighborhood.[6]

Emigrating to the United States thrust Poles into a new urban-industrial milieu and shifted gender roles. Polish immigrant women often arrived at a young age and were free of the restrictions of ancient traditions. Many had left because they saw economic opportunity for themselves, and migration meant agency for these young women. They had more control over their lives. In Poland, parents, especially fathers, with the aid of matchmakers, picked spouses for their daughters. In Chicago and in America in general, women found their choices greatly expanded and could choose spouses with less interference. Also, once married, they took on more responsibilities than in rural Poland. For one, the village tradition that a bride join her husband's family household and become subservient to his parents no longer proved possible. In the diaspora, married couples established their own households. Also, in the new setting, men most likely worked away from home and were absent daily for long periods of time. The tasks of dealing with financial matters and disciplining children fell solely on women. Suddenly, women found themselves in a more independent position and more aware of their rights. Unlike in Poland, women with abusive husbands could turn to police and courts for aid. They set up female networks that aided them in this new setting, as traditional resources such as grandparents, aunts, and cousins often no longer existed. By surrounding themselves with other Polish women, they more easily navigated the new American industrial state of affairs.[7]

Before 1914, the vast majority of unmarried Polish women in America were employed outside the home. Roughly 20 percent continued to work after marriage. This resulted from the types of industry located in the various Polish American neighborhoods and from working-class realities. Men often did not earn enough wages to support their families; therefore, women and children had to work. By 1900, 38.7 percent of Polish women employed in Chicago worked in the garment trades and 7.3 percent labored in laundries, while only 1.9 percent held professional positions—patterns that appear to have been common in other cities. Twenty years later, women, many of whom were Polish, made up roughly 20 percent of the labor force in Chicago's packinghouses.

Each member contributed to the family's survival. After marriage, wives helped with finances by taking in boarders, often family members or *rodacy*, people from the same village or region. Many Poles considered themselves "birds of passage" who intended to return to the rural homeland and expand their family holdings. These single men sought out places where they could board with a family member or neighbor from Poland. The fact that all family members contributed to its survival also meant that children often went to work at an early age, as they had on

Polish farms. The difference was, of course, that in America children often worked in factories.[8]

By the twentieth century, St. Stanislaus Kostka parishioners could boast of a beautiful church decorated by the paintings of Tadeusz Żukotyński. The pastor Rev. John Kasprzycki and his nine assistants ran an extraordinary Polish Catholic institution. The parochial school, headed by Mother Superior Sister Mary Rogiera, was the largest in the world, with forty-four nuns, four laymen, and ten parish priests teaching thirty-eight hundred children. Priests celebrated five masses every Sunday, assisted by one hundred altar boys. These *ministranci* (i.e., altar boys) received ten cents a month in a higher education fund that they could use to attend St. Stanislaus College, which offered both a commercial and classical high school curriculum. Forty-five men's societies enrolled ninety-five hundred members, while seventeen women's societies had more than seven thousand members. The parish's White Eagle Sokol Hall provided the first gymnasium for the community and fielded an undefeated football team from 1900 to 1903. The boys from St. Stanislaus Kostka even trounced the University of Chicago, at the time a football powerhouse, during a practice game. Parish boundaries stretched from the Chicago River on the east to Humboldt Park on the west and from North Avenue south to Augusta Boulevard.[9]

Despite this growth, Polonia faced various problems. Subpar housing conditions, as well as poverty, drunkenness, and a growing problem with crime, haunted the neighborhood. Robert Hunter's 1901 *Report by the Investigating Committee of the City Homes Association* pointed to extensive overcrowding in the ten-block area just to the west of St. Stanislaus Kostka Church, which included the Black Spot.

The district surveyed covered the area bound by Division Street on the south, Blanche Street (now Le Moyne Street) to the north, Noble Street to the east and Ashland Avenue to the west. Small frame houses, seen as the characteristic home of the working class, remained but were often moved to the rear of the lot with a newer large brick tenement erected on the front of the parcel. The new buildings often cut off sunlight for the rear dwellings. At times, one large structure covered from 80 to 100 percent of the lot. In other cases, two or three buildings covered the standard Chicago lot, which generally ran twenty-five feet wide and one hundred and twenty feet deep in working-class neighborhoods.

Landlords divided old wooden frame buildings and rented them out to two or more families, which made matters worse. This resulted in the creation of small, dark, and inadequately venti-lated apartments. In general, owners did not maintain these older rear buildings, which suffered from terrible conditions caused by uncollected trash, rodents, and other vermin. Windows opened directly over garbage and manure boxes. Ground floors stood near ill-smelling outhouses, and backyards often contained rubbish of all sorts. The rear buildings made up over 30 percent of those in Stanisławowo surveyed by Hunter and the housing committee. In the block bound by Holt, Cleaver, Blackhawk and Bradley Streets, the aforementioned Black Spot, investigators found thirty-six rear dwellings out of a total of eighty-five structures. In these rear houses lived 432 persons of whom 211 were adults and 221 children. In the fifty-two-acre area surveyed, 2,716 families lived with a total population of 13,825 people or 339.8 individuals per acre. The average building contained three apartments. Houses at the front of the lot in Stanisławowo averaged 4.27 apartments per building. Most apartments contained three to four small rooms with over five persons per apartment. Of course, Poles often took in borders to help pay rents and had larger families. Investigators found that overcrowding was one of the most important reasons for unsanitary conditions in these dwellings.

Many houses in working-class districts were built before the city raised the street level to help with drainage. In other cases, developers simply saved money by not filling in the lots to the height of the streets and built on the lower levels. On Cleaver and Holt Streets, investigators found unsanitary conditions in these low lots, as basement dwellings accumulated water after a rain shower. About 20 percent of the people of the district to the west of St. Stanislaus Kostka lived in basement or cellar apartments. Canvassers found some of these adequate for residents, but also saw Poles to be the most wretchedly housed group in the city.

Investigators found one tenement on Noble Street covering almost the entire lot with a dark and damp cellar where three people resided. Bad odors permeated the rooms, probably from the toilets under the vaulted sidewalks, which Poles called *Jan Pod Sidewalkiem*, Chicago Polish slang for the "John" under the sidewalk. Vaulted sidewalk privies, outlawed nine years earlier, contained fifty-nine out of sixty-nine toilet facilities. The report found two kinds of these water closets, both banned by the city in 1894, but still in use in the Stanisławowo neighborhood by almost 20 percent of the families canvassed. The first was simply a hole dug into the ground without any connection to the sewer system. The other, a vault connected to the sewer and flushed out on occasion by rainwater from the roof or with water brought from a fire hydrant. Only one bathtub was found in the homes inspected. Bathhouses, or a hardly private washtub in the kitchen, provided the only choice for most working-class Chicagoans. The city operated four widely used public bathhouses, but most were privately owned.

Unpaved or poorly maintained and broken up streets ran through the district. At times, residents pried up the cedar street paving, known as Nicholson blocks, and used them for firewood. Many unsafe and poorly maintained wooden sidewalks existed near St. Stanislaus Kostka Church. Unpaved alleys made up a large portion of the neighborhood, as they did of much of the city then. In 1900, the Polish district still had no public playgrounds or parks. Alleys and the dark passageways between houses, called gangways, provided playgrounds for children.

In 1900, the horse provided the primary means of transportation of goods in the city. Many in working-class wards used them to make deliveries, to pick up rags and metal, and for hauling. The

The entrance to the *Jan pod Sidewalkiem* (John under the sidewalk) was located on the right of this residence at 1419 Emma Street (now Cortez Street) in the Polish downtown district in 1914. Notice the below-grade apartment which could be entered on the left. (Northwestern University Settlement Association Records Photographs, Series 41/6, Northwestern University Archives, Evanston, IL.)

Polish district housed 202 horses in 108 stables. In addition, several homes kept chickens, hogs, pigeons, and ducks. Investigators bemoaned this "village" custom still prevalent across Chicago's neighborhoods. Manure boxes presented sanitary and health problems throughout the neighborhood. One house on Noble Street kept horses in the basement of the front building. Caretakers threw animal excrement directly into the alley, attracting flies and rats. The stench made it impossible for the residents of the rear dwelling to open their windows. Filthy alleys and streets as well as poor garbage pickups affected both front and rear dwellings. Poorly maintained wooden garbage receptacles stood in alleys. Monthly rents in Stanisławowo averaged $5.66 per apartment ($156 in 2017). Unskilled workers made up 58.3 percent of residents, 37.5 percent were skilled workers, and 4.2 percent were commercial or "special" workers.[10]

Shown here is a typical backyard in the Polish district on the Northwest side, ca. 1900. Notice the wooden balloon-frame buildings. (Northwestern University Settlement Association Records Photographs, Series 41/6, Northwestern University Archives, Evanston, IL.)

Ten years after the publication of Hunter's findings, sociologists Sophonisba Breckenridge and Edith Abbott revisited the housing issue in a series of reports. These not only looked at some of the same areas explored by Hunter and his group but also expanded to include other districts, many of which contained large Polish populations. They resurveyed the entire ten-block area in the Polish district originally canvassed by the City Homes Association. Their findings reflected those made ten years earlier, with one major exception: the outlawed privy had virtually disappeared. Also, the district seemed slightly less densely populated, as the city demolished tenements on the 1400 block of North Cleaver Street to build the Kosciuszko School. The 1911 study did not yet reflect the fact that the block directly in front of St. Stanislaus Kostka Church would soon be replaced by the 3.8-acre Pulaski

Park and fieldhouse in 1912. Industrial and commercial concerns had replaced housing on almost every block. Breckinridge and Abbott counted 574 lodgers on the ten blocks resurveyed in 1911 but had reason to believe that more boarders actually lived in the area, as household heads lied for fear that the survey might result in the forced eviction of lodgers.

The buildings in the Polish neighborhood tended to be built before the 1902 tenement code and contained more apartments than in most other districts. One hundred and forty-one structures contained six apartments in Stanisławowo, with 846 apartments. One building held seventeen apartments and another twenty-three. As in 1900, the four-room apartment predominated. Investigators found one-third of the rooms surveyed to be dark and gloomy, with nearby structures often blocking light. Landlords charged a median rent of $8.00–$8.50 in 1911 ($200–$213 in 2017).[11]

Breckenridge and Abbott surveyed other neighborhoods containing large Polish American populations, especially Back of the Yards and South Chicago. In both of these South Side industrial neighborhoods, they looked at specific blocks dominated by Poles, as well as others. While the two districts differed in many ways from the Northwest Side enclave, overall they resembled each other. Both had been recently settled. The Back of the Yards had only emerged after the location of the packinghouses to the west of the stockyards in the late 1870s. In South Chicago, real growth took place after 1880 when the North Chicago Rolling Mill Company constructed its South Works on Lake Michigan. In 1901, Hunter wrote about these areas in a limited manner. Both contained wooden frame houses, whether two-flats or single-family dwellings. Also, housing rarely covered the entire lot, and few alley tenements existed as compared to the older sections of the city. Both neighborhoods nestled up against the two great industries that dominated them. In South Chicago, this meant the steel industry just to the east of the predominantly Polish area known as the Bush. In Back of the Yards, Polish blocks stood south of the meatpacking houses and Forty-Seventh Street just east of Ashland Avenue.[12]

Hunter regarded conditions in Back of the Yards and South Chicago to be so atypical as to be unsuitable for his study. The 1901 study found outside conditions to be especially bad. Canvassers found the worst environment to be in the Bush from Eighty-Third Street to Eighty-Seventh Street and between Ontario (Brandon) and Green Bay Avenues, a neighborhood almost entirely inhabited by Polish immigrants and their families. Neglected and dilapidated wooden homes prevailed, and the city had not put in sewers. The privy remained in general use. Backyards, streets, and empty lots stood filled with garbage of all sorts. Smoke from the steel mills covered the entire neighborhood. Investigators found the entire area to be dreary, ugly, and unhealthy. Hunter found no large area in Back of the Yards to have such terrible conditions, but again Hunter found outside conditions to still be deplorable. He noted a lack of sewers and standing pools of sewage around many of the houses. Heavy clouds of smoke and the stench from the packinghouses, stockyards, and Bubbly Creek (nickname of the South Fork of the Chicago River's South Branch), which acted as an open sewer for the meat packers, blanketed the area.[13]

Breckenridge and Abbott did a much more thorough study of these two areas in 1911. In South Chicago, they visited the Bush, which they considered typical of the poorest section of South Chicago. The area contained wide streets and blocks divided by twenty-foot-wide alleys. Narrow gangways separated buildings and resulted in dark and poorly ventilated rooms. The majority of structures covered less than 50 percent of the twenty-five-foot-wide and one hundred and forty–foot-deep lot. One- and two-story wooden houses and four-room apartments predominated. Investigators found South Chicago's homes to be in the worst condition of all those chiefly occupied by Poles. The density of population in the Bush, however, was less than any of the other neighborhoods surveyed, including Back of the Yards. While Poles heavily inhabited the area, people of other nationalities also lived

This photograph, taken about 1900, shows Commercial Avenue in South Chicago looking north from Eighty-Eighth Street. The Church of Immaculate Conception, BVM, pictured here, was the first of four Polish churches in South Chicago. At this time, the street contained a mixture of businesses. (Chicago Public Library Special Collections, WCE/SC, box 3, plate 71.)

in the neighborhood, including other Slavic groups, Germans, Hungarians, Irish, and Swedes.

Lodgers also presented a problem in the Bush, where they often slept in rooms occupied by family members including children. Investigators wrote that 72 percent of all sleeping rooms had less than the minimum amount of space for the number of inhabitants. The median rent of $9.00 per month in South Chicago ($225 in 2017) was higher than in any other neighborhood canvassed in 1911. In addition, Bush residents kept chickens, ducks, pigeons, goats, and even pigs. Many people brought these animals into the house during the winter season, often storing them in the attic or basement, resulting in even worse sanitary conditions.[14]

Surveyors found that conditions had somewhat improved in Back of the Yards since Hunter's 1901 report. Cement sidewalks

Reverend Francis J. Karabasz. As Polonia quickly grew, young Polish American priests were often called upon to establish new parishes. In 1910, Rev. Karabasz organized the Parish of the Sacred Heart of Jesus, the third Polish parish in the Back of the Yards neighborhood. Previous to his appointment as pastor, the young cleric, born in Lemont, Illinois, had served at other Polish parishes in South Chicago and Back of the Yards. (From the collection of the Polish Museum of America, x2005.001.0818.)

replaced many of the wooden walkways, and streets had been paved. The city also extended the sewer system and enlarged Bubbly Creek. Still, the packing industry, with its offensive conditions, dominated the neighborhood. As in other neighborhoods, Polish residents, while they tended to cluster and dominate some parts of the district, lived with other ethnic groups. The largest group of male household heads worked as unskilled labor in the meat industry, but skilled workers, tradesmen, businessmen, and others were found among the population. Most of the male and female lodgers also worked in the stockyards. On the predominantly Polish blocks, investigators found 387 lodgers out of a total population of 2,873 residents or about 13 percent. Once again, however, the actual number may have been higher, as residents notoriously underreported boarders.

Typically, wooden frame buildings that held two four-room apartments and did not cover a large portion of the lot dominated the housing market. Lots with more than one house on them remained rare. Back of the Yards gave the impression of not being densely populated, but the congestion problem could be seen within the houses themselves. Residents often slept in rooms not generally recognized as bedrooms, and apartments contained small, poorly ventilated, gloomy rooms. Outhouses and privies were still in use. Most apartments that included a separate toilet facility had them open onto a kitchen, a not very sanitary setup. Buildings, except for those on Whiskey Row—a strip on Ashland Avenue that contained more than forty saloons—were generally well maintained.[15]

Poor housing conditions in all of the Polish neighborhoods looked at in both 1901 and 1911 resulted from Chicago's rapid industrialization. The city grew, as massive factories, mills, and packinghouses dominated neighborhoods. Developers hastily put up the wooden balloon frame buildings, which were built at a low cost. In the older districts, such as the Northwest Side, massive industrialization brought larger tenements and a higher density of population per acre, as Polish and other immigrants needed to live as close to the manufacturing district along the North Branch of the Chicago River as possible. The ability to walk to work proved necessary for the underpaid unskilled workers who made up the bulk of the population of these neighborhoods.

Though Polish immigrants lived in small, crowded apartments that lacked adequate sanitary facilities, they actually yearned to own their own homes. To own one's own home afforded a source of pride and status. Land ownership in the Polish countryside was a thing of great social significance and connoted a higher social standing. This attitude was carried over with them when they emigrated. Another element in the wish for home ownership was a sense of security, which again proved to be an important factor in Poland. Land provided tangible evidence of prosperity and economic security. Investment also proved to be an important factor. Many also saw the purchase of a home as a sign that their move to the United States had become permanent. Home ownership demonstrated a greater identification with the host society.[16]

Boarders often helped pay off mortgages or helped save on rent for future homes. Also, while conditions may have looked bleak to housing reformers, they often reflected a kind of communal solidarity. Renters often took in lodgers who came from the same village and needed a place to stay when they arrived in Chicago. This was seen as an act of kindness to the newly arrived. It did create overcrowding, but it was a natural part of a communal obligation to many in Polonia. Immigrants reported similarly crowded conditions in villages back in the Poland. An extra person in the household might have caused some difficulty, but it was nothing unusual.[17]

The two great industries that ruled over these neighborhoods employed the bulk of the men and, in the case of meatpacking, many of the women. The Northwest Side, however, contained a more varied industrial base. Polonia sat close to Goose Island and to the Halsted Street industrial corridor. The North Branch of the Chicago River attracted a diverse lot of manufacturers. Nearly a score of tanneries were located on the west bank of the North Branch and provided a stench much like the South Side's packinghouses from which these tanneries received most of their hides. The men who worked in these plants provided the leather that was used for shoes, purses, and other consumer products across the country.[18]

Nearby, the Halsted Street industrial corridor contained not only tanneries but also foundries, coal companies, boiler factories, shipbuilding firms, and various other industries that lined the river and filled adjacent neighborhoods from North Avenue to Erie Street. At Grand Avenue and Halsted, south to Harrison

The Herman Bottle Works on Augusta Boulevard, ca. 1914. Chicago's industrial neighborhoods held a wide variety of manufacturing plants, often interspersed with residential structures. (Northwestern University Settlement Association Records Photographs, Series 41/6, Northwestern University Archives, Evanston, IL.)

Street, stood some of the greatest wholesale and mail order establishments in the world. Many Polish women worked in these and in the garment trades. Others found jobs in shops along Milwaukee Avenue, one of the most cosmopolitan streets in the city. That street also housed many saloons. As early as 1888, some sixty bars operated on the strip from Lake Street to California Avenue, a four-mile stretch. Milwaukee Avenue soon became known as the "Polish Broadway," and it linked various Polish neighborhoods that grew out of the original settlement.[19]

To Live among Others

While the Northwest Side held the largest concentration of Poles, it did not contain only Polish speakers. The 1911 survey listed 2,785 household heads in the ten blocks canvassed. The overwhelming majority were Poles (2,649), but native-born whites, Czechs, Germans, Lithuanians, Jews, and others also lived there. The same was even truer for the other Polish districts across the city. Pilsen, Bridgeport, Back of the Yards, South Chicago, and Hegewisch all contained large and varied ethnic populations. In Pilsen, and across the Lower West Side, Poles mingled with Czechs, Jews, Lithuanians, Slovaks, Croats, Germans, Irish, and others. More than thirty Roman Catholic parishes surrounded the stockyards and served many different nationalities in Bridgeport, Canaryville, McKinley Park, and Back of the Yards; the same proved to be the case for South Chicago, Hegewisch, and the entire Southeast Side of the city. Ethnic diversity marked working-class Chicago owing to the city's large industries needing more and more workers.[20]

From the beginning, Poles tended to settle near Germans and Czechs in Chicago. On the Northwest Side, Polish immigrants often attended services at the German Catholic parish of St. Boniface on Noble Street, south of Division Street, or at another German parish that welcomed them, St. Joseph's. Father Joseph Molitor, pastor of St. Wenceslaus Parish, a Czech church on the Chicago's Near West Side, greeted Poles in the 1860s and 1870s. The priest spoke Polish and helped the Polish community early in its settlement in the city. It was the beginning of a long-lasting relationship between the two Western Slavic groups in Chicago.

By the Civil War, the Czech community had already developed an institutional base. Besides the parish of St. Wenceslaus, the Czechs created saloons, clubs, and a nascent political organization, which the newly arrived Poles joined. In 1865, Poles and Czechs came together to mourn the death of President Lincoln. On September 23, 1871, they held a joint meeting at the Bohemian Gymnasium on DeKoven Street pledging support for the Republican ticket and advocating the nomination of Frank Novak, a Pole, for collector of the West Division to enforce city tax laws on the West Side. Ethnic leaders pointed out that if the two nationalities would unite they could accomplish all of their political goals. Poles and Czechs often referred to each other in their newspapers as "brothers." In the early years of the immigration, Polish Chicagoans frequently used Czech semipublic spaces to rally or protest, and they often celebrated together. On June 16, 1878, the Gmina Polska held a picnic marked by a parade that began at Twenty-Second and Canal and proceeded to Silver Leaf Grove near Douglas Park. The Bohemian Sharpshooters escorted the procession.[21]

The two ethnic groups worked closely together during the period prior to 1918. The Czechs, as an older and established group, often presented a model for Poles as they built their own institutions. In the early 1870s, Bohemians (as Czechs were referred to before 1918) created several building and loan associations modeled after similar German American associations. The first of these was the Chicago Bohemian Building and Loan Association, No. 1. Czechs quickly withdrew their savings from American-owned Chicago banks and invested in the new organizations. Within fifteen years, the Czechs had organized fifteen such societies, designed to help their membership purchase homes. In 1883, Polish Chicagoans could boast of the Sobieski Savings and Loan Society as the first Polish building and loan association to be established in Polonia.[22]

Financial ruin threatened both communities during the depression of the 1890s. On August 25, 1893, as visitors enjoyed the Columbian Exposition, unemployed workers marched through downtown streets. Czechs and Poles made up a large portion of these demonstrators. At one point, the crowd reached about four thousand at the Columbus statue in Grant Park, with hundreds of onlookers milling about. At 3:30 p.m. over a thousand men formed a line and marched north on Michigan Avenue carrying the American flag and a banner that read "We Want Work." At the corner of Wabash and Randolph Streets, a teamster attempted to drive a wagon through the crowd, which in turn attacked the driver. The police rushed to save him. Afterward, the march continued to city hall and returned to the Columbus statue, where speakers again addressed the crowd in English, Polish, Czech, and German. That September, the *Chicago Tribune* reported a large number of immigrants returning to their homelands as economic conditions worsened.[23]

Many adherents of socialism were attracted to the United States in the years after the Civil War. Cities like Chicago had long been centers for socialist activity, and the Czechs played an active role in the movement. In 1896, one hundred Polish and Czech socialists met at Pulaski Hall for more than two hours and presented resolutions to Congress condemning Spanish actions in Cuba and in support of Cuban revolutionaries. Speakers included Polish socialists Joseph Grondzieniewski and George Duzewski and the Czech Frank Malc. Several nonsocialist speakers also addressed the meeting, which ended in a march through the streets.[24]

Poles and Czechs proved especially sensitive to the German and Austrian occupation of Poland, Bohemia, and Moravia. In 1902, both groups objected to the visit of Prince Henry of Germany to the United States. The protests included the singing of patriotic songs and the delivering of speeches and resolutions. While Czechs had often cooperated with Chicago's Germans, they felt that the German community ignored their political ambitions. Also, Czechs objected to German being taught in the city's public schools. Bohemians saw this as counterproductive for their children. In turn, in 1900, Chicago's German politicians succeeded in stopping the adoption of Czech, Polish, and Italian language classes in the public schools.[25] Some German Catholics in the nineteenth century tried to prevent Poles from attending services at St. Boniface Church on Noble Avenue. In 1908, the pastor of that parish, Fr. Albert Evans, cautioned parishioners about nearby Polish taverns and dance halls. He feared the church's hosting of Polish weddings, claiming that celebrants would drift over to the newly constructed Eckhart Park and hold drunken orgies.[26]

While conflict occasionally broke out between Germans and Poles in Chicago, they also often worked together. When the Polish Catholic Church of Immaculate Conception, BVM, burned down in South Chicago, the parishioners of St. Peter's German

Catholic Church welcomed them at services. German Catholics also helped the Poles on the North Side, especially in the early years of the settlement, when Poles from the German-occupied partition of Poland predominated in the immigration. Still, on various occasions before the First World War, the Polish and German communities clashed. An especially hostile clash that even involved German newspapers from New York City and St. Paul, Minnesota, revolved around the teaching of the Polish language in Chicago high schools. Germans called Polish a dead language and claimed Poland had no literature. In 1908, Poles organized a boycott of German goods in Chicago.[27]

Dealings with other immigrant neighbors from East Central Europe also often proved tense and mirrored events in the homeland. Lithuanians and Poles at first interacted well, but as nationalism raised its ugly head, these old allies argued. Lithuania and Poland had united in the Middle Ages and at one time formed the largest political entity in Europe. In the late eighteenth century, both fell prey to Russian expansion. Many Poles felt Lithuanians were simply a Polish regional folk group. Lithuanian national consciousness rose in the years after the 1863 rebellion, and soon Lithuanians saw both the Poles and Russians as oppressors. As both groups set down roots in Chicago, they became rivals. Mary McDowell, of the University of Chicago Settlement House in Back of the Yards, reported that Polish and Lithuanian young people refused to date or participate in events with each other.[28]

Lithuanian newspapers often spoke out against the Poles and the idea of Poland. The editors of *Lietuva* appealed to their readers not to Polonize names, a popular custom, especially among the upper and professional classes back in Europe. *Lietuva* called for loyalty to Lithuanian organizations, such as the Lithuanian National Alliance, rather than joining Polish fraternal organizations. In 1908, *Lietuva* praised Lithuanian church organists for forming their own organization and refusing to play in Polish churches. The next year, an article by Dr. Antanas Rutkauskas portrayed the Poles as the eternal enemy of Lithuania and com-

Kilinski's Ice Cream Parlor. Polish-owned businesses appeared up and down the main and side streets of Polonia. (Photograph by W. Rozański. From the collection of the Polish Museum of America, x2007.001.0012.)

mended the work of Dr. Jonas Šliupas, a physician, publicist, and national liberationist for helping to separate Lithuanians from Poles in America. Rutkauskas complained that the Poles constantly called the Lithuanians Polish, "but only a Pole is a Pole." At the time of the First World War, *Lietuva* complained about A. Zemaitis, a printer, who marched in a parade commemorating the one hundredth anniversary of the death of Thaddeus Kosciuszko, who himself had been born in Lithuania. The cavalcade sent off five hundred volunteers to the Polish Army in France. *Naujienos*, another Lithuanian newspaper, charged that Polish American census takers refused to register Lithuanians as Lithuanians but counted them instead as Poles.[29]

The *Dziennik Związkowy* reported an incident involving Lithuanian nationalists and the Polish organization Unya Lubelska (Union of Lublin) in May of 1918. The newspaper claimed that Lithuanian Bolsheviks upset the proceedings of the group's meeting at Pulaski Hall. The journal complained that the Lithuanian newspaper *Draugas* scandalously attacked Poland. After World

War One, the struggle between Poles and Lithuanians in Chicago continued, especially as the two nations fought with each other in Europe over the predominantly Jewish city of Wilno (Vilnius).[30]

Like the relationship with Lithuanians, that with the Jewish community, another large group with whom Poles shared the Polish lands, was strained. Here, too, the complicated interaction between the two groups developed over centuries. Interactions between Polish peasants and Polish Jews proved especially intricate. Jews and Poles in Europe often lived in the same cities and villages and interacted on many levels. Nevertheless, events in both Europe and the United States combined to increase misunderstandings between the two throughout their shared history in Chicago. The city's English-language newspapers often pointed to Polish anti-Semitism.[31]

The role of Jews as economic intermediaries in the Polish lands was transported to America. Polish peasants in particular preferred Polish Jewish businesspeople over Polish Americans, who they felt had little business acumen. Jews saw peasants in Poland as customers, and peasants saw Jews as outsiders and viewed them with both disdain and admiration. The saying to be as "smart as a Jew," for instance, was common among peasants. Polish Jews played an intrinsic role in both Poland and Polonia. In Poland, Jewish musical bands, *klezmorim*, played for peasant weddings. Jewish midwives helped pregnant Polish women. Peasant girls worked in Jewish homes as domestics, and Polish neighbors acted as *Shabbat goyim*, performing household chores forbidden to Jews during the Sabbath. Indeed, Polish Catholics and Polish Jews lived side by side for centuries in what the sociologist Ewa Morwaska has called "distant proximity." In America, too, they often lived together in neighborhoods but lived apart as far as institutions and cultures were concerned. This spatial integration but social segregation was typical of many groups in the American industrial city.

Polish peasants referred to Jews as *Żydki* or in the singular as *Żydek*, which translated as "Little Jew." This term implied the reality that Jews, while rooted in the Polish countryside, where still seen as alien and therefore as vulnerable. For peasants at the bottom of the social ladder, Jews could be seen as social objects susceptible to violent victimization. Jews often felt that Polish peasants were uncouth and uncivilized and exerted a kind of brutish power. Nevertheless, Jews also expressed pity toward Polish peasants for their wretched living conditions. Jews felt both a sense of fear and mistrust reinforced by the threat of their neighbors. Immigrants brought these relationships to America.[32]

The intricate relationship, while frequently strained, was on an individual basis friendly, even close. Polish Chicago's business and journalist class, conversely, often attacked what it saw as Jewish economic power, a frequently expressed bias. As early as 1888, the *Zgoda* complained that, while Polish businesses along Noble Street went bankrupt, Jewish businesses prospered. The paper complained that Jewish businesspeople bargained with Poles, especially Polish women. *Zgoda* encouraged Polish Chicagoans to avoid Jewish stores and patronize only those of Polish Christian owners. In 1896, as two Jewish-owned banks collapsed, the *Dziennik Chicagoski* lectured its Polish and Lithuanian customers and wrote that Poles rush to the Jews "as if to a fire" to buy steamship tickets, to seek out medical advice, and to trust them with their money. Despite such objections by the growing middle class in Polish Chicago, Polonia's working-class residents continued to patronize Jewish businesses. The *Dziennik Chicagoski* lamented, "And still the Poles do as they please. And you see what happens— tears and gnashing of teeth!" The PRCUA's newspaper *Narod Polski* lambasted Jewish-owned businesses and their Polish patrons in 1901. The Polish socialist press, in contrast, decried anti-Semitic attitudes, but their voice remained a minority one.[33]

As Polish newspapers lashed out against Jewish-owned establishments, the ideological divide between the Polish National Alliance and the Polish Roman Catholic Union also resulted in charges by the *Dziennik Chicagoski* that Jews and socialists had undue influence over the PNA. In 1896, the newspaper claimed that the PNA leadership was attempting to turn Polonia away from Catholicism and toward the Jews and anarchism.[34] For many Polonia leaders, Jews who had lived side by side with Poles for centuries became "the other."

Despite Polish Christian antagonism toward Jews, the Polish press on occasion offered grudging admiration for them. In 1911, the *Dziennik Związkowy* chastised Polish Chicagoans for not sending their children to school. The PNA newspaper stated that Polish fathers often felt that an elementary school education was sufficient for their children and that they should go to work at the age of fourteen. The Polish daily wrote, "Let us take, for instance, the Jews. Every Jew, even a very poor one, tries by all means to educate his children. High schools, colleges and other institutions of higher learning are filled with Jews, and this is the reason why they have such strong influence in this country." The paper further admonished Polonia: "Only one generation was necessary for Jews in America to create an intelligent class. We Poles had the same chance, but we did not take advantage of it."[35]

This clash resulted from various factors such as antagonistic ideologies, economic competition, traditional anti-Semitism, and the policy of the Russian government, which promoted conflict between Poles and Jews. In addition, the pre–World War One boycott of Jewish businesses by the National Democratic Party led by Roman Dmowski in Poland resulted in clashes in the United States. The outbreak of war in 1914 and the eventual emergence of an independent Poland further exacerbated relations in Chicago and across the United States between the two groups.[36] All in all, the relationship between Jew and Pole remained a complicated one, especially in Chicago. The city considered itself the second largest Polish city in the world and stood behind only New York and Warsaw in the number of Jewish residents. The relationship between Poles and Jews in America, and in Chicago in particular, shifted over time, and the era during World War One and its aftermath proved to be especially dangerous.

While the Polish relationship with Lithuanians, Jews, Germans, Czechs, and other East Europeans was historically a long one, Polish immigrants quickly came into contact with groups that they had not been familiar with in Europe. At first, chief among these was the Irish, a well-established group in Chicago. The exchange between these two groups revolved interactions in the Catholic Church and on the factory, tannery, mill, and slaughterhouse floors. The Irish controlled the Catholic Church in Chicago and across the United States. They also worked their way up in the city's political and labor union structure. Indeed, in many ways the Irish introduced the Poles to life in Chicago. An argument can be made for the "hibernization" (i.e., the process of making Irish) of Poles and others in American cities as occurring before Americanization. Irish American street gangs certainly had an influence on their Polish counterparts in Chicago, particularly on the South Side where they came most in contact and, on occasion, in conflict.[37]

The relationship with African Americans and with Mexicans developed more fully after World War One. This also occurred primarily on the South Side, where these groups came largely into contact after the Great Migration of African Americans took place around 1915 and after Mexican immigration increased after 1920. World War One proved crucial for many of the dealings Poles had with other groups across the city. Fighting on the eastern front devastated Polish lands, while in the United States, and particularly in Chicago, the Polish community attempted to navigate its relationship with the homeland as well as with the ethnic groups and the power structure in Chicago and the nation.

World War One

A Turning Point

For a universal war for the Freedom of the Peoples,
We beseech thee, O Lord.
For the arms and the eagles of our nation,
We beseech thee, O Lord.
For a happy death on the field of battle,
We beseech thee, O Lord.
For the burial of our bones in our own land,
We beseech thee, O Lord.
For the independence, unity, and freedom of our Fatherland,
We beseech thee, O Lord.
In the name of Father, Son, and Holy Ghost. Amen.
—ADAM MICKIEWICZ, "The Pilgrim's Litany"[1]

In 1896, the editor of *Dziennik Chicagoski*, Stanislaus Szwajkart, stated that a "decisive moment" approached that would bring about the resurrection of the Polish state. Szwajkart decried the political and ideological divisions that plagued both Poland and Polonia and called for unity, urging Polonia to be prepared for this rebirth, "which will follow a war." On June 2, 1910, the PNA news-paper *Zgoda* proclaimed on the front page that there would be no peace without a free and independent Poland. At that moment, the clouds of war had not yet gathered over Europe and the world, but many felt that conflict would be inevitable as the empires of the old continent maneuvered for power. Three of those empires—Russia, Germany, and Austria-Hungary—occupied the Polish lands. In December 1912, *Zgoda* asserted that Poles in the United States would be prepared to aid the fatherland in its quest for independence. The following February, *Zgoda* proclaimed that Polonia was prepared for combat and that the question of Polish independence remained a factor in the search for peace.[2]

Indeed, in the Polish lands, leaders in all three partitions hoped to restore the Polish state. In 1905, Poles in the Russian partition actively took part in the revolutionary struggles of that year. They and their Russian allies lost their battle, but the hope of change remained as the czarist state continued to totter. The 1912 war between the allied forces of Serbia, Bulgaria, Greece, and Monte-negro, who fought the Ottoman Empire, further agitated Polish patriots. The Balkan War seemed to presage another conflict that might embroil the three empires that ruled over Poland, as well as and most of Eastern and Central Europe. In the Austro-Hungarian Empire, the soldier and Polish patriot Józef Piłsudski agitated and prepared his militia for a future struggle against Rus-sia. The future "George Washington" of independent Poland saw himself as the heir to the traditions of the old Polish-Lithuanian Commonwealth and desired the resurrection of that multiethnic state. Piłsudski became the leader of the Polish Socialist Party and supported the revolutionaries in Russia in 1905. During World War One, he at first supported the Central Powers with the hope of defeating Russia. Later, he then hoped for the Allies to defeat Germany and an independent Poland to rise from the conflict. To many observers, all of this would seem to be a pipe dream in 1914.

Piłsudski's main rival, Roman Dmowski, organized a political movement of National Democrats, or Narodowa Democracja, popularly known as the Endecja (the Polish pronunciation of the organization's initials ND) and hoped for a Russian war against Germany that might reunite all the Polish lands under the czar and eventually lead to independence. Poles conspired everywhere, and the Fourth Partition along with its capital, Chicago, proved to be no exception. Dmowski and his followers, including the pianist Ignacy Jan Padereweski, would have a major impact on the Polish independence movement, as seen by the Allies.[3]

1914: Annus Horribilis

Naturally, Polish political and ideological differences influenced Polish Chicago. When war broke out on July 28, 1914, it placed Poles in an awkward position. Poland saw its youth fighting on both sides of the struggle. Józef Piłsudski immediately supported the Austro-Hungarian Empire, while those who sided with Edmund Dmowski condemned Germany and hoped for the victory of the Entente composed of France, Great Britain, and Russia. Polish Chicagoans had a mixed reaction. While all hoped that the end of the war would result in a free and independent Poland, most feared that the country would be devastated by the fighting and that none of the clashing empires had Poland's interests in mind.

In Chicago, on August 3, a gathering sponsored by Polish National Defense Committee, or Komitet Obrony Narodowej, of roughly two thousand Poles at Walsh's Hall burned the picture of Czar Nicholas II and copies of the *Dziennik Naródowy*, which had called for Poles to side with Russia in the event of a general European war. The Polish National Defense Committee, a supporter of Piłsudski and his legion in Austria-Hungary, put forth a resolution condemning Russia as the mortal enemy of Poland. It also condemned Germany and concluded by saying, "What we want and hope that Poland will achieve through this war is freedom and independence; not a part of Poland, but the whole." The PNA newspaper *Dziennik Związkowy* called the meeting with its demonstration a childish prank.[4]

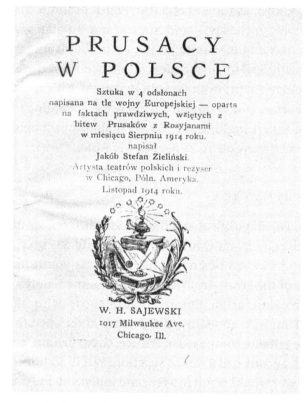

The script for the play *The Prussians in Poland*, by Jakób Stefan Zieliński, which described the events of August 1914 on the Eastern Front. It was distributed by the W. H. Sajewski Publishing Company, which published many Polish books in Chicago. (Author's collection.)

The following week, the Polish National Alliance held an annual picnic at Pulaski Park to benefit the PNA library. More than a thousand people gathered in what became a demonstration in support of Poland, now suffering from the horrors of war. A notice at the entrance to the park surprisingly announced that there would be no dancing at the picnic. At 5 p.m., Michael Kmieciak, chairman of the Library Department and a director of the PNA, addressed the crowd and thanked them for their support of the library fund. He then introduced John F. Smulski, who spoke about the situation in Europe and stated that the immigrant community could not simply stand by and ignore Poland's plight.

As he spoke, several women went about the crowd and collected money, about $48.00 ($1,174 in 2017) for aid to those suffering in Poland. The band then played a medley of Polish songs. Casimir Zychlinski, president of the Polish National Alliance, explained that there would be no dancing at the picnic because it was not fitting to dance "while our brothers in Poland are dying from the sword and from starvation, when cannons are playing funeral music for women and children." The PNA leader condemned all three of Poland's occupiers and called for the resurrection of the Polish state. The crowd responded with another collection that came to $59.18 ($1,449). The meeting sent a cablegram to the Belgian nation lauding their stand against German aggression and condemning the Prussians as the eternal enemy of Poland.[5] While both the picnic and the gathering sponsored by the Polish National Defense Committee called for the reconstitution of Poland and condemned the occupying powers, their differences also highlighted the division within Polonia and Poland as to what side should be supported in the hostilities.

The *Dziennik Związkowy* lamented this lack of unity in both Polonia and Poland, declaring that every Pole was a born politician and that if every Pole was allowed to govern according to his own ideas "we would have at least twenty-five million governments and twenty-five million systems of government, with as many countries, monarchies, and republics." The paper complained that this curse hung over both the nation and the diaspora. The *Dziennik Związkowy* protested that those who called it and the PNA "Moscowphiles" forgot that the Russians are a Slavic people, and the war that was raging was between Teuton and Slav. Earlier, the newspaper had stated that Germany was the enemy of every Slav and cited the historic victory of the combined Polish and Lithuanian forces against the Teutonic Knights at Grunwald in 1410. While wishing for a Russian and Slavic victory, the *Dziennik Związkowy* also hoped that the war would weaken Russia so that Poland could rise and settle her score with the Russian Empire. Furthermore, the *Dziennik Związkowy* proclaimed, "we see in the defeat of Germany the defeat of our everlasting oppressors, the defeat of monarchism and, by the same token, the defeat of Russian czarism, which, although it will emerge victorious from the war with the Germans, will be weakened and will pave the way toward revolution!" The newspaper thus predicted the destruction of all three empires, something that could only be considered a Polish fantasy in 1914. The daily foresaw a future in which Poland would be a neutral country dividing Germany and Russia.[6]

The *Dziennik Związkowy*, in an August 20 editorial, bemoaned the fact that Polonia argued over which course to take and called for unity. The newspaper proclaimed that the diaspora had only two tasks: to collect as much money as possible to help the homeland and to encourage as many people as possible to return to Poland after the war and help rebuild the country. The paper, echoing *Endecja*'s right-wing leanings, also warned against the Jews, recalling the 1912 boycott of Jewish businesses led by the Dmowski party. "The Jews will not rest but will immediately endeavor to get control of the commerce, industry, and handicraft of a free Poland." Polish nationalists quickly turned against the Jewish minority as they attempted to build support among the masses both in Poland and in the diaspora.[7]

As Polish hopes for independence rose, rallies took place across Chicago's Polonia. On Sunday, September 13, commune (or chapter) 39 of the PNA held a meeting at Słowacki Hall (Columbia Hall) on Forty-Eighth and Paulina. Leaders complained about the small turnout and that Polish Chicagoans did not comprehend the importance of the war for Poland. The Back of the Yards Polonia turned out in greater numbers for another rally organized three weeks later. That meeting adopted a resolution condemning Germany and demanding the reunification of the Polish lands. It also pledged to support the independence fund of the Polish National Alliance.[8]

As winter approached, Chicago's Polish press appealed to Polonia to help those caught in the war zone. The war in the east raged primarily in the Polish lands, as Poles faced a bleak Christmas. All of the fraternal organizations made emotional appeals to send funds to Poland so that children might have a bit of Christmas joy as the imperial armies marched across the countryside. The *Dziennik Związkowy* put this in terms of "Prussian barbarism."

Poles from the German Partition dominated the leadership of Chicago's Polonia and they harbored a special hatred toward Germany because of Otto von Bismarck's Kulturkampf, which persecuted both Poles and Catholics in the 1870s. The twentieth century brought more anti-Polish actions on behalf of Berlin, which wanted more ethnic German settlers in the Polish lands. Indeed, Polish Americans knew of attempts by Berlin to assimilate Poles or replace them with German colonists. These attempts included the forced Germanization of the school system in parts of the German Partition, which resulted in a school strike by Polish students in Wreześnia in 1901. That year, various reports appeared about Poles being dismissed from the German military and civil service or of having to confess to priests only in the German language. Reports circulated of German administrators dismissing Polish students from secondary schools and universities for partaking in Polish cultural initiatives. In Wreześnia, German teachers punished Polish students and caned them for insisting on speaking Polish. The *Naród Polski* reminded readers that the Prussian government made religious instruction in German mandatory on every level.

Demonstrations erupted in Chicago and across American Polonia. In December 1901 and early 1902, protest resolutions were adopted in the Chicago parishes of St. Stanislaus Kostka, St. John Cantius, and St. Mary of Perpetual Help. Poles planned a series of protest meetings in five parishes across Chicago. These occurred on January 26, 1902, in the parishes of St. Adalbert, St. Mary of Perpetual Help, Holy Trinity, St. Joseph, and Immaculate Conception. Activists immediately adopted resolutions in Polish and English asserting the sanctity of one's native language. The anti-German resolution was a protest in the name of two hundred thousand Polish Chicagoans and two million Polish immigrants in the United States.[9]

As a result of this history, when war broke out in Europe, many saw Germany as Poland's primary enemy, but Russian persecution of Poles complicated the issue. Most saw the Austro-Hungarian Empire as under German influence despite the fact that Austria's Poles had been given the most freedom and Polish nationalism most fully bloomed in Galicia. The issue of whom to support in the war continued to befuddle many Polish Chicagoans. By 1914, all three partitions were represented among the many immigrants who had arrived, with those from Galicia making up a large percentage of most recent immigrants. To many, Russian promises of unifying all of Poland under the Russian scepter did not bode well for Poland. The struggle between Piłsudski and his Polish Socialist Party and Dmowski and his National Democrats continued to divide Polonia. The Polish tradition of insurrection also played a part, as many Polish Chicagoans identified with Piłsudski's plan to create a Polish army to fight the Russians. Nevertheless, opinion makers and fraternal leaders in Chicago, especially those who led the Polish National Alliance and the Polish Roman Catholic Union, leaned toward Dmowski and his increasingly important ally in the United States, the renowned pianist Ignacy Jan Paderewski. Also, public opinion among Americans in general tended to favor the Entente.[10]

Polish leaders in Chicago continued to ask for support for Poland and framed it within anti-German language. Leaders within the PNA, in particular, reproached Polonia for being stingy and not raising enough money for Polish relief. In an editorial, the *Dziennik Związkowy* reprimanded its readers for false promises and chided them for giving so little to the cause: "Will we not blush that we who are millionaires in comparison to our brethren on Polish soil—we who are well fed and clothed, we in our comfortable 'parlors' and warm bedrooms—have not been able together to contribute even $100,000 to help our homeland at a time so full of hope!"[11]

Of course, the war had just begun and the majority of Polish Chicagoans remained as unskilled workers with few extra funds.

That they donated what they did spoke to their continuing concern for Poland, as did the money they sent back to their families in Poland. The coming years of fighting saw a growing response from the American Polonia and especially from Chicago, its capital.

Polonia Organizes

One of the first displays of organized reaction to the fighting occurred on Polish Day, Sunday, January 24, 1915. Planned under the auspices of a new group that came into being in Chicago the previous October, the Polski Centralny Komitet Ratunkowy (Polish Central Relief Committee), it received support from all major Polish American organizations. Leaders told Polonia to reach out to other ethnic groups to raise money.[12] Earlier, on January 20, Mayor Carter Harrison II of Chicago issued a proclamation encouraging all the people of Chicago to take part in tag days to raise money for Polish relief on January 23 and 24. The mayor, who had learned ethnic politics from his late father, the former mayor of the city, said that no country suffered more from the fighting than did Poland. He established a Polish Days committee that included a wide cross-section of Chicago's Polish clergy, aldermen, and leaders as well as prominent non-Poles, such as Julius Rosenwald and Charles M. Dawes. Polish Days raised $250,000 ($6,119,650 in 2017) for humanitarian aid for the devastated Polish lands.[13]

While Polonia took up the issue of Polish relief, many hoped to raise an army. Polish American organizations contacted the British and French governments, which, however, refused to aid them, because the United States remained neutral and they did not want to embarrass Washington. Poles in France spoke of forming an army, but this soon collapsed. Talk of a Polish legion in Russia emerged, but this, too, failed. Polish Chicagoans and others who hoped to reach the Piłsudski legion faced an expensive and almost insurmountable problem because of the British blockade of German and Austrian ports. So as long as the United States remained neutral, no Polish army could be effectively raised in the diaspora.[14]

Meanwhile, divisions within Chicago's Polonia and across the Polish settlements in the United States continued to fester. The fifteen Chicago communes (chapters) of the Polish National Alliance, which included about one-fourth of the national membership, adopted a resolution on March 12, 1915, condemning the "remnants" of the Polish National Defense Committee for attacking the PNA and undermining its influence. The Chicago communes further implored the PNA leadership not to come under the influence of the socialist faction that represented Piłsudski and the Polish Socialist Party.[15]

As the war continued, it became more and more evident that physical destruction and famine had devastated the Polish lands. The Nobel Prize–winning author Henryk Sienkiewicz made a personal appeal to the United States to send aid to the stricken country. He represented a group organized in Vevey, Switzerland, allied with Dmowski and served as president of the General Relief Committee for the Victims of War in Poland. Paderewski acted as vice president. The committee appealed for American aid, pointing out that Poland was the eastern equivalent of Belgium, which had also been ravaged by the fighting. Sienkiewicz explained that all labor and industry had been swept away by the invading armies. Paderewski arrived in Chicago in 1915 and addressed some fifty thousand Polish Chicagoans in Humboldt Park marking the annual celebration of the anniversary of the Polish constitution adopted in the eighteenth century. The Polish Roman Catholic Union encouraged its members to take part in an international singing contest to be held at Riverview Park on the city's North Side on June 13 to raise funds for Polish relief. In an astonishing show of solidarity, eighteen different ethnic groups promised to take part in the event.[16]

Paderewski, as the representative of the Vevey committee, named Mrs. Lynde Aldis Lathrop, wife of the wealthy insurance and real estate businessman Bryan Lathrop, to lead the Chicago Polish relief movement. Switzerland, Austria, and Russia sanctioned Paderewski's committee. The Lathrop's gave a luncheon at the Blackstone Hotel to organize the Chicago committee for Polish relief at which they raised $2,350 ($57,525 in 2017). Paderewski arrived to confer with the committee on May 29. Unfortunately, the renowned pianist did not seem to have a deep understanding of American politics, as his committee had no Democratic Party members at a time when the Democrats controlled the White House. While Paderewski is often mentioned as the force behind involving the United States in the Polish cause, the maestro made major mistakes and also favored large public gestures over more detailed behind-the-scenes political activity. Nevertheless, Paderewski came to the United States to garner the country's aid in the cause of Polish relief and his efforts created a major public relations campaign that brought the Polish question to the American public and its politicians.[17]

As a result, the humanitarian disaster that befell all three partitions during the fighting brought Polish statehood up before the court of American public opinion. Poland's suffering helped mobilize American support for the country's resurrection. While the international politics of attempting to send relief to Poland proved complicated and eventually, by the end of 1916, ended in defeat, the effort gained massive public sympathy for Poland. The failure to aid the starving Polish population promoted the idea of the rebirth of the Polish state in the American public's eye.[18]

Chicago's Polonia greatly involved itself in these matters. President Wilson proclaimed January 1, 1916, Polish Relief Day. Polonia leaders sent a telegram of thanks to the White House. The *Dziennik Związkowy* addressed the question in February with an editorial calling for American aid to the Polish people. In March, Archbishop George W. Mundelein proclaimed Sunday, April 2, as Polish Day in the Chicago Archdiocese, and all parishes, regardless of ethnic identification, made collections for Polish relief. Mundelein also made a personal contribution to the cause.

John Smulski and Ignacy Jan Paderewski, ca. 1917. Smulski acted as Paderewski's agent in Chicago as both struggled to organize Polonia in support of Polish independence during World War One. (From the collection of the Polish Museum of America, x2005.001.0462.)

On May 28, 1916, Chicago's Poles celebrated the 125th anniversary of the May 3 Constitution and paid tribute to Thaddeus Kosciuszko. A parade of roughly thirty thousand people made its way through the Northwest Side of the city and ended at the Kosciuszko monument in Humboldt Park. The rally put forward a resolution demanding Polish independence. That evening, Polonia celebrated further with a banquet in the Auditorium Hotel on Michigan Avenue.[19]

Later that year, as international diplomatic efforts at coordinating relief for the beleaguered nation failed, the major Polish organizations, nearly all headquartered in Chicago, again sent a message asking for President Wilson's aid. Manifestations of Polish patriotism and concern for those suffering in the Polish lands appeared across Chicago's Polish neighborhoods. On Sunday, December 3, the Poles in Back of the Yards held a commemoration of the November Uprising at Słowacki Hall. Speakers honored the writer Sienkiewicz, who had recently died, spoke of the tribulations that Poland endured, and collected $57.15 ($1,233 in 2017) for Polish relief. As 1916 came to an end, the Polish Central Relief Committee in Chicago called for Polonia's participation in a great bazaar on January 10, to be held at the Chicago Coliseum on South Wabash Avenue, to raise more funds. The committee requested that representatives of all Polish societies attend an organizational meeting at the Polish Women's Alliance Building. The appeal pointed to similar bazaars held in Detroit and New York City. The Polish Central Relief Committee drew attention to the fact that local Polish efforts would share in the proceeds to help the people of the beleaguered nations.[20]

As a result of Poland's partition among Germany, Russia, and Austria-Hungary, the Polish political response to the war remained fragmented in both Europe and the United States. Nevertheless, the orientation of Chicago's Polonia increasingly favored the Entente and, therefore, Poland's Dmowski faction. Late in 1915, Dmowski left Russia and moved his operations to western Europe. He began to assert more authority over the Poles in France and Britain and, consequently, in the United States as well. Meanwhile Paderewski, always a popular figure in the United States and especially in Chicago, emerged as the voice here not only of Polish relief but also of Polish independence. Despite his shortcomings, he played a major role in Polonia politics. In addition, Chicagoan John F. Smulski, the inheritor of his father's publishing empire as well as a successful businessman and politician in his own right, arose as a powerful ally of Paderewski. In general, the pro-Entente forces seized the day, as the Polish

National Defense Committee and those who favored the Central Powers declined by the end of 1916. In the long run for Polonia, this was a good result of the internecine struggles, as the United States increasingly favored the Entente and would soon join it as an ally.[21]

Polonia Goes to War

On April 6, 1917, the U.S. Congress declared war on Germany and the Central Powers. Chicago's Polonia quickly answered the call to arms. The announcement had many ramifications for the diaspora on local, national, and international levels. It solidified the position of the Paderewski-led faction and put American Polonia firmly within the camp of the Entente (now known as the Allies). In addition, the end of American neutrality freed the Polish community to raise a Polish army in North America to fight on the Western Front. Third, with the declaration of President Wilson's Thirteen Points, an independent Poland with access to the sea became an allied goal. The successful Bolshevik Revolution took Russia out of the war later that year and the Central Powers now occupied all of historic Poland, which enabled the Allies to promote the objective of Polish nationhood if they could defeat Germany.

Polish men volunteered in large numbers for the American armed forces. One estimate claimed that Poles, both European-born and American-born, made up forty-two thousand of the first hundred thousand men to volunteer. Eventually as many as three hundred thousand Polish Americans served in uniform. On April 7, the National Department of the Central Polish Relief Committee, with its Chicago-dominated Executive Committee, telegrammed President Wilson offering their loyalty and their willingness to place at his disposal all the strength and resources at their command. Polonia obviously wanted to assure Wilson of its loyalty to the American and Allied cause, especially now that Polish independence with access to the sea had become a goal of the Allies.[22]

On Sunday, June 3, 1917, Chicago's Polonia showed its organizational strength and patriotism with a huge parade and demonstration to mark the annual Kosciuszko and Polish Constitution Day celebration. Marchers assembled at the PNA Headquarters on Division and Noble Streets at 1:00 p.m., which was decorated in Polish and American national colors. Mary Sakowski, president of the women's division of the Polish National Alliance, distributed badges to some eighty women who had volunteered to sell them to raise money for civilian victims of the war as it raged across the Polish lands. Polonia organizations formed their ranks under the guidance of Chief Parade Marshal R. Kaszubowski and his assistant marshal, L. Panka. Thousands filled the streets, boulevards, and Humboldt Park at the site of the Kosciuszko monument, where a platform stood filled with dignitaries. American and Polish flags decorated the parade route. The procession caused streetcar service to be temporarily suspended, as the long line of marchers made passage along Division Street impossible.

Adam Majewski, commissioner of the Polish National Alliance, rose to open the program at 3:30 p.m. After a few words of introduction, he called on the demonstration's chairman, Julius Śmietanka, to address the crowd. Applause broke out during his speech, in which he called for the full support of Polonia for the American war effort and for an independent Poland. He summoned youth to enlist in the U.S. Army as volunteers and urged the purchase of Liberty Bonds. The orchestra followed with a rendering of "America" and the Polish hymn, "Patrz Kosciuszko Na Nas z Nieba" (Watch us from heaven, Kosciuszko"). The activist and Polish patriot cleric, Rev. Władysław Zapała, reminded the immense throng that Kosciuszko donned the peasant cloak and fought for their liberty as well as for Poland's. Speakers called for sacrifices in both America's and Poland's name. The gathering adopted a resolution in the name of the estimated crowd of forty thousand Polish Americans in attendance and vowed to sacrifice everything for the freedom of both countries. The gathering ended with the singing of "Boże Coś Polskę."[23]

Polish American aid to a Poland still starving, and occupied by the Central Powers, continued after the American declaration of war. On July 10, Laura de Gozdawa Turczynowicz, author of the book *When the Prussians Came to Poland*, visited PNA Headquarters. A well-known vocalist, she had been born in Canada and married Stanisław de Turczynowicz, Count Gozdawa. Turczynowicz fled the German incursion with her children and arrived in New York on September 30, 1915. She went on a speaking tour to promote her book and to raise funds to support the Red Cross in Poland and Lithuania. Casimir Zychlinski, the president of the Polish National Alliance, assured Turczynowicz that Polonia would come to the aid of their stricken homeland. After the author's speech, a discussion began on the prospect of forming a committee for the reconstruction of Poland. The next day, organizers held the first meeting.[24]

On August 5, a mass demonstration at Pulaski Park called by the PNA condemned the arrest of General Piłsudski and Wacław Sieroszewski, as well as the internment of the Polish Legions in the east, because of their refusal to swear allegiance to Germany's kaiser. The Philaret Choir sang a rendition of "Jeszcze Polska Nie Zginęła" (Poland is not lost) and "The Star-Spangled Banner." The initial speaker, Anthony Czarnecki, a member of the Chicago Board of Education who also worked on the *Chicago Daily News*, spoke out against the arrests and the German treatment of Poles. He lauded Piłsudski and said, "The Polish legionnaires refused to take the oath of allegiance to Germany, knowing that this would be a violation of all the most sacred feelings in Poland, it would be a curse upon the nation." Despite previously opposing Piłsudski, Chicago's Polonia now embraced him and his legion. This would be important in the years to come as Piłsudski took on the mantle of Poland's savior.[25]

That October 25, the annual meeting of the Polish Central Relief Committee opened at the Polish Women's Alliance Hall on Ashland Avenue. Delegates from major Polonia centers attended. The president of the relief committee, Teodor M. Helinski, stated

Polish Women's Alliance Hall on North Ashland Avenue, 1917. The hall provided a gathering place for many manifestations of Polish American unity in the name of Polish independence. The first recruiting station for the Blue Army was also located in this building. (Postcard, author's collection.)

that funds had not been flowing in recently but that this probably resulted from the fact that Polonia faced various economic and social demands. In addition to collecting funds to help those suffering in Poland, funds were also allocated to aid German-held Polish prisoners. The relief committee further passed a resolution to create a Polish army to fight side by side with the Allies. The motion also requested Polish priests to issue the call to arms from every pulpit and further expressed thanks to the Allied Powers and especially to the United States and France for allowing the creation of the Polish Army.[26]

The organization of a Polish army in the United States instantly became a cause célèbre in the Polish community. While only a small minority of Polish Americans volunteered for what became known as the Blue Army or Haller's Army, it provided a potent symbol for Polonia to prove its allegiance to the cause of Polish independence. On June 4 1917, the French government permitted the creation of an independent Polish army on its territory. The U.S. War Department agreed that the recruitment for the Polish Army could take place within the United States and its territories the following October. On October 10, the first volunteers gathered at the Polish Women's Alliance Building, where a recruitment office had been organized.

Over thirty thousand Poles in the diaspora volunteered for the Polish Army. The federal government, however, stipulated that only those born outside the United States who had not yet taken out citizenship papers, were not heads of families, not in the process of volunteering for the American armed forces, and were not within the age range of the draft, that is twenty-one to thirty years of age, could join Haller's Army. By November, the Polish Army opened recruiting centers in eighteen states and Canada. Training facilities operated at Fort Niagara-on-the-Lake, Ontario, and St. John, Canada. By December, a second training camp opened at Fort Niagara, New York. The first contingent shipped off to France in February 1918.[27]

On Sunday, September 9, 1917, thousands marched to the Kosciuszko monument in Humboldt Park to receive the visiting Franco-Polish military mission and to honor Kosciuszko yet again as the Polish hero of the American Revolution. American, French, and Polish colors decorated neighborhood homes. At nine o'clock in the morning, Polish organizations gathered on Division Street to conduct the visitors from France to St. Stanislaus Kostka Church. Reverend Francis Debiński, pastor of the church, celebrated Mass and Rev. Rector Władysław Zapała delivered the sermon. During his homily he said, "We welcome the Polish Army here on this free soil, where we are permitted to pray in our churches in Polish, where we are permitted to speak in Polish, where our national growth is not impeded." After Mass, organizers took the visitors to the Washington Monument in Washington Park on the South Side. When they returned that afternoon, a parade took place to the Kosciuszko monument. Despite the rain, about ten thousand spectators followed the procession. The French representative, Henri Franklin Bouillon, and Lt. Wacław Gąsiorowski of the Polish Army in France placed wreaths on the Kosciuszko monument. Bouillon declared that the Polish Army would be independent and that it would fight for the resurrection of the Polish state. He proclaimed, "We shall in as full measure as possible, make reparation for the criminal partition of Poland." A telegram pledging the support of four hundred thousand Chicago Poles was sent to French president Raymond Poincaire. The importance of this cannot be underestimate: it bound American Polonia in general, and Chicago's Polonia in particular, to the Polish war effort. Those men who would volunteer and be sent to France and later to Poland served as Polish soldiers, under Polish command, and now fighting in an undeniably Polish cause.[28]

On October 14, 1917, between twenty-five and forty thousand Poles and their supporters gathered at the Dexter Park Pavilion (International Amphitheater) in the Union Stock Yard to celebrate the one hundredth anniversary of the death of Kosciuszko and to present the first battle flags to the Polish Army. At 1:00 p.m., crowds began to fill the streets around St. Joseph's Parish in Back of the Yards as marchers arrived at Słowacki Hall (Columbia Hall), which had been designated as the starting point for the parade to the pavilion at Forty-Third and Halsted Street. Recent volunteers for the Polish Army and members of various Polish societies took part in the spectacle. Representatives of the Polish Army in France—Lt. Gąsiorowski, Stanisław Prince Poniatowski, and Sergeants Włodzimierz Szaniawski and Henryk Rzekiecki—marched along with the volunteers. Reverend Stanisław Cholewinski, the pastor of St. Joseph's, officiated at vespers, assisted by other Polish pastors from Back of the Yards, including Fr. Francis Karabasz of

Recruits to the Blue Army taking physicals in Chicago, ca. 1917. (From the collection of the Polish Museum of America.)

Sacred Heart Parish and Fr. Louis Grudzinski of St. John of God Parish. Reverend Edward A. Kowalewski, pastor of St. Mary Magdalene Church in South Chicago, gave the sermon in which he stated: "We, the 'fourth partition' of Poland, pledge ourselves to give you all possible aid within our means and, as today, so later, we shall encourage the Polish clergy to pray God that you may carry these Polish colors to victory."

At 3:30 p.m., the parade began on its route to the Dexter Park Pavilion. A living American flag made up of Polish girls dressed in red, white, and blue led the way. The Dexter Park stage held the representatives of allied governments and the armies of the United States, France, England, and Poland. Paderewski addressed the crowd for over an hour, stating that "America cannot be a stepmother to the Polish people, she must be a real mother." He presented the flags to the troops. New recruits took their oaths. At the conclusion of the ceremony, which lasted until after 9:00 p.m., the assembly collected $13,560 ($259,129 in 2017) to support the Blue Army.[29]

In March 1918, Poles from Back of the Yards held a similar celebration and reveled in the unfurling of the colors of the Fourth Regiment of the Polish Army. Again, crowds gathered along Forty-Eighth Street as civilian and military societies from the South Side Polish neighborhoods gathered on a cold Sunday to march to St. John of God Church, where Rev. Kowalewski again preached. Afterward, Emily Napieralska, leader of the Polish Women's Alliance, admitted with sadness that relatively few young men had enlisted in the Polish Army. She said that the recruits numbered about twenty-five thousand, while out of a population of four million, there should be at least a million recruits. By March 1918, recruitment in Chicago to the Polish Army continued to fall off to just a few men daily, causing concern among Chicago's Polish leadership.

Polish settlements across the city held rallies. At times, attendance was rather disappointing to organizers, as in the case of the gathering held at Holy Trinity Parish on March 12. Even the slightly more successful rally at St. Hyacinth's Parish in the Avondale neighborhood saw only $36.11 ($691 in 2017) collected for the Polish Army. Nevertheless, an assembly over a thousand people gathered the same day at St. Mary of the Angels Parish in the Bucktown neighborhood and collected $169.46 ($3,241) to support the Blue Army. A Sunday, March 17, rally in Back of the Yards at St. Joseph's Parish again proved disappointing. The next day, the local Citizen's Council in Bridgeport held an assembly for the Polish Army in Bridgeport at Mickiewicz Hall on South Morgan Street in the heart of the Polish community. The meeting collected $254.16 ($4,861). In addition, the gathering sent off eleven recruits for the Polish Army. On March 25, Madame Helena Paderewska spoke to Polish women from across the city at Pulaski Hall. The schoolchildren of nearby St. Adalbert's Parish greeted the wife of the Polish pianist and leader with a rendition of the American national anthem and a medley of Polish songs. She spoke to the crowd on behalf of the children of war-torn Poland and asked for contributions to the Polish Army. Madame Paderewska, like her illustrious husband, had worked fervently for the Polish cause. Earlier, she had sold dolls, made by Polish artists in France, to raise money for relief for her war-ravaged homeland. She also organized the Circle of Girls for Girls, a group of young Polish women who dressed in traditional Polish folk costumes and sold Polish and American flags at various events to raise funds.

The International Red Cross had refused to organize a Polish Red Cross unit. As a result, Polonia, with the urging of Helena Paderewska, organized a group called the Polish White Cross to support the Blue Army.[30]

While the formation of a Polish army to fight in France heightened Polish expectations, Polish American volunteers and draftees to the American armed forces greatly outnumbered those to the Polish Army. American regulations prevented many, especially those born in the United States, from enrolling in the Polish Army. Others found it easier to join the American Army or were drafted. On April 24, 1917, the first 120 Polish volunteers for the U.S. Army left for boot camp. A week later, the Polish community sent off another two hundred Polish recruits. The young men joined others at Camp Jefferson near St. Louis for basic training. By that time, some five hundred Poles had been recruited in Chicago.

On Sunday, May 27, 1917, a parade made its way through the streets of Chicago's Bucktown neighborhood. Saint Hedwig's parishioners showed their support for the war by encouraging enlistments in the U.S. Army. Chicago police lieutenant Palczynski and a platoon of police including eleven Polish policemen headed the parade. Saint Hedwig's scout band and a troop of scouts followed them in procession. A rally was held in St. Hedwig's Hall afterward, and nineteen men enlisted in the U.S. Army. By September 1918, 2,439 members of the PNA who lived in Back of the Yards had joined the U.S. Army. Seven of those had already been killed in France. Polish Blue Army recruits from the neighborhood stood at 754 for a total of 3,193 PNA members serving in the allied armed forces just from this one South Side neighborhood.

Roughly ten thousand Chicago Poles served in the U.S. military during World War One. The first Chicagoan to die in combat was Peter Wojtalewicz of Company G of the Eighteenth Infantry. Two Polish American soldiers, one from Chicago and the other from Milwaukee, captured the first American-held German prisoner of war. Although no official numbers exist, the *Literary Digest* estimated that Polish names made up 10 percent of the casualty lists, while the proportion of Polish Americans in the population of the United States stood at 4 percent.[31]

Not only did Polish Americans join the armed forces, they also participated in Liberty Loan Drives. Polish involvement in the various drives played an important role in the war effort. Jan Smulski reported that, during the war, American Polonia purchased $150,000,000 ($2,431,649,007 in 2017) dollars' worth of bonds. The PNA alone procured $500,000 ($8,105,497) of the bonds. The *Dziennik Związkowy* pointed out that every dollar used to purchase Liberty Bonds contributed to the struggle to defeat Germany and thus spared the blood of those fighting. In South Chicago, the newspaper *Polonia* encouraged laborers to work hard, buy bonds and stamps, and save fuel and food, all in the name of defeating Germany and the Central Powers, thus liberating Poland. By April 1918, the Polish Liberty Bond office on Division Street alone had sold over $10,000 worth of bonds. The Polish press used patriotic language to rally the community to buy the bonds and stamps, proclaiming that those who could afford the bonds but did not buy them were cowards with no place in Polonia.

On April 10, 1918, the St. Stanislaus Kostka Liberty Bond Committee held a meeting in the church hall to rally parishioners to join the third Liberty Loan Drive. Judge Edmund Jarecki addressed the crowd and explained the need for yet another bond drive. He and other speakers reminded the Polish community that they had already proven themselves to be great supporters of the war effort, but they had to give yet more. F. S. Barc, editor of the newspaper *Naród Polski*, said the drive would send Kaiser Wilhelm to hell as quickly as possible, while claiming that when that occurred Lucifer and all his devils would be so repulsed by the German monarch as to flee.[32]

Polish Chicagoans further demonstrated their devotion to the United States and the war effort with loyalty parades. On the Fourth of July, 1918, Chicago's Polonia held a massive parade pledging allegiance to their new home in America. Ludwik Panek acted as grand marshal as representatives from across Chicago's Polonia gathered under Polish and American flags to once again parade across the Northwest Side. The various groups included the Chicago Police, Polish Falcons (*Sokoły*), Polish members of the Illinois Militia, the Mothers of Polish soldiers in France, the Polish National Alliance, the Polish Roman Catholic Union, Polish Women's Alliance, various Polish parishes, and other groups.[33]

Chicago's Wartime Pan-Slavic Alliance

The good relationship between the Polish and Czech communities continued into the twentieth century. When war broke out, the two communities began to grow closer together as increasing numbers of Chicago Poles recognized Germany and Austria-Hungary as enemies of Polish independence. The Czech and Moravian lands had long bristled under Austrian rule, and in 1915 the Czech newspaper *Denni Hlasatel* appealed for "brotherly agreement" between the two communities and declared that it should be easier for them to cooperate as the liberty of both nations was at stake in the Great War.[34]

Beginning as early as 1915, the two Slavic groups campaigned against what they called "Kaiserrized" textbooks in the public schools. They felt that the textbooks showed a definite pro-German bias and championed Germany's kaiser Wilhelm. In

August 1917, superintendent of Chicago Public Schools, John D. Shoop, after promising new books for two years, refused to remove offending texts. Both the Bohemian (later Czech) National Alliance and the Polish National Alliance planned massive demonstrations against the offending texts. Finally, thousands of Slavic students tore out the offending pages from textbooks in a show of solidarity against the Central Powers. Czechs and Poles also petitioned to have German names removed from public schools and streets. Poles, in particular, objected to the name and bust of Otto von Bismarck, "The Iron Chancellor," on a Chicago Public School located in the heart of Logan Square, a largely Polish neighborhood. In July 1917, Mrs. Lu Lu Snodgrass, a member of the school board, tabled a motion to change the school's name made by a Polish member, Anthony Czarnecki. She stated that Bismarck was dead and should be respected. Czarnecki responded that Bismarck might be dead but so were Nero and Attila, yet they did not deserve a school named after them. Czarnecki further argued, "Bismarck was just as much a tyrant as they. And yet in this free country we ask a child from Poland or from Alsace-Lorraine to go to a school labeled after Bismarck, the man who crushed their national life." He suggested the name of a German who had fought for America, such as the Revolutionary hero Friedrich Wilhelm von Steuben, as a compromise. Superintendent Shoop explained, "We do not want to hurt the feelings of anyone." The Chicago Public School Board, handpicked by Republican mayor William "Big Bill" Thompson, who still hoped to court German Americans politically, refused to remove the bust. In August 31, 1917, riding a wave of anti-German sentiment, Czarnecki presented and had passed a school board resolution that ended more than a half century of German-language instruction in the city's public schools. During this time, the German language claimed parity with English in the school system. Finally, in March 1918, after a petition of Polish students, the school board renamed the Bismarck School name after General Frederick Funston, who had fought in the Philippines and led relief efforts during the 1906 San

Francisco earthquake. In April, Czarnecki fought off an attempt by Chicago school board member Albert H. Severinghaus to change the name of the Kosciuszko School as revenge for his successful fight to change the Bismarck School name. Changing the name of a school might seem unimportant, but it had great symbolic meaning for the Polish, Czech, and German communities.[35]

Poles and Czechs moved closer politically. On March 3, 1918, at the Chicago Coliseum, an overflow crowd of thirty-five thousand Polish people cheered Paderewski as he said: "As long as a united, independent Poland is not resurrected, as long as the Czechs, Moravians, and Slovaks are not free, as long as Serbia and the Southern Slavic peoples are not freed and united, as long as the great, terrible war now raging from the Baltic to the Adriatic—a war involving more than fifty-four million highly civilized Slavs—is not won; so long will Prussian ambition remain uncurbed." The maestro called for a united Slavic response to Germany and a mighty Slavic wall stretching from the Baltic to the Adriatic seas. Slavic unity was also supported by Jaroslav J. Zmrhal of the Bohemian National Alliance and by other Slavic groups. Twenty-five men from the Polish Army in France, who had fought on the Western Front, acted as a guard to the Polish military mission in attendance. Clarence Darrow, the legendary Chicago lawyer, addressed the crowd and stated that America stood "with Poland in all her longings, dreams, hopes and aspirations."

A week later, the Polish Falcons (*Sokoły*), a gymnastic-patriotic organization, called a meeting at the Polish Women's Alliance Hall, again emphasizing the need for Slavic unity. Representatives of the Czech Falcon organization—Dr. Rudis-Jicinsky, editor of the Czech *Sokol Americky*, and Mr. Paskowsky, commandant of the Czech Falcons—attended. The hall, filled to capacity, shook with applause for the various speeches given by the Czech guests and for the singing of the hymn "Gde Domov Moj" (Where my home is). Dr. Rudis-Jicinsky's statement that Poles and Czechs must fight together to bring about Slavic unity also brought an enthusiastic response. Rybicki, president of Circuit II of the Polish Falcons' Alliance, called for a union of Polish and Czech Falcons in Chicago. The Polish audience rose to applaud the proposal. The *Dziennik Związkowy* called for a United Slavic States to be established in Europe.[36] Such a United States of Slavic Europe never materialized, but the roots of Czech and Polish cooperation ran deep in Chicago, and both sides saw it as a possible way of influencing politics both in the city and in Europe. Events in Europe soon caused tension between the new states of Czechoslovakia and Poland, but as immigrants in general came under attack in America, the two largest Slavic groups in the city continued to cooperate.

The conclusion of World War One saw the resurrection of Poland and the creation of the Czechoslovak Republic. Poland had been devastated by the war. Millions of Poles, especially children, now faced starvation. The United States reached out to help the new republic, with future president Herbert C. Hoover leading the American Relief Agency, in an attempt to alleviate famine in the Poland. The new republic was a bleak desolate land that suffered from the aftermath of the war. Polonia, too, responded, donating millions of dollars in relief. The Polish Gray Samaritans, a group of women trained by the Young Women's Christian Association to deal with poverty and famine in Poland, volunteered to work with Polish children. These young women served under the auspices of the American Relief Agency with the Polsko-Amerykańska Komitet Pomocy Dziecom (Polish American Committee to Aid Children) for the distribution of relief material from the United States. Agency officials and the Gray Samaritans supervised food shipments and their distribution across the Polish countryside. Gray Samaritans went to rural Polish villages to organize the so-called Children's Kitchens to feed Polish youth during this time of crisis. These women did a yeomen's job and, in some cases, physically protected the bales of clothing and other materials in order to save a generation of Polish children.[37]

Poland now struggled to establish its frontiers. Many wanted the old Polish-Lithuanian Commonwealth restored. Haller's Army joined the Polish struggle as the fighting in eastern Europe continued until finally the country stabilized its borders. The newly established Soviet Union invaded Poland and the fighting did not end until the Treaty of Riga in 1921. Poland had not been restored to its pre-partition glory as the largest state in Europe, but it had regained its independence. Recruiting in the United States for the Polish Army continued until February 15, 1919. By that time, the United States had established diplomatic relations with the new Polish Republic that it had helped create. That year would, however, bring new trials for Chicago's Polonia as the United States sought something known as "normalcy."

Interwar Polonia

Years of Stress and Change

While we are proud of the country of our forefathers, we consider
ourselves first and foremost as Americans. We feel that we can best
help Poland by being better American citizens.
—FRANK ŚWIETLIK, Polish National Alliance, 1934.[1]

On November 11, 1918, Chicago's Polonia celebrated both the
armistice and Poland's declaration of independence. The end of
the fighting brought isolationist and anti-immigrant attitudes
in America to a head. A race riot and then a massive steel strike
rocked Chicago the year after the cease-fire. Gains made by Polish
and other working-class Chicagoans disappeared as the Red Scare,
and an antiunion movement marked the immediate postwar era.
Relations between Polish Chicagoans and their neighbors broke
down as events unfolded in Europe. In addition, Polish Americans,
who had offered so much aid to the Polish independence movement, felt shut out and without influence in the new Poland. Polonia turned increasingly inward into a defensive position vis-à-vis
both American and Polish society. A new maxim, "Wychodźstwo

dla Wychodźstwo" ("The emigration for the emigration"), had a special meaning for Polish Americans who now had to look after their own interests in what was increasingly becoming their permanent home. The pressures to assimilate increased as a result of the war and with the eventual cutting off of immigration by congressional fiat. Everywhere the community's sense of *Polskość* seemed under attack. What did it mean to be Polish in Chicago after the "war to end all wars" had finally brought about a resurrected homeland? What did it mean to be American for a generation born in the city?

The Search for Stability

Chicago celebrated a joyous New Year's Eve after the Armistice. Mayor William H. Thompson and Police General Superintendent John J. Garrity promised to strictly enforce laws closing down establishments at 1:00 in the morning, but Chicagoans always accepted such statements with a wink and a nod. War weary revelers spent over $1,000,000 ($16,210,993 in 2017) during the night's celebration. Loop hotels and cafés reported receipts doubling those of the previous year. Thirteen downtown establishments forgot about the 1:00 a.m. closing rule, including the Hotel LaSalle, the Hotel Morrison, and the Palmer House. Complaints flooded police stations that more than one hundred bars and hotels across the city ignored the law. At Milwaukee and Crawford (now Pulaski Road) the Milford Theater presented the "All Star Vaudeville Show—a Riot of Fun" and a New Year's Eve celebration. The Paulina Theater at 1335 North Paulina, in the heart of the Northwest Side's Polonia, offered Harold Lockwood in the movie *Pals First*, while the nearby Strand Theater at Milwaukee and Hoyne staged a midnight show that featured four vaudeville acts and a six-reel movie. Polish Chicagoans joined in the festivities as John F. Smulski proclaimed that Polish immigrants had a right to feel justly proud of the part they had played in gaining Poland's independence.

The year 1919 proved to be a taxing one, as the United States attempted a return to normalcy. What that meant was anyone's guess. The economy began to readjust as heavy wartime orders disappeared. During the conflict, both the meatpacking plants and steel mills employed large numbers of Poles. The wartime need for manpower resulted in both the arrival of African Americans from the South and the rebirth of the labor movement. The city's black population doubled in response to growing opportunities in the city's major mass production industries, and so racial tension spread across the South Side. That year, Mayor William Hale Thompson won a second term, as the city wondered how Prohibition would be imposed in 1920. Organized labor had made tremendous strides during the war. The return of men from Europe, the growth of the African American community, and the decline of the immediate postwar economy put pressure on unions. Meanwhile in Europe, fighting continued as Poland, her borders not yet secure, had to repel neighbors who did not want to see a strong independent Polish republic. An editorial in the *Chicago Tribune* asked the potent question, "What Do You Mean, Peace?[2]

Polish Chicago remained optimistic as the future promised great things for the homeland. The hope of the founders of the Gmina Polska and the Polish National Alliance that many Polish Chicagoans would remigrate back to Poland seemed possible. When the war broke out, leaders made numerous calls for the diaspora to return and rebuild Poland once peace had been established. While most remained in the United States, some hundred thousand persons returned to Poland. The interwar era became a defining moment for the diaspora. Few could imagine the problems that the diasporic community would face in the upcoming years.[3]

As 1919 progressed, tragedy haunted Chicago. On July 21, a blimp, *Wingfoot Express,* burst into flames over the Loop and crashed into the Illinois Trust and Savings Bank. It was just one event in what turned out to be a stressful and disastrous time for the city.[4] That year, Chicago witnessed horrific accidents, labor strife, racial and ethnic fighting, strikes, and, while then yet not widely known, the most famous baseball scandal in major league history. The following years brought more bad news as "normalcy" seemed not all that normal.

In 1919, Chicago still saw itself as a city of immigrants. The war, however, had cut off immigration and encouraged the movement of African Americans from the rural South to the North. Not only the expansion of wartime industries but also the promises of freedom and mobility attracted these long-exploited Southerners. When the war ended, blacks and whites both saw job opportunities diminish, and competition between the races over jobs, housing, and politics increased. Wartime tensions among Poles, Czechs, other Slavs, and German Chicagoans also remained intense. So did growing feelings of anti-Semitism, specifically among Catholic ethnic groups. The Irish and Poles remained at odds with each other, especially in the Stock Yard District. All of this made Chicago a powder keg. On July 27, less than a week after the crash of the *Wingfoot Express*, a massive race riot rocked Chicago's streets. It began with the killing of Eugene Williams, a young African American boy, in Lake Michigan off of the "white beach" at Twenty-Ninth Street and quickly escalated. The anger and frustrations of the war bubbled up to engulf the city.

There were various conflicting claims as to the ethnicity of the white gang members involved in the fighting. Many newspaper reporters did not fully comprehend the complexities of the human and institutional geography of the South Side between Twenty-Sixth and Sixty-Third Streets. The question of who the white rioters were is a complex one, but evidence points to the Poles, for the most part, not taking an active part in the fighting. Twenty-three blacks and fifteen whites died in the riot. Most of the riot-related casualties took place east of the Union Stock Yards in neighborhoods dominated by Irish, German, and other northwestern European groups. A look at the backgrounds of the whites who died gives a more complete picture of at the socioeconomic basis of the riot. The facts point to the riot being a primarily lower-middle-class event, with participants from what was then considered old immigrant stock. Irish, German, and Swedish names appear among the lists of rioters killed in the fighting.

Polish Americans were not blameless, for they had been involved in anti-Jewish riots in the Douglas Park area just before the race riot. West Side Polish and Jewish gangs actively battled each other. Polish newspapers were divided on the issue of the race riot. The *Dziennik Związkowy* took a rather neutral stance, while the *Naród Polski* took a more anti-black and anti-Semitic stand. It claimed that Germans and Bolsheviks controlled both groups. But it, too, cautioned the Poles to remain calm and stay out of the fighting.

Early on Saturday morning, August 2, a fire broke out in a Polish and Lithuanian section of Back of the Yards. Local Polish priests and Polonia newspapers immediately accused Irish gangs and not African American rioters. Later, a grand jury blamed Irish-dominated social athletic clubs for the fire in an attempt to incite East Europeans against African Americans. They had started the fires early that morning while wearing blackface.

The assertion that no Poles took part in the race riot is not correct. That some Polish Americans hated blacks is without a doubt true. For the most part, however, Poles showed more anger at Jews, and as long as African Americans belonged to the stockyard and steel mill unions, Polish Chicagoans felt little animosity toward them. This changed as the 1920s progressed. As black migration increased, and as the curtailing of immigration reduced the number of young European-born workers, Poles began to feel keenly the competition with African Americans for work in the city's industries. The 1919 steel strike and the 1921–22 packinghouse strike hastened that process, as many whites regarded blacks as strikebreakers. Animosity between Poles and African Americans grew in the cauldron of events surrounding the immediate years after World War One.[5]

In the September 1919 steel strike, steelworkers, in a strike centered in Chicago, stopped work in major steel plants across the country. Walkouts heavily affected Polish neighborhoods and towns south from Seventy-Ninth Street along the lakefront and into northwest Indiana—especially Gary. Wartime organizational campaigns, government intervention, and labor shortages had established unions as a potent force. Polish workers saw their incomes rise and felt secure in their jobs. Management waited until the postwar reaction set in, and in November 1918, Bethlehem Steel announced it no longer felt obliged to recognize decisions of the War Labor Board. Companies counteracted the labor movement with the creation of employee representation plans and hoped these would draw employees from union-organizing efforts. For management, the plans also offered a refuge from interference from Washington. Anti-Soviet sentiments, in turn, ran high and steel companies used anti-Communist rhetoric against union leaders.

Chicago's Polonia took an active part in this conflict, which began on September 22, 1919, as well as in the ill-fated packinghouse strike during the winter of 1921–22. These two strikes can be seen as communal events in which neighborhood residents united to fight the management of the steel mills and packinghouses. Both clashes ended in defeat for organized labor. Polonia saw itself under attack, and despite Poland's war against the Soviet Union, which lasted until 1921, many, if not most, Americans, in the aftermath of the Bolshevik Revolution, painted Polonia and all East Europeans as Red sympathizers.[6]

Polonia and the Intellectuals

For many in the United States, immigration had long been a topic of concern. The so-called new immigration from eastern and southern Europe after 1890 raised fears further. The unpronounceable names, exotic traditions, and religions of what many already-established Americans saw as unassimilable immigrants brought about a reaction across U.S. society. Various studies conducted by members of Congress and academia gave the nativist response a veneer of credibility. Chicago, in contrast, had always been receptive to immigrants. By 1910, these newcomers and their children made up roughly 80 percent of the city's population. Many U.S.-born Protestant whites wondered if cities like Chicago or New York could even be called American.[7]

In response to immigration concerns, the Field Museum of Natural History in Chicago approved in 1919 a three-year trip around the world by Professor George A. Dorsey. He planned to send reports to the *Chicago Tribune* and to comment on the immigration issue. Dorsey, the first person in the United States to earn a PhD in anthropology, was well known in Chicago and across the country. He had served as supervisor of the Archaeology Section of the Columbian Exposition, was curator of the museum's Physical Anthropology Department, and had been on the faculties of both Northwestern University and the University of Chicago. Few could match Dorsey's academic credentials at the time.[8]

The anthropologist planned to visit Austria-Hungary and Galicia with the goal of finding out just who these immigrants were and what they wanted. He sent regular reports in the fall and winter of 1910. A frequent criticism of Dorsey was that he suffered from the misconceptions of someone not familiar with other countries' local history and customs. Earlier, he had argued that immigrants from eastern and southern Europe differed vastly from those from northern and western Europe. Dorsey saw northern European types as fully assimilatable into American society, while he viewed eastern and southern Europeans oppositely. The professor seemed fascinated and perhaps entertained by these "primitive" people.[9]

Dorsey attempted to recount Poland's history to his *Chicago Tribune* readers. He retold the usual stereotypical claims of the greediness of the nobility (gentry) and of the backwardness of the peasants. He suggested that Poles were "strong in intensity, but weak in action" and that they lived in the past and yearned for the sixteenth century. He claimed that he had met no Pole who believed in a future for Poland. Dorsey felt that it was most unlikely that Poland would ever regain its independence. Furthermore, he doubted the physical strength and the mental capacity of the Polish peasant. Also, the professor saw little hope for assimilation of the Polish contingent in the United States.

Dorsey concluded that immigration from eastern Europe should end. He made the misguided assertion that the United States needed farmers not industrial workers. He further believed that immigration should be restricted to the point of exclusion of certain groups. Dorsey maintained that while he had preferences as to whom should be allowed to enter the country, he held no hostility toward any one person, group, or nation. He claimed that his objections were directed toward the masses that transplanted European conditions to American cities and retarded the development of American culture. Dorsey feared that immigrants from southern and eastern Europe were refashioning American cities in their own image rather than being assimilated. In this way, he reflected the attitude of many others who shared his cultural, class, and educational background.[10]

While Chicago's Polish Americans felt particularly attacked, this argument was part of a larger societal assault against immigrants. The enormous 1911 study commonly known as the Dillingham Commission, authorized by the U.S. Congress, set the parameters of the critique. In turn, the lawyer and eugenicist Madison Grant wrote the 1916 best seller titled *The Passing of the Great Race*, which also stressed the inferiority of eastern and southern Europeans. Grant wrote that these "lesser races" should be compared to non-European, and therefore subservient, peoples. He espoused social Darwinism and the superiority of the Aryan race, especially the superiority of Anglo-Saxon culture.[11]

These investigations led to more outrages after the war, including passage of the Eighteenth Amendment prohibiting the sale of alcohol. This law was particularly directed at immigrants, especially those from a Roman Catholic background. This seemed especially true in light of nineteenth-century native-born Protestant campaigns against the "Continental" Sunday, a day that included the visiting of beer gardens, picnics, and other such festivities. These pursuits had long been the target of blue laws prohibiting all types of activities on the Sabbath. Immigrant and ethnic communities, however, routinely ignored such laws, especially in cities such as Chicago, which often did not enforce the regulations. Urban ethnic politics made such enforcement particularly difficult. As pro-prohibition sentiments surged during the years before World War One, the Czech American leader Anton Cermak (or Čermák, in Czech) rose through the ranks to lead the United Societies for Local Self-Government in defending against prohibitionist politicians. Poles and Germans as well as Czechs and others supported this movement, and it became the basis for Cermak's ascent in the Democratic Party.[12]

Since 1896, Massachusetts senator Henry Cabot Lodge had campaigned for a literacy test for immigrants. Finally, in 1917, Congress passed a literacy test bill over President Woodrow Wilson's objections. After the Republicans Party took control of Congress in 1919, Representative Albert Johnson of Washington State, a friend of Madison Grant, a supporter of the Immigration Restriction League, and the head of the Eugenics Research Association, became chairman of the House Committee on Immigration and immediately called for curbing immigration. The House of Representatives again held hearings from 1919 to 1921 and proposed the limitation of immigration. Wilson pocket vetoed the measure. The law finally passed in 1921, with Republican President William G. Harding's approval, and was designed to reverse recent immigration trends. This was the first bill to curb European immigration and was aimed particularly at eastern and southern Europeans. In 1924, the National Origins Act succeeded the earlier law, which was based on the 1910 Census, and used the 1890 census as a baseline for immigration quotas. This cut eastern and southern European arrival numbers to a trickle. Years of social Darwinist theory, nativist diatribes, academic and popular attacks, and a general American fear of outsiders finally closed the door to immigrants from Poland and other countries of eastern and southern Europe by the end of the 1920s.[13]

The publication of W. I. Thomas and Florian Znaniecki's five-volume *The Polish Peasant in Europe and America* beginning in 1918 proved to be an important landmark in the creation of what came to be known as the Chicago school of sociology. The study implied that American Polonia was in disarray and the Polish family unable to deal with the vast changes brought about by capitalism and the modern industrial state.[14] Indeed, Polonia would bear the brunt of other studies emanating from the University of Chicago. Frederic Thrasher's *The Gang: A Study of 1,313 Gangs in Chicago*, which appeared in 1927, claimed that Chicago's working-class neighborhoods provided a breeding ground for street gangs and criminal activity. In particular, Polish neighborhoods appeared ripe for such pursuits, according to Thrasher. Clifford Shaw published *The Jack-Roller* in 1930, which studied the life of a Polish American juvenile delinquent from the Back of the Yards neighborhood. Over and over again, it seemed to Chicago's Polish American leaders that sociologists portrayed their children in a negative light. Many felt this began with Thomas and Znaniecki's study. Both Thrasher and Shaw, however, saw the neighborhood environment as more influential than any ethnic culture. Still, since Poles made up a good deal of the population of Chicago's working-class wards, Poles felt that sociologists had targeted their community. When seen as part of a general nativist attack on immigrants and their communities, Polonia's defensive reaction can seem credible. The subject of Polonia's youth proved especially troubling.[15]

Juvenile Delinquency and Polonia's Response

It did not take a close reading of either the daily newspapers or the sociological literature to know that crime, vice, and social malfunction disturbed the settlements in which most immigrants lived. Polish American youth were actively involved in the street life of the city. They adapted to the gang culture that had long thrived in working-class neighborhoods. While Polish gangs did not play an important role in the 1919 race riot, the 1920s saw their growing importance in the social and political life of the city's poorer wards. Increasingly, these children of immigrants became known as part of the city's underworld.

Perhaps the most notorious young Polish American criminal to emerge was John "Dingbat" Oberta from Back of the Yards. He rose quickly in the organization run by "Polak" Joe Saltis, a Slovak American, who ran the Prohibition Era beer trade on the Southwest Side. Saltis and Oberta aligned themselves with Hymie Weiss's organization. Weiss, who's birth name was Earl J. Wojciechowski, was born in Poland. Although many in Back of the Yards saw Oberta as a kind of Robin Hood character who doled out gifts and favors to poor packinghouse families, both Saltis and Oberta had violent masochistic temperaments. In addition, Oberta has often been credited with the dubious distinction of inventing the "one-way" ride. Ironically, in 1930, other gangsters took Oberta and his driver on a one-way ride outside the city to 103rd Street and Roberts Road.[16]

Polish American members of organized crime presented one type of problem, but the fate of young boys and girls who grew up on the same streets and often looked to men like Oberta as heroes were of more concern. The outside world closely identified the Polish community with a high crime rate and juvenile gangs. Back of the Yards, South Chicago, Pilsen, Bridgeport, and the Polish Downtown area (Stanisławowo-Trójcowo) all ranked high among indices of juvenile crime. In fact, as Thrasher and others noted, these areas had long harbored such activities. Native-born whites, Irish, German, and other western European immigrant groups had all been involved in criminal activity.

Polonia's extensive social network provided a type of fortress for the community and helped it to attempt to provide a stable communal life. Nevertheless, the Polish American community could not counteract every influence in the city. Street life proved

Classroom, Sacred Heart Parochial School, Back of the Yards, 1920s. Polish parochial schools were designed to maintain a sense of Polishness. They also acted as a bridge to the larger American culture. (From the collection of the Polish Museum of America, x2013.002.0011.)

to be a magnet for Polonia's youth, attracting them in ways that proved difficult to thwart. As early as the 1890s, the *Dziennik Chicagoski* bemoaned the fact that Polish boys took part in criminal activities. The newspaper claimed that robberies in Polonia happened as almost a daily occurrence. Crime seemed rampant, and even the local church was not immune. In 1908, John Rasmarowski robbed and then set fire to the parish house at St. Hyacinth's in the Avondale neighborhood. Some robberies ended up with shootings and murder. That same year, the *Chicago Tribune* reported that three Polish boys stood accused of two murders and several robberies in the Stanisławowo neighborhood. The newspaper further reported that the boys seemed rather proud of their accomplishments.[17]

Polish bars on Milwaukee Avenue and Division Street proved especially problematic. Quarrels, physical fights, beatings, stabbings, and sometimes murders occurred in these establishments. Residents formed a "vigilance committee" in 1902 to deal with the problem. Neighborhood saloons often had a hall in the rear, which the *Chicago Tribune* described as small and dark and as breeding grounds for vice where young Polish Americans formed so-called pleasure clubs that held dances that lasted well past midnight. Of course, alcohol flowed freely, and the festivities often ended with young men and women arguing and fighting. These places attracted a mix of both the respectable and hoodlum elements in the community. The halls centered on Noble Street between Bradley Street and Milwaukee Avenue. From there, saloons and dance halls branched out along both Bradley and Division Streets.

Nine saloons operated on Noble Street between Division and Milwaukee Avenue. One of these was John Konwinski's Polish Hall at Noble and Division, which has been described as a low and dilapidated building, with windows covered in colored calico and a worn-out bar. Benches and tables surrounded the hall floor, where young girls and boys attended dances. Father J. Kruzinski of St. Stanislaus College, a local Polish Catholic secondary school and a member of the local vigilance committee, stated that he had no objection to these places when used properly for wedding receptions and the like, but they often provided sites that were disgraceful and breeding places of crime.[18]

Such places existed throughout working-class districts in Chicago and provided much needed public space for residents who lived in overcrowded neighborhoods. While they did often cater to activities that some found unacceptable, they also provided space for people to celebrate or gather and discuss local issues important to the community. The back halls of taverns provided places for unions, political parties, fraternal groups, and patriotic societies to meet and organize. Indeed, these saloon halls played an important part in the development of a web of communal feeling that created a public sphere for local residents. It was poverty that posed the real threat to Polonia.[19]

In 1911, six young Polish Americans encountered Fred

Guelzow Jr., a twenty-six-year-old truck farmer near Lincoln and Patterson Avenues as he took a load of vegetables to market at about 8:00 p.m. on October 20. The boys robbed him of seven dollars. They then stabbed Guelzow six times and crushed his skull. Later, they abandoned the cart and took his horses to Abe Klee and Son's auction grounds and asked $200 ($5,000 in 2017) for the team. Klee bargained with the boys, and they quickly came down in price to $85.00 ($2,118). He then became suspicious and called police. When they arrived, police arrested the three boys and noticed Guelzow's name etched on the boots worn by Walter Shiblawski, who also had the truck farmer's association card in his pocket. When he could not explain the boots, Shiblawski panicked and confessed, implicating his brother Frank and four others: Leo Suchomski, Frank Kita, Thomas Schultz, and Philip Somerling, Shiblawski's brother-in law and the oldest of the defendants.[20]

The murder raised the question of how environment, class, and crime might be associated. The *Dziennik Związkowy* editorialized that the boys had been corrupted by the streets and the negligence of the law that allowed hoodlums to gather at all hours of the night to do mischief and argued that, if these young men had been brought up in Poland, they would have grown up as useful members of society. The *Dziennik Związkowy* blamed American society and lamented that the accused had little money to hire a good defense lawyer and so would hang. The newspaper further stated that "racial hatred" played a role in the condemnation of the Polish youths. The paper chided the American judicial system and claimed that money often played a more important part in it than did justice. Jane Addams agreed that the environment in which the Polish boys grew up was as much to blame as anything else. In an address to the American Sociological Society at the Raleigh Hotel in Chicago, the famed settlement house founder proclaimed that the city's slums produced these murderers.

Various Chicagoans pleaded for mercy for the young Polish Chicagoans, who were found guilty on December 2, 1911. Four of the young men were scheduled to hang on December 22. Kita and Suchomski, both sixteen years old, were given life sentences. Late in December, the defendants were granted a reprieve until February 16, 1912. Jane Addams made a personal plea to the governor. Letters from Rev. Casimir Sztuczko of Holy Trinity Parish, the Polish National Alliance, and others pleaded for the youths' lives. Julius Rosenwald, the philanthropist and head of the Sears Roebuck & Company, sent a lawyer, S. A. Lewinsohn, to work on their case and to go to Springfield to plea for mercy. Rosenwald personally called Governor Charles S. Deneen, asking him to commute the sentences of two of the prisoners, Frank Shiblawski, age twenty-one, and Thomas Schultz, age eighteen. Many Chicagoans asked for mercy, including John Smulski. Even Judge Adelor J. Petit, who sentenced four of the young men to death and two to life imprisonment, spoke out against the death penalty. Nevertheless, on February 16, the four young men hung for Guelzow's murder. Three bodies laid in state at Joseph Jarembowski's funeral home on Blackhawk Street. Thomas Schultz's family waked his body at their home. A near riot broke out as crowds gathered outside the funeral parlor. Ten police officers arrived to preserve order. St. Stanislaus Kostka Church held funeral services for the four convicted Polish Chicagoans. Protestant preachers, rabbis, and Catholic priests called for Chicago to clean up the slums and prevent more such events[21]

Studies of the juvenile delinquency problem dated back to the years before World War One. One 1907 study of juvenile delinquent boys found they came from families where one or both parents had died, where the parents had divorced, or where one or both suffered from alcoholism. Poor housing conditions and the presence of street gangs helped shape juvenile delinquents. Much of this delinquency was actually youthful behavior of a rather minor character, simply "adventurous wrongdoing," including minor burglaries and breaking into railroad cars. Polish and other immigrant groups tended to live close to railroad freight yards, which proved a significant temptation. The average offender was a little over thirteen years of age. Many of these delinquent occurrences happened during the summers, when boys were not attending school. In 1905, the category of adult offender included any youth over the age of sixteen.[22]

Generally, minor crimes prevailed among Polonia's youth. A cursory look at the case file of the Northwestern University Settlement on Augusta Boulevard in the later 1920s and early 1930s clearly shows this trend. The boys tended to have little education and went to work early in their lives. One such juvenile delinquent, arrested in October 1929, had an eighth-grade education and worked as a bakery helper. Police charged him with robbery. Police held some as runaways after parents complained. Often, minor infractions lead to recurring problems. One eighteen-year-old male first broke into a relative's house and, later, was held twice for stealing cars. Stolen automobiles frequently provided boys with so-called joyrides that at times ended in accidents. Other cases of delinquency resulted from underage boys playing pool. At times, infractions included breaking windows or playing ball on school grounds.[23]

Northwestern University Settlement case workers frequently found poor home conditions among those charged with delinquency. One account told of a very poor living environment, where suspicious parents refused to talk with investigators and would not give the names and ages of their other children. While the boy had no previous court record, police charged him with riding in a stolen car, and he was held on a $10,000 bond ($249,155 in 2017). Investigators complained that one Polish American boy had a bad work attitude. He'd had thirteen jobs since quitting high school the previous year. The boy was eventually found guilty of stripping a car and given six months supervision.[24]

Poles had long attempted to deal with poverty and crime in their neighborhoods. On Sunday, February 7, 1892, fifty-five Polish Chicagoans gathered at the Polish Hall to discuss the problem. The following Sunday, neighborhood leaders formed the Polish Welfare Association No. 1 of St. Stanislaus Kostka Parish to address neighborhood poverty. Dues for the new organization ran one dollar per quarter or four dollars per year. The association also welcomed donations of money, food, and clothing for the neighborhood poor. Board members wrote a constitution that provided for not only the physical but also the spiritual and moral needs of the poor. It also stated that, should for any reason the association be disbanded, all remaining monies would go to Holy Family Polish Orphanage in Chicago. Staff interviewed applicants and helped as quickly as possible, while turning away some who tried to cheat the system. Funds for the poor began to run out by July, and the society appealed for more members and donors. The call went out to Polish businessmen, especially grocers, bakers, shoe store owners, druggists, and doctors to donate goods and services for the poor.

As money for the Polish Welfare Association No. 1 ran out, the *Dziennik Chicagoski* editorialized against what it called materialism and scolded parents for being greedy and sending children to work at an early age. It bemoaned the stinginess of the community for not supporting the association. The arts, too, were underfunded, and the newspaper predicted the end of the national group unless Poles opened their pocketbooks. Community leaders planned "Opera in a Room" recitals conducted by Stanisław Szwajkart to raise funds. In September, the *Dziennik Chicagoski* editorialized that Chicago's various Polish clubs should tax their members twelve cents a month to contribute to the association, as well as to the Kosciuszko Monument Fund and the Polish Emigrant Home in New York City.[25]

All of these early attempts to relieve poverty in the Polish community were short lived. Juvenile crime remained an issue. From December 1, 1914, to November 30, 1915, Polish youths made up roughly 21 percent of 2,326 boys who appeared in juvenile court. This percentage represented a great increase over the previous year. *Naród Polski* blamed this on boys leaving school at too early an age to work or make a dishonest living on the street.[26]

The most successful attempt to deal with the problem of poverty and juvenile crime began on August 16, 1922. Members of the

Northwestern University Settlement House, 1400 West Augusta Boulevard, ca. 1940. This settlement house opened in 1892 in a rented apartment on Division Street in the Stanisławowo-Trójcowo neighborhood and continues to serve the community today. (Northwestern University Settlement Association Records Photographs, Series 41/6, Northwestern University Archives, Evanston, IL.)

Chicago Society of the Polish National Alliance active in politics, business, and education came together to create a new Polish Welfare Association. Julius F. Śmietanka, the association's first president, insisted on professionalism in the quest to deal with juvenile delinquency. About twenty persons held an organizational meeting on January 9, chaired by Judge Edmund Jarecki. They aimed to provide help for Polish juvenile delinquents, who often received stiff sentences and severe punishment for minor crimes. Indeed, a 1915 study found that many of the boys and young men had been arrested on insignificant charges and received extreme sentences due to incompetent or unscrupulous lawyers and bondsmen. Life membership in the Polish Welfare Association cost $200 ($2,914 in 2017), and people could join as active or honorary members. Young and upwardly mobile members of Polonia made up the bulk of the membership, and the decidedly secular and professional nature of the new organization reflected the maturity of Polonia as it developed in the twentieth century.

In 1926, the Polish Welfare Association joined the Council of Social Agencies and hired a professional staff under the leadership of Mary Midura. The next year, in addition to the fifty-nine cases handled in juvenile court, the association involved itself with eighty-nine cases heard in various courts, such as the Court of Domestic Relations, Boy's Court, Municipal Branch Court, Indifferent Parent's Court, or Federal Court. Midura complained that, due to a lack of staff, the association could not address the roughly one thousand cases of Polish youth handled by the juvenile court during 1926 and 1927. In January of 1927, the Polish Welfare Association held a ball and reception in the Palmer House to raise funds. The following year, the organization's budget was $12,000 ($171,780 in 2017). Much of this raised on January 18, 1928, when the association again held a formal reception and benefit ball at the Stevens Hotel (now the Chicago Hilton and Towers). In 1929, the stock market crash put an end to much fundraising in Polonia. As the Depression ensued, Midura and one caseworker tried to carry on, but by 1933, the budget fell to $2,000 ($37,659), while the caseload of the overburdened Polish Welfare Association expanded to include much more than juvenile delinquency. Midura established the interpretive service that aided agencies in working with Polish clients. In addition, the association sponsored educational, publicity, recreational, and group work.[27]

The Urge to Organize: Neighborhoods

By the 1930s, Polonia had spread outside the original immigrant enclaves to outlying neighborhoods and suburbs. Polish Downtown, along with Pilsen, Bridgeport, Back of the Yards, South Chicago, and Hegewisch remained high crime and juvenile delinquency areas. The Polish Welfare Association had a presence in these neighborhoods, but the Depression overwhelmed its efforts.

Baskets for Polonia's poor, 1927. Even before the outbreak of the Great Depression, Chicago's Polonia organized to help poor families in the community. (From the collection of the Polish Museum of America, x2007.001.0172.)

In turn, grassroots organizations developed particularly in the steel mill and packinghouse districts during the New Deal era. Polish priests and residents joined others to deal with social problems exacerbated by the economic crisis.

The work of Ernest W. Burgess and the Chicago school of sociology highlighted juvenile delinquency. His students went out into the industrial districts of the city in search of an answer to what sociologists saw as a problem of family disintegration. Many studied South Chicago's steel mill area and the Stock Yard District. Both of these had large Polish American populations and a reputation for gangs. In the 1930s, the Sociology Department at the University of Chicago launched a program designed to encourage local communities to organize and deal with their own problems. Clifford Shaw, who had studied with Burgess, looked for a new way to deal with juvenile delinquency. He rejected the

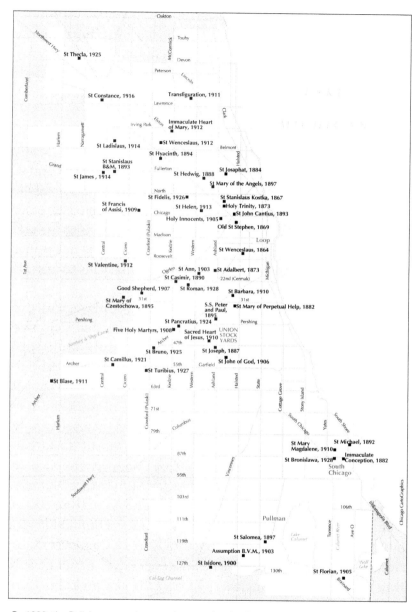

By 1933, the Polish community spread across the city. This map lists Polish Roman Catholic parishes and the date of their founding. (Courtesy of Chicago CartoGraphics.)

imposition of middle-class values on working-class communities and attacked the problem from the inside by trying to enable neighborhood people to deal with problems on their own terms. This resulted in the Chicago Area Project, with the first experimental phase taking part in South Chicago's heavily Polish Bush neighborhood.

The Bush lay adjacent to U.S. Steel's South Works, and for all of its drabness and problems, it maintained an institutionally rich base with a Polish Catholic parish, St. Michael's, at its center. Wooden frame buildings and occasional brick two-flats lined the streets. The mill's red glow dominated the nighttime sky. Saint Michael's, as it soared toward the heavens, competed with the mill for domination of the skyline. While Shaw at first did not realize its importance, this parish proved crucial to his plans to provide agency to members of the community.

Investigators originally intended to align themselves with two social settlement houses: Neighborhood House and Common Ground. Neighborhood House, founded by Baptists in 1911, had strong attachments to the Baptist community living near the University of Chicago. E. A. Connover came to the Bush in October 1931, along with psychiatrist Dr. T. Burling, and worked out of Common Ground's facilities. They familiarized themselves with the gang life of the Bush and the neighborhood's institutional culture. The first two youths interviewed by Connover attended St. Michael's Parochial School. The principal, Sister Mary Olympia, cooperated with the researchers and let the boys out from classes to be interviewed. In the spring of 1932, Connover brought in various street social workers including Saul Alinsky. Connover found a local public school, Thorp, to be less cooperative, although Sullivan Public School's principal supported the new program. Over time, the project developed the idea of there being such a thing as natural leaders. If boys, often heads of local street gangs, could be brought into the project, then so could other gang members. Shaw wanted to take an organic approach, one that would emerge out of the neighborhood itself, to the problem of juvenile delinquency.

He then turned away from the local social settlements and moved toward working with St. Michael's pastor, Fr. John Lange.

Lange had worried about the project's connection with the Baptist-dominated social settlements and feared that this relationship might lead to the proselytization of the local Catholic youth. While Lange saw the attractiveness of the sports programs being put in place by the settlement houses, his fear of children being lost to Protestantism prompted him to forbid his parishioners to participate in Neighborhood House activities. The activists soon realized that St. Michael's obviously held the key to the largely Polish Catholic neighborhood.

James McDonald, who had replaced Connover as Shaw's primary representative in the Bush, worked cautiously and recognized that residents did not trust outsiders, especially those from Hyde Park and the University of Chicago. He attempted to set up the "Bush Conference," a summer baseball league. Eventually McDonald reached out to Dr. Adam Mioduski, a neighborhood chiropodist close to Fr. Lange, who arranged for McDonald and Lange to meet. The social worker and the priest quickly came to an understanding. McDonald guaranteed the nonsectarian nature of the project, and Lange offered support. Still other obstacles remained, as many in the Polish community distrusted outside social workers. The main objection rose out of various leaders of the Polish Welfare Association and the PNA who wondered why the Bush had been chosen and feared that any published report might shame Polonia. The Polish community resented earlier studies and objected to the poor public image resulting from these "scientific" investigations. The community felt it had been slandered during the Red Scare and the anti-immigrant movement of the 1920s as well as by Shaw's *The Jack-Roller*.

On December 22, 1932, Lange and Mioduski's leadership proved crucial at a meeting of Polish fraternal and neighborhood leaders. Shaw's work and an earlier study of South Chicago by Burgess troubled the community. The so-called Sullivan School Experiment, conducted by University of Chicago faculty, worried

some leaders. Broadsides appeared warning the Polish community of a threat to their reputation and took a strong working-class
stand that argued that industrialists exploited the neighborhood
and endowed universities and research in order to hide rather
than solve social problems. The author of the flyer implied that
only the community could heal itself and did not need the help of
outsiders.

Ironically, this gave Shaw an opportunity to explain the project. An open forum took place, and while local residents chal-
lenged Shaw and Burgess, they did not want to attack a project
that already had Lange's and Mioduski's blessings. The Bush
Area Project, as it was then known, opened the St. Michael's
Boys Club in 1933. Shaw and his colleagues held an optimistic
view of human nature. They believed that change could occur
if residents willed it. This was exactly what Polish leaders in the
Bush wanted to hear. Local control meant that Lange, Mioduski
and others had a deciding say in important decisions. Lange and
Shaw cooperated to reach common goals in what turned out to
be a successful arrangement. By 1935, Shaw alleged that there
had been a reduction in juvenile delinquency in the Bush and
called for a citywide program to combat the problem. McDonald
recruited Stephen Bubacz as a natural leader, and he became the
driving force behind the Russell Square Community Committee,
an outgrowth of the Bush Project and a powerful neighborhood
organization. Bubacz helped evolve the idea of "curbstone coun-
seling" in which Chicago Area Project staff spent time on street
corners and in alleys to get to know local youth, eventually iden-
tifying natural leaders and get them to participate in the project's
programs.

The Russell Square Community Committee and the St.
Michael's Boys Club continued to organize the Bush, and in 1939
opened Camp Lange outside of Michigan City, Indiana, a largely
Polish American community, to send local youth out of Chicago
for the summer. Camp Lange proved to be a genuine community

Saint Michael's Church, seen from Russell Square Park on Eighty-Third Street. The neo-Gothic structure was built during the pastorate of Bishop Paul Rhode, the first Polish American Bishop of the Catholic Church. In the 1930s, the parish proved to be crucial for the development of the Russell Square Community Committee. The St. Michael's Boys Club met in the parish facilities. (Chicago Public Library, Special Collections, SSCC 1.37.)

project. Money raised from across the neighborhood built the camp and proved the communalism of the Bush community.[28]

The efforts in the Bush neighborhood inspired the citywide expansion of the Chicago Area Project. Saul Alinsky, however, felt that Shaw and McDonald's efforts were too conservative. He soon left the project and eventually made his way to the Back of the Yards neighborhood. Here, too, Poles made up a large percentage of the population; three Polish parishes stood near the packinghouses. Alinsky successfully organized that neighborhood and went on to take his program to working-class neighborhoods across the country. The Back of the Yards Neighborhood Council became a prime example of a local organization having an impact on the day-to-day lives of residents. It also became a major supporter of the United Packinghouse Workers of America–CIO in the union's successful effort to organize the meatpacking industry at the heart of that community.[29]

Spectacle and Politics

The Chicago Society, besides establishing the Polish Welfare Association, founded the Polish Day Association, which recalled the Columbian Exposition's Polish Day. Like many of the other projects of the Chicago Society, it aimed at the problems of poverty and education among Polish Chicagoans and evolved into a separate institution. Created in 1926, the association had collected over $55,000 ($1,035,633 in 2017) by 1933 toward these efforts. It combined its charitable efforts with the general Chicago Polish propensity to celebrate and held Polish Day annually at Riverview Park, the city's premier amusement venue. Major Felix Streyckmann, the chairman of the Foreign Language Division of Chicago's 1933 Century of Progress Fair, invited the Polish Day Association to plan for a Polish Day at the fair. The association then decided to hold a Polish Week of Hospitality from July 16 to July 23, 1933.[30]

Before Polish Week, three thousand Polish Americans participated in athletic programs at Soldier Field, sponsored by the Polish Falcons. On the final day, ten thousand Polish Americans gathered in the stadium to witness drills, calisthenics, and athletic contests. On Sunday, July 16, the Polish Roman Catholic Union celebrated its sixtieth anniversary with a Solemn High Mass at St. Adalbert's and held a banquet for members and friends of the organization at the Morrison Hotel. The next day, the Polish Week of Hospitality officially opened with a Polish Festival of Music featuring performances by the Chicago Philharmonic Orchestra in the Auditorium Theater, conducted by Jerzy Bojanowski of Warsaw's Grand Opera. The Polish medical, dental, and legal societies also opened their conventions, while the Congress of Polish Women met on that Monday and Tuesday. At noon on Saturday, Polish Day at the fair commenced with a parade of twenty thousand marchers and fifty floats down Michigan Avenue to the fairgrounds along the lakefront south of Roosevelt Road. There, various music and dance festivals were held, along with a Miss Poland

Polish Day Parade, Century of Progress Exposition, 1933. This float from St. Hedwig's
Parish commemorated the victory of King Jan Sobieski at Vienna in 1683. (From the collection
of the Polish Museum of America, x2011.002.0080.)

beauty contest, won by Irene Napientek. At eight in the evening,
a five thousand–person pageant in Soldier Field commemorated
one hundred years of Polish immigration to the United States
and Chicago. The following day, Polish parishes held special services to close the week of hospitality, followed by a grand finale at
Riverview Park.[31]

Chicago extended the Century of Progress Fair another year,
and Polonia celebrated Polish Day again, on August 26, 1934,
with some sixty thousand Polish Americans in attendance. Emily
Napieralska, a veteran of Polish Chicago's affairs and longtime
president of the Polish Women's Alliance, acted as chairman. The
Polski Gorale or Polish Highlanders delighted the crowd with their
traditional folk songs and dances. Included among the honored
guests were Andrew Bohomoloc and Geroge Świechowski who
had sailed the *Dal*, a twenty-seven foot one-masted boat from
Poland to Chicago.[32]

The same year, Frank Świetlik, representing the PNA at a
conference in Warsaw convened by the World Alliance of Poles

Living Abroad (Światowy Związek Polaków z Zagranicy, or Świat-pol) refused to join the alliance. Świetlik told the members of this Polish government organization that Polish Americans no longer considered themselves Poles living abroad but, rather, Americans of Polish descent. The incident took place in the hall of the Polish Senate before a number of members of the Polish cabinet. This rebuff by the largest diaspora put the Polish government in a difficult position and so it cancelled the formal signing of the worldwide Polish constitution in Kraków's Wawel Castle. Warsaw had established Światpol to prevent the assimilation of Polish immigrants in various host countries and to tie them to the Polish Republic. The organization hoped to compel the use of the Polish language abroad by increasing the number of Polish schools and language classes and by insisting that all Polish organizations overseas use only Polish in meetings and official documents. Światpol also promoted the idea that Poles living abroad should put their savings in Polish banks. Warsaw saw Polonia as an outpost of Poland, but in the years after 1918, the Polish American community had moved in a much different direction.

The American delegation headed by Świetlik reminded Polish officials that Poland's prestige in the United States had fallen considerably since Warsaw repudiated its World War One war debt. Świetlik explained that Polish Americans remained proud of their heritage but considered themselves Americans. The movement that began with the saying "Wychodźstwo dla Wychodźstwo" ("The emigration for the emigration") had borne unexpected fruit. Polish Chicagoans, and Polish Americans in general, felt more integrated into American society. The cutting off of immigration from eastern and southern Europe in the 1920s influenced this perception, but so did the growth of an American-born generation. Reports of constant political squabbling in Poland and conflict with neighbors and minority groups within Poland, especially Jews, had also affected Polonia, particularly in Polonia's capital, as Polish Americans attempted to take a larger part in Chicago's diverse economic, cultural, and political life.[33]

The Sacred Heart Hearts baseball team at Davis Square Park in Back of the Yards, ca. 1935. Polish American youth embraced baseball and other American sports. Polish parishes fielded teams, and by the 1930s, Polish newspapers often covered sports in English in order to maintain their growing American-born readership. (*Sacred Heart of Jesus Church Fiftieth Anniversary Yearbook.*)

Importantly, the American-born generation desired political power in Chicago, and their relationship with the Czechs played an important part in this process. The Czech community's ability to build bridges across ethnic lines allowed Anton Cermak's rise politically. For Polonia, this proved crucial, despite the fact that political and military tensions existed between the Czechoslovak Republic and Poland. The alliance between Poles and Czechs in Chicago was a long and fruitful one, and neither group wanted to lose that connection due to European events.

On December 11, 1930, Polish Democrats nominated one of their own, Superior Court Clerk Mieczysław S. Szymczak, for mayor. Fifteen days later, three hundred and fifty of Chicago's leading Polish Democrats, including Szymczak, met at the Sherman Hotel to pledge their undivided support for Cermak's candidacy for mayor. In March, they organized the Polish American Cermak for mayor organization to promote Cermak's election. This group quickly developed into a rebirth of the Polish American Democratic Organization (PADO). Officers included Frank V.

Zintak, manager; Julius F. Śmietanka, president; and Emily Napieralska as one of four vice presidents. Szymczak, also a founding
member, sat as the only Polonia representative on the Executive
Committee of the Democratic Party of Cook County.

The Chicago-born Szymczak provided leadership for PADO.
The recipient of multiple bachelors, masters, and law degrees, he
taught at both St. Mary's College and DePaul University. In 1922,
he organized the Guarantee Mortgage and Security Corporation.
Szymczak helped launch the Ridgemoor Building and Loan Association in 1925 and served as director and as vice president of two
North Side banks. He worked for the Cook County Forest Preserve
District as a Cermak appointee from 1926 to 1928. Obviously, a rising star in both the political and business world, Szymczak tied his
future to Cermak and his nascent Democratic machine.[34]

As early as 1922, Szymczak had promoted American citizenship
classes for Polish immigrants and served as president of the Natu-
ralization League of Illinois, an organization dedicated to getting
Polish immigrants to apply for citizenship. The league eventually
opened more than fifty citizenship schools across Chicago and
planned to provide correspondence classes to Poles nationwide.
Szymczak realized that Polish immigrants had to become citizens
and vote if they were to have any chance at political power or, in
Chicago parlance, "clout."

That same year, Szymczak became involved in Judge Edmund J.
Jarecki's campaign as member of the Polish Fellowship League.
The league, supposedly a nonpartisan organization whose goal
was to unite all Polish organizations to promote good citizenship,
supported Jarecki, Frank P. Danisch, and John Prystalski, all Democrats, as candidates for judgeship. Participants in a mass meeting
on October 15 at Pulaski Hall voted to support the entire Democratic ticket, as the Republican Party had not listed any Polish
candidates for office. Szymczak and Stephen Kolanowski planned
assemblies in every Polish neighborhood to get out the vote. At
Walsh's Hall on the Northwest Side, speakers included Congressman Stanley Kunz and other Polish American politicians. Polo-

nia began to feel it had at least some influence in the Democratic Party.

As Cermak's star rose in the Democratic Party, so did Szymczak's. Attempts at organizing the community began to bear fruit beyond ward boundaries. In 1927, Szymczak ran for the Office of City Treasurer. He received the support of Democratic Party boss George Brennan, who promised the support of the regular organization. Szymczak took advantage of the new medium of radio and addressed Chicago in March and April. Despite these efforts, he lost the race, though he nevertheless drew the most votes on the Democratic ticket. The victorious Republicans offered the young Pole a job in an attempt to split the emerging Democratic alliance with Polonia, but he refused the position of assistant city treasurer. Cermak then appointed him general superintendent of the Cook County Forest Preserve District. In November 1928, Szymczak became the Democratic nominee for Clerk of the Superior Court. This time Szymczak won and emerged as a major voter attraction and ally of Cermak.[35]

After defeating Mayor Thompson, Cermak became mayor in 1931 and firmly established the Democratic machine, and Szymczak became an even more important force in Polish Chicago's politics. The Czech-born mayor appointed Szymczak to his cabinet as city comptroller in April. As comptroller and as the head of PADO, Szymczak found himself in the maze of Chicago politics. The machine ran on patronage, favors, and loyalty. The Polish American Democratic Organization, with Szymczak at its head, emerged as a citywide powerbroker. Polish Chicagoans approached the organization for both jobs and favors in return for political support.[36]

Szymczak kept a running log of those he recommended for positions in his files. Many job seekers had been victims of the financial collapse. They pleaded with Szymczak and claimed the support of several Polish politicians. The frustrations of the Great Depression became quite clear in such appeals. Szymczak understood the steps one took to obtain patronage jobs for his constit-

uents, who now numbered all the Poles in Chicago. He always
reminded those who approached him to first contact their local
Democratic committeeman.[37]

The election of Franklin Delano Roosevelt to the presidency
in November 1932 further fueled Polonia's aspirations, as Chicago
and the Polish community became important to the Democratic
coalition. Almost immediately, the Polish community agitated for
Szymczak to be placed in Roosevelt's cabinet. As early as December 1932, Polish organizations headquartered in Chicago petitioned Roosevelt for the cabinet post of secretary of the treasury.
When Anton Cermak died after being shot in an assassination
attempt on President Roosevelt's life, Polonia urged Szymczak to
take over the office of mayor.[38]

The attempt to name Szymczak mayor failed, and Edward Kelly
became Cermak's successor. Polonia's ambitions for Szymczak,
however, did not end. Efforts continued to have him placed in
a cabinet post or some other position in the Roosevelt administration. Finally, in June 1933, Roosevelt named Szymczak to the
board of governors of the Federal Reserve, the highest position
a Polish American had yet obtained in the federal government.
Polonia rejoiced at the honor, but Polish Chicago lost its most tal-
ented politician to the federal bureaucracy. The Polish American
Democratic Organization, as a vehicle for Szymczak's ambitions,
was successful, but it could not take control of the Chicago Democratic Party as it hoped to during the Cermak years and directly
after Cermak's death.[39]

Szymczak left for Washington, DC, and PADO continued to
support Polish interests in Chicago. In the fall of 1934, it turned
to the airwaves. *The Polish Hour of Education* or *Godzina Oświaty*
ran from 6:00 p.m. to 7:00 p.m. every Sunday on WCFL radio,
"The Voice of Labor." The Polish American Democratic Organization planned an hour of music, information, and education to
tie Polonia with the local Democratic Organization and introduce
candidates for office. The first script called for W. F. Walkowiak,
the organization's secretary, to give a brief explanation of the pro-

gram, followed by Polish music and several talks by PADO members in English and in Polish, as well as a listing of current events. Musical performances, humorous sketches, and news also filled the hour. Walkowiak acted as the master of ceremonies, introducing the various performers and Democratic notables to the radio audience. Like other Polish American organizations, PADO also closely watched events in Poland and raised one hundred dollars for Polish flood relief in September 1934.[40]

Polish Chicago continued to create various institutions and extended itself citywide. Despite the Cermak model, Polonia, often divided internally, found it difficult to maintain alliances with other ethnic groups in Chicago. Conflict between Polonia and the Jewish community demonstrated itself to be a constant problem, and Szymczak had to intervene. News from Poland in the 1930s did not help matters. Chicago's English dailies reported the constant outbreaks of anti-Semitic riots in Poland and territorial clashes between Poland and both Lithuania and Czechoslovakia. They also carried stories about conflicts with Poland's Ukrainian minority. Polonia divided internally over many issues and, often in a hostile relationship with its Chicago neighbors, had little power to change the Democratic Party's political structure. Nevertheless, its influence did expand between the wars. As the 1930s came to an end, Chicago's Polonia again began to fear for the homeland. War seemed probable, as Poland's neighbors agitated for changes in the structure of postwar Europe.[41]

6

Apocalypse Again

World War Two and Its Aftermath

I want you Americans to remain loyal citizens of the United States. Today the unity of the Polish people is fighting and will fight until the very last.

—GENERAL WŁADYSŁAW SIKORSKI, speaking at Chicago's Soldier Field, April 20, 1941[1]

On September 1, 1939, Nazi Germany attacked the Polish Republic. Sixteen days later, the Soviet Army invaded Poland from the east and crushed any chances that Poles could hold off the German onslaught. Just twenty years after the nation had reestablished its independence, another partitioning of Poland occurred. For American Polonia, who had often quarreled with the Second Republic and felt itself under attack in the United States, this event brought the homeland back to the center of attention. Chicago's Polish community immediately responded, as it read the headlines of that September day and the months following the brutal Nazi attack.

This time, there would be no raising of a Polish army in the

United States. Polonia's efforts, organized from Chicago, would focus on aid to the Polish population. Not only had the relationship with Poland changed, but Polonia's younger generations were increasingly American born. The cutting off of immigration in the 1920s had a profound effect on Polish Chicago, as did the successful struggle to regain Poland's independence. The community now saw itself as a permanent part of American society. Even the Polish National Alliance, whose original leadership thought all immigrants would return once Poland regained independence, now celebrated the diaspora's permanence.

Naturally, Chicago's Polonia looked on in horror at events in Poland. The immediate response included meetings, organizing efforts, political efforts, and raising funds for those suffering in Nazi- and Soviet-occupied Poland. As France and Great Britain responded to the attack by declaring war and the Nazi assault spread across Europe, many in Polonia hoped that the United States would eventually become involved. That would take more than two years, however, while Hitler's forces seemed unstoppable as they crossed the continent.

Over the next six years of war, the Polish nation suffered terrible losses and the Holocaust destroyed Polish Jewry. Afterward, in a radical turn of events, Germany invaded the Soviet Union, which then became an ally of the West in its struggle against fascism. After the war, Poland fell into the Soviet sphere of influence and remained a satellite of the USSR for more than forty years. Chicago's Polish Americans were caught up in a worldwide struggle that forever changed Poland, the United States, Chicago, and Polonia.

Chicago Polonia's Initial Response

Even before the invasion, it became evident that Hitler would not back down from his demands on the Polish state, and Chicago's Poles raised funds for Polish defense. On July 13, 1939, the *Dziennik Chicagoski* ran a front-page political cartoon of a Nazi soldier staring across a barbed wire fence at some well-fed cattle on a farm called Poland while a small skinny dog named Danzig looked at him. The soldier remarks that the little dog does not interest him, but the butter and the fat is what he wants. The Free City of Danzig gained semiautonomous status in 1920 after World War One. It included Danzig and surrounding towns inhabited primarily by Germans. Poland, in turn, created a new port on the Baltic Sea, Gdynia, to ensure the republic's access to the sea as assured in the Treaty of Versailles. This Polish Corridor divided Germany from East Prussia. Danzig was claimed by Nazi Germany, and much of the city's populace yearned for a return to German control. The *Dziennik Chicagoski* rightfully understood that Hitler's aims went well beyond the Baltic port and the contested Polish Corridor that connected the country to Gdynia. The weekly *Zgoda* posted names of those PNA members who donated money to the Polish cause.[2]

On August 25, Casmir Frenzel of the Polish Army Veterans Association claimed that thousands of Polish Americans would volunteer to fight for Poland. Joseph Liszka, president of the Polish American Business Association, and Teofil Sawicki, of the Polish Falcons (Sokoły), held beliefs diametrically opposed to those of Frenzel. Liszka felt that not more than one out of thousand Polish Americans would fight for Poland. Sawicki pointed out that Poland was now an independent country and that Polish Americans should not meddle in its affairs. The advice of the Falcons was "stay here."

The next day, Chicago's Polish American organizations announced they had received $250,000 ($4,402,625 in 2017) in contributions from their members for use by the Polish government in the crisis. The Polish National Alliance alone had received over $200,000 ($3,522,101) in donations. Meanwhile, the Polish American Council (Rada Polonii Amerykanskiej or RPA), which represented the major fraternal organizations, promised to help Poland should war come. The RPA originated in 1935 as the Polish American Interorganizational Council in Chicago to bring together the leadership of the Polish National Alliance, the Polish

Roman Catholic Union of America, and the Polish Women's Alliance to coordinate charitable activities in Polonia and Poland. It acted as a counter to those who would have joined Światpol (the World Alliance of Poles Living Abroad). Some felt it should be a political organization, but leaders primarily saw its purpose as charitable, and, once the fighting began, it championed war relief for the Polish population.[3]

A concert held in Grant Park on August 29 featured Jerzy Bojanowski conducting the orchestra and George Czaplicki, of the Chicago Opera Company, as baritone soloist. Dr. Wacław Gawronski, the Polish consul general, attended the concert, as did many Polish Chicagoans. Last-minute program changes eliminated several German items from the program, replacing them with works by the Polish composers Stanisław Moniuszko and Frederic Chopin. Organizers did retain compositions by Weber and Wagner, though, to make the point that politics and art were not to be confused. The audience heartily applauded Czaplicki and called him back to the stage for repeated encores. As the summer ended, Polish Chicago held its breath as it hoped for peace between Nazi Germany and Poland. The RPA held a meeting the day of the Grant Park concert at the Polish Women's Alliance Hall and pledged funds for Poland's defense. Hitler gave Poland an ultimatum on August 30, and twenty-four hours later, the Nazi onslaught began.[4]

On September 1, the *Dziennik Chicagoski* headline screamed "War Explodes." Warsaw and Częstochowa had been bombed. The paper printed an appeal by the RPA titled "Our Countrymen!" The call went out to all of American Polonia asking them to sustain their efforts to help Poland. Meanwhile, on the corner of Chicago Avenue and Hermitage Street, a group of children hung Hitler in effigy as news of the war spread through the city's neighborhoods. The newly appointed rabbi of KAM Temple on the city's South Side, Dr. Jacob Weinstein, pointed out that the large number of East Europeans in Chicago could not help but be affected and that Jews in particular would be caught between the "hammer and the anvil." Polish Americans across the Chicago area prayed for peace. They met in Cicero's Osinski Sokol Auditorium to protest the bombing of Polish cities. The meeting, held under the auspices of both the PNA and PRCUA, began a drive to collect funds for Polish war relief. Some worried that there might be street battles between German and Polish Chicagoans, but police felt no need to increase neighborhood patrols.[5]

On Sunday, September 3, at a Czechoslovak Labor Day rally in Pilsen Park on Twenty-Sixth Street and Albany, nearly five thousand of the Chicago Polonia's traditional allies, the Czechs and Slovaks, gathered to support Poland. Polish Chicagoans planned a meeting at the Coliseum the following Sunday to raise funds for Polish defense. That same day, more than five hundred delegates joined twenty directors of the Council of Polish Organizations in America in Chicago and promised the aid of five million Polish Americans for the beleaguered republic. They opened a nationwide drive to create a $10,000,000 ($179,516,722 in 2017) relief fund for the Polish Red Cross to alleviate the suffering of Polish women and children. The Polish American Veterans Association condemned German barbarism and called for Polonia to remember its common Polish heritage and to maintain Polish traditions during this difficult time.

On September 6, 1939, the Polish National Defense Fund, which had been collecting money for the Polish armed forces, terminated activities and the Polish American community focused on humanitarian aid. The efforts of the Polish Red Cross also ended in the United States, when the American Red Cross agreed to organize charitable assistance to Poland. The United States' status as a neutral country prohibited more active military support. On September 7, 1939, U.S. Federal Reserve Board governor, and Chicagoan, M. S. Szymczak, met with representatives of the State Department and received their support for the Polish American Council's efforts. From that point on, the council became the primary organization in charge of raising funds for Polish aid. That night, five thousand representatives of Polish American societies met in the Ashland Boulevard Auditorium to plan a collection of funds for civilian relief in Poland. Judge Edmund Jarecki told the crowd that while America remained neutral they had "no restrictions on what they feel in their hearts." That same day, at 3535 West Roosevelt Road, four hundred members of the Federation of Polish Jews in America appointed a committee to solicit funds for Poland and encouraged members to pray for a Polish victory. The Polish Women's Alliance made an appeal to the women and mothers of the world, calling for a declaration that it was immoral to murder the innocent. The organization sent their plea to all of the English-language newspapers and claimed that children's hospitals had been bombed and balloons were being used to attract children with poisoned candy. By mid-September, the PNA elected Charles Rozmarek as president and donated $100,000 ($1,763,453 in 2017) to Polish relief. In October, Rozmarek enjoined Polonia to use all its strength to support the Polish people in their time of need. The PNA leader, Świetlik, who held the important position of censor in the organization, which meant he presided over meetings of the PNA's congress (*Sejm*), the ultimate authority in the organization, proclaimed that no one should starve in Poland. It was obvious that all Polonia could do was offer financial aid as the reality of a Polish defeat seemed overwhelming.[6]

As Poland fell, Poles formed a government-in-exile in France. Rumors had it that the ailing Paderewski would assume the presidency. A group of Chicagoans formed a local branch of the American Commission for Polish Relief to administer assistance to Poland and to refugees in the West. The commission organized in New York with President Henry Noble McCracken of Vassar College as national chairman and Chicagoan Chauncey McCormick, the first representative of the American Relief Association to be sent to Poland after the 1918 armistice, to serve on its board of directors. He soon accepted the chairmanship of the Chicago committee. McCormick promised that a local office would open and formal organization of the committee would be completed. One of the first tasks of the association was to dispatch a group of

Quakers to supervise relief in and about Warsaw. As winter had begun to set in, conditions in the Polish capital turned for the worse, with an estimated six hundred thousand homeless. The national committee hoped to get the British to lift their blockade of Germany in order to ship two hundred thousand woolen blankets to Poland.[7]

Polonia, led by the Chicago-based fraternals, continued to raise funds. The national convention of the *Sejm* (ruling senate) of the PNA held in September in Detroit donated $100,000 ($1,761,050 in 2017) to the Polish cause. On the last day of the meeting, Alexandra Rytela, the director of the Wolski Hospital in Warsaw, spoke about the conditions in Poland and told the group that Poland would fight to the last. *Zgoda* proclaimed that Polonia must be prepared to help Poland and the Polish people. Świetlik and the outgoing president of the PNA, John Romaszkiewicz, sent a missive to the U.S. Congress saying that the nearly three hundred thousand–member organization fully supported President Roosevelt's position to repeal the embargo provision of the Neutrality Act.[8]

Meanwhile, General Władysław Sikorski, the new premier of the Polish government-in-exile, called for the raising of a two hundred thousand–man Polish army in the United States and Canada. While Sikorski would raise an army in Europe, it would not primarily be made up of Poles living in the United States and Canada as he had hoped. The Polish Army in the West consisted largely of Polish soldiers who had made their way to Rumania and then France, and years later, many who had been captured by Soviet forces and allowed to go to Britain once the Soviets themselves had been invaded by Nazi Germany.[9]

Świetlik suggested that all funds they raised be sent to the American Red Cross for the relief of the Polish population. Both Rozmarek and Świetlik traveled to Washington, DC, to present the Red Cross with a check for $150,000 ($2,641,575 in 2017). In his first address as president, Rozmarek called for unity and proclaimed that the protest against the attack must be made before the entire civilized world. On October 8, the Legion of Young Polish Women sponsored a symphonic event of Polish music seldom heard in the United States, including a Paderewski nocturne. Czaplicki again performed, along with violinist Michael Wilkomirski and pianist Thaddeus Kozuch, at the Civic Opera House. The money raised went for Polish relief.[10]

While America warily watched events unfold in Europe in 1940, Chicago's Polonia continued to raise money to aid those caught in the fighting. In January, PNA censor Świetlik, in an address on Chicago's radio station WCFL, called for a million-dollar fund for the suffering Polish people. Meanwhile, more than ten thousand of Chicago's Polish women joined the Polish Civilian War Relief Unit, which represented seventy-two parishes and Polish organizations. By early 1940, they had converted $12,000 ($209,817 in 2017) worth of materials into clothing and supplies for the Polish Army in France. The women completed more than nine thousand sets of clothing and medical supply kits, and then outfitted the hospital and ambulance corps of the new army with necessities such as operating gowns, convalescent robes, bandages, and surgical supplies.[11]

On February 6, the Legion of Young Polish Women held their annual Red and White Ball in the Gold Room of the Congress Hotel and earmarked proceeds for Polish war relief. Four days later, Jan Kiepura, the Polish tenor, sang a concert before a crowd of more than twenty thousand in the Chicago Stadium for the benefit of the Polish Relief Fund. General Józef Haller proclaimed to the crowd that "we live and we will win!" Former president Herbert C. Hoover joined him and Frank F. Świetlik. Hoover pleaded for help for the millions of Poles in dire want and facing starvation as a result of the war. He called for the sending of $20,000,000 ($349,694,286) worth of food and supplies. The president added that the supplies could not be forwarded unless the belligerents agreed on a program to distribute the goods. Hoover blamed the British blockade and hoped an accord could be reached to guarantee that only civilians would be helped and neutral parties would administer funds. The Chicago Stadium Corporation donated its fee of $5,000 ($867,424) to the relief fund. The rally sent a strongly worded resolution to President Roosevelt to take steps to answer Poland's cry of distress. Not trusting the aggressors, the resolution called for American control of the distribution of aid to both those in Poland and those who had fled the country.[12]

Meanwhile, the Commission for Polish Relief reported in late February that no word had been heard from the German Foreign Office on allowing relief to reach needy Polish civilians. The British demanded American supervision of distribution as a prerequisite for securing immunity from the blockade. Commissioners proposed a staff of fifteen Americans to administer aid. The Germans would allow only one American to regulate the distribution of goods. McCormick stated that he doubted that the group could accept this. In the interim, America's Polish Jews sent ten million pounds of clothing to Hungry to aid forty thousand Polish refugees. The Chicago Society Auxiliary sponsored a luncheon and fashion show for the benefit of the Chicago Polish Civilian War Relief Unit in the Loop's Hotel Sherman. March saw more fundraisers for Polish relief. That May, roughly fifty thousand took part in the Polish Constitution parade that culminated in Humboldt Park. Świetlik, in a fiery talk, called for Polish Americans to unite around one goal: to relieve hunger and suffering in Poland.[13]

By June 1940, the RPA had raised, nationally, $529,053.29 ($9,176,769 in 2017) for Polish relief, especially for food and medicine. *Zgoda* listed the donors and the amounts collected. Many of the donations came from Polish Catholic parishes, from local groups of fraternal organizations, and from individuals. For example, the RPA received $475 from Chicago's St. Fidelis Parish in Humboldt Park, and the Legion of Young Poles in America donated $500. Individuals donated what they could, from a dollar or two to more substantial donations.[14]

On July 28, 1940, *Zgoda* ran several photographs showing the shipment of food to Poland on behalf of the RPA. The newspaper reported that shipments had reached their destination in Warsaw, Lublin, and Radom. Local committees distributed the consignment, which included scarce materials such as wheat, milk, and other foodstuffs. One photograph showed John Hartigan, a representative of the American Commission to Aid Poland, along with Princess Tarnowska, director of the Polish Red Cross, and Dr. Sane of the German Red Cross inspecting the shipment. The state of Illinois donated the most funds to the RPA, over $208,000 ($3,607,894 in 2017) in total. Funds also assisted Polish refugees across Europe.[15]

Chicago's Poles kept up their efforts and attempted to maintain community life. In late January 1941, Polonia honored Mrs. Anna T. Strojny, who had helped five thousand Polish Chicagoans gain American citizenship, with a testimonial dinner attended by some five hundred people. Strojny conducted her classes at Kosciuszko Park on the Northwest Side and began a second class at the Polish Veterans Home on North Wood Street. Since childhood, she had helped Polish immigrants by translating letters and official papers for customers in her father's grocery store. While Polonia celebrated Mrs. Strojny, it continued efforts to help those in occupied Poland. In February, the Legion of Young Polish Women again dedicated their annual Red and White Ball for the benefit of the Polish War Relief Fund. On March 2, the Polish Women's Alliance sponsored a recital by the Polish tenor Jan Kiepura at the Civic Opera House to benefit the Paderewski Food Fund. On the cultural front, the Polish Opera Society presented Moniuszko's *The Haunted House* at the Civic Opera House on March 26. The society hoped to preserve Polish arts in America as the Nazis attempted to destroy the nation's cultural heritage.[16]

In April, the prime minister of the Polish government-in-exile, General Sikorski, visited Chicago for two days, the first of three wartime visits to the United States. He arrived in Chicago on Saturday, April 19, and held a press conference. At noon, the Chicago group Friends of Poland hosted a lunch for him and other Polish dignitaries at the Racquet Club. Sikorski's busy schedule included an afternoon visit to the headquarters of the Polish Roman Catholic Union of America and a reception at the Drake Hotel to greet delegates of Czech American organizations. At 8 p.m., he attended a board meeting of the Polish American Council. The next day, Sikorski attended a solemn High Mass at St. John Cantius Church, and at 1:30 p.m., despite rain and a blustery wind, an estimated seventy-five thousand Chicago Poles gathered at Soldier Field to honor the general. A banquet in the Palmer House concluded the visit. In July, a Polish mission headed by Major General Bronisław Duch arrived in Canada to raise an army of volunteers. Duch prophesized that many would volunteer, but the response failed to meet expectations, as only 722 men enlisted.[17]

On Sunday, June 29, 1941, Paderewski died of pneumonia in New York. Chicago's Archbishop Stritch celebrated a solemn High Mass for his soul at St. Stanislaus Kostka Church on July 3. In November, four thousand persons attended a memorial service at the Chicago Civic Opera House, where Stritch praised the deceased pianist. Świetlik announced that the American government offered temporary burial of Paderewski's remains in the Arlington National Cemetery until they could be moved to a free and independent Poland. Polish Chicagoans created a memorial room for the fallen hero in the Polish Museum. It included various memorabilia, including the furnishings of the room in the Hotel Buckingham in which the pianist had died. The museum also displayed his piano, music notes, and books, as well as the pen used to sign the Versailles Treaty.[18]

Some accounts claim Polonia was unprepared to respond to the outbreak of war in Europe.[19] Nevertheless Polonia, and Chicago's Polonia in particular, raised funds to help those in need, including the Polish Army in exile. Politically, Polonia had little power nationally and remained internally divided. Ideological, political, and regional conflict, as well as disagreements particular to Chicago, hindered efforts and marked the response to Poland's tragedy. While some hoped that an enthusiastic response for a Polish army raised in North America might develop, this did not transpire. Polonia's young men identified with their American homeland, and the twenty years of Polish independence had not tied Polonia more closely to their land of origin. They might have a rudimentary knowledge of the Polish language and of the country's history, but they were not as attached to Poland as their parents and grandparents had been. They saw themselves as Polish Americans with the emphasis on America. Perhaps this was a result of the cutting off of mass immigration in the 1920s, disappointment in politics back in Poland, or increased assimilation. Most likely it was a combination of all these influences and others, such as intermarriage. Also, no support for a military response emerged from the large Chicago-based fraternals, as it had during World War One. The Polish National Alliance's reaction to Światpol in the early 1930s gave evidence to this break with the homeland. While Poland would still be a major concern, and Chicago's Polonia would raise relief and later political efforts on behalf of the country, this connection to the Polish Republic was a sympathetic one in the context of an American reality. Polonia provided assistance when it could, but Chicago was the capital now, not just of the Fourth Partition but of Polish America in its entirety. According to the 1940 U.S. Census, Polish foreign stock (i.e., both foreign-born and American Poles) in Chicago numbered 359,984. The focus of Polonia would be on aiding Poland but also on defending the United States. The time for that would come soon enough.[20]

Chicago's Polonia Goes to War

President Roosevelt imposed the first peacetime draft in American history on September 16, 1940, as the United States prepared for war. The *Zgoda* reported that, despite the fact that Polish Americans, both foreign and native born, made up roughly 4 percent of the country's population, they accounted for 17 percent of those who had already volunteered for the American Army. The number of Polish Americans serving would be even larger if it included all branches of the service. The newspaper stated that

Polish Americans wanted to serve their country, and as the draft order went into effect, the number of Polish Americans in the armed services continued to grow.[21]

The United States officially entered World War Two on December 8, 1941, after the Japanese attack on Pearl Harbor the day before. The first member of the Polish National Alliance to be killed in battle died during the attack. The *Dziennik Chicagoski* encouraged Chicago's Polonia to play a major role in the war, urging its sons and daughters to join the armed forces. Furthermore, it asked workers to give up striking and offer their labor for the common cause. Five days later, the Polish government-in-exile declared war on Japan. It then petitioned the U.S. government to conscript all Polish nationals in the United States to serve in a Polish military force under American command. As in World War One, this proved impossible, but Polish Chicago along with Polish Americans across the country eagerly joined the U.S. armed forces. Earlier in that same year, Nazi Germany invaded the Soviet Union. Suddenly, the Axis powers saw themselves at war with two of the most powerful nations in the world. Great Britain no longer stood alone, as it did after the fall of France in the summer of 1940.

For Chicago's Polonia, the war meant a call to arms. On December 20, Świetlik urged Polish Americans to buy bonds and defense stamps, to volunteer for the Red Cross, and to join civilian defense. The PNA censor and the president of the RPA declared that the entire American Polonia, united and strong, would serve the country in this crisis. The RPA asserted that Polish Americans stood as one in defense of the United States and that they would fight for the same ideals for which Poland continued its struggle. The appeal reminded Polonia that efforts must be carried on in factories as well as on the battlefield.[22]

Chicago's draft boards in largely Polish neighborhoods reported their quotas filled. The English-language youth section of *Zgoda* encouraged young Polish Americans to invest in America's future by buying bonds to finance the arming of the American military. Polish National Alliance president Rozmarek

Pictured here are Polish National Alliance women who volunteered to aid the American Red Cross during World War Two. (Courtesy of *Zgoda*.)

announced that the organization had already purchased $2,385,000 ($39,399,389 in 2017) worth of U.S. Bonds and had donated $5,000 ($82,598) to the American Red Cross. The board of the PNA inaugurated first-aid classes for Polish American youth and planned classes for civil defense volunteers.[23] The community continued its attempt to save Polish culture, now under vicious attack by the Nazi regime. In February 1942, the Polish Arts Club of Chicago presented a Polish ballet at the Civic Opera House. Felix Sandowski, formerly of the Warsaw Opera, directed the troupe, which featured the ballerinas Janina Frostowna and Nina Juszkiewicz, while Jerzy Bojanowski conducted. It presented a program largely devoted to native Polish dances and choreographed to music by Polish composers.[24]

The PNA gave $750,000 ($11,263,160 in 2017) to Polish relief through the RPA. Of the PNA's three hundred thousand members, some 197,000 lived in Chicago. The Polish Roman Catholic Union of America supported Red Cross first-aid training, civilian defense, and other wartime activities. Members of the PRCUA bought $500,000 ($7,508,773) in war bonds and $3,500,000 ($525,614,110) of other government securities. The Polish Alma Mater pledged to buy $25,000 worth ($375,439) of war bonds. They donated $1,300 to the ambulance fund for the Polish Army. The Polish Women's Alliance purchased $100,000 ($1,501,755) in war bonds and gave $41,000 ($615,719) to the Paderewski Food Fund, $30,000 ($415,526) to the RPA, and $4,000 ($60,070) to the

In April 1942, the Northwestern University Settlement House players reenacted a Polish wedding pageant or *Poprawiny*. More than fifty players, almost all of Polish descent, made up the cast. Efforts were made throughout Polonia to maintain Polish traditions during World War Two. (Northwestern University Settlement Association Records Photographs, Series 41/6, Northwestern University Archives, Evanston, IL.)

American Red Cross. Since December 1939, the women's organization had been sending food packages to Polish war prisoners in Germany, France, and elsewhere. Every weekend, the PWA arranged dances for soldiers and sailors in Chicago. The American entry into the war complicated Polish relief efforts. Wartime rationing made the collection of foodstuffs and the shipment of goods to war-torn Europe difficult. Yet with the aid of the Red Cross, the RPA sent approximately twelve thousand food packages per month to Polish prisoners of war in Germany.[25]

On May 3, 1942, Chicago's Polish Americans celebrated the 151st anniversary of the adoption of the Polish Constitution. Some hundred thousand Polish Chicagoans heard Illinois governor Dwight H. Green, PNA president Rozmarek, and other speakers address the Humboldt Park gathering. The day's events began with Mass at fifty-five Polish Catholic churches in the archdiocese. A two-mile-long parade preceded the festivities. Green told the crowd that "we in America recognize our debt to Poland, a debt we have tried to repay and have repaid in part by our amicable relations and our earnest prayers that Poland's independence be restored." Green told the gathering that Polonia had nourished the true values of Americanism.[26]

By the end of the month, in an event that occurred countless times across the city's neighborhoods, the Bridgeport Civic League gave a send-off fete to seventy-six draftees leaving from Draft Board 96, located at 3205 South Morgan in the predominantly Polish section of the neighborhood. Speakers included Charles Kulikowski, president of the league, and Rev. Raymond Płoszyński of St. Mary of Perpetual Help Parish. The bugle corps of council 80 of the Polish National Alliance and the St. Mary High School Girls' Glee Club provided musical entertainment. A similar program occurred at Good Shepherd Parish at Twenty-Eighth and Kolin on the West Side. Parishioners held a parade and program that afternoon to honor those who marched off to war. The program included the blessing of three flags—the American flag, the service flag, and the flag of Poland.[27]

On July 19, Chicago's Polish community along with the city's other Slavic and East European communities marked the 532nd anniversary of the Battle of Grunwald in which the combined Polish, Lithuanian, and Czech forces defeated the German Teutonic Knights. Slavs throughout the world planned to celebrate the past triumph and dedicate themselves to the future defeat of Nazi Germany. All Polish, Czech, and Lithuanian churches began the day with a special memorial service and prayers for an Allied victory. The American Slav Congress sponsored the Chicago rally, to be held in Soldier Field. Celebrations began with a parade of army, navy and Red Cross units, boy scout troops, and groups representing many nationalities. The gathering emphasized the role of Slavic Chicago in the war effort both in the armed forces and on the home front, where Slavs made up an estimated 53 percent of workers. More than two hundred organizations participated in

Float sponsored by St. James Parish at the American Slav Congress rally at Soldier Field on July 19, 1942. Notice the two men dressed in Polish and U.S. Army uniforms guarding a woman representing Poland wearing a crown. Also pictured are Red Cross volunteers, children in traditional folk costumes, and Uncle Sam, along with other figures from Polish and American history. The message on the float reads "Poland is not lost," the title of the Polish national anthem, and portrays the "V for Victory" emblem with words "God Bless America" along the front of the float. (Courtesy of *Zgoda*.)

the event, including the PNA, the Polish Alma Mater, the Polish Highlanders Alliance of North America, and the PRCUA, among others. Polish American volunteers continued to join the armed forces as 1942 dragged on, and in November, the Polish groups of the American Legion sponsored a recruitment drive among Polonia's young men aged eighteen to nineteen years old. The Polish Day event took place at 333 North Michigan Avenue in the heart of the city. Later that year, residents of the heavily Polish Avondale neighborhood honored all residents in the armed services with the dedication of Victory Hill at Oakdale and Pulaski Road.[28]

In December, General Sikorski returned to Chicago and spoke at the Polish Women's Alliance hall. More than a thousand per-

General Władysław Sikorski (*left*) is picture here meeting with the Polish ambassador
Jan Ciechanowski (*center*) and Chicago's Mayor Edward J. Kelly (*right*) in 1942. (From the
collection of Polish Museum of America, x2005.001.0639.)

sons packed auditorium as another thousand gathered outside the
hall. Sikorski reiterated that Poland wanted her prewar boundaries restored and wanted to create a federation of all the central-
eastern European countries after the war. He also said that the
Baltic Sea could no longer be a German "lake" and must be placed
under control of the Baltic nations, Britain, and the United States.
Meanwhile, the RPA reported at the end of the year that seventy
thousand Polish American women were working with the organization as it continued to send food, clothing, and toilet articles
each month to Polish war prisoners and to Polish refugees across
the world. The RPA reported that at least seven hundred thousand pounds of clothing had been shipped overseas since October
1939.[29]

Polish Chicago and the Polish-Soviet Question

In 1943, relations between the Polish government-in-exile and the
Soviet Union became strained. Świetlik condemned the USSR's

statement that the lands captured in 1939 would not be returned to Poland after the defeat of Nazi Germany. The intentions of the Soviet Union seemed clear, and Chicago's Polonia attempted to rally American support for the prewar borders. President John Olejniczak of the Polish Roman Catholic Union of America stated that the Soviet attitude was contrary to everything the Allies were fighting for. In March, Chicago's Polish leaders wired President Roosevelt to protest Soviet territorial demands on Poland.

Tensions between the Poles and the USSR increased over the Katyn Forest massacre of Polish officers and intellectuals. The Soviets denied culpability and blamed Germany, but Poles persisted in their accusations. The Polish government demanded the release of Polish citizens imprisoned in the USSR and accused the Soviets of attempting to create a Soviet Poland. General Sikorski died suddenly in an airplane crash in Gibraltar in July, and his death complicated Allied relationships for the duration of the war.[30]

As 1944 began, Chicago's Polonia continued to keep the issue of postwar Poland before the larger public. That January, the Council of Polish American Professional Organizations sponsored a series of lectures to be held in the Loop. The talks aimed to foster good will between the United States and Poland. Meanwhile, Polish American students at Harrison Technical High School raised money to help purchase five Fairchild PT-15B Cornell training planes for U.S. naval cadets. The event took place on January 12, recognized nationally as Polish Unconquerable Day. The Tau Sigma Pi and Sigma Gamma sororities of the Polish Women's Alliance sponsored a spring social at PWA headquarters for the benefit of Polish war refugee children. In September, the Polish Civilian War Relief unit of the Chicago Chapter of the Red Cross held its fifth annual convention at the auditorium of St. Mary Magdalene Parish in South Chicago. That October, Polonia Society volunteers gathered more than ten thousand pounds of clothing and shoes to provide aid to recently liberated Polish civilians.

The community celebrated returning war heroes such as Chicagoan Lt. Bruno Godlewski, who, the previous March, at the age of nineteen, lost his right hand and most of his left arm in a Free Polish Air Force bombing mission over Essen, Germany. The Polish National Alliance raised $13,000 ($180,931 in 2017) for Godlewski, who had joined the Polish Air Force in Canada in 1941 after the U.S. Army Air Force rejected him as too young. He served as a tail gunner in a Wellington bomber operating out of England. On his eleventh mission, nine German fighter planes attacked the bomber. During the attack, the young man shot down three German planes before passing out from wounds in both arms and chest. Godlewski received Poland's highest award, the Virtuti Militari medal, as well as the American Distinguished Flying Cross and British Distinguished Flying medals. He returned to Chicago after spending seven months in various hospitals.[31]

In January 1944, the Soviets announced that they would accept the 1919 Curzon Line as Poland's eastern border, thus guaranteeing Soviet control over most of the territory seized by the USSR in 1939. It placed the previously Polish-held cities of Lwów, Wilno, Pinsk, and Tarnopol in the USSR. The treaty of Riga (1921) had established the Polish border some 120 miles to the east of the Curzon Line. Moscow suggested that Poland could be compensated with land originally part of pre-1939 Germany. Both the London Polish government and American Polonia vehemently opposed such a border adjustment.[32]

As the war continued, Chicago's Polonia worried about possible outcomes for postwar Poland. On Sunday, February 6, the PNA held a large public meeting to discuss the Polish situation at the Chicago Civic Opera House. An overflow crowd of Polish Americans and their supporters jammed the theater to hear Świetlik, Rozmarek, Governor Green, Mayor Edward Kelly, and Dr. Wacław Lednicki among, others, address postwar issues. Various speakers condemned the aggressive attitude of the USSR and called for Washington to support Polish territorial claims. The crowds loudly applauded Governor Green as he called for American support for Poland. Rozmarek reminded the rally that the Soviets had been Hitler's ally for twenty-two months. Mayor Kelly paid tribute to Poland as the first to fight against aggression. The meeting assailed the Soviet Union's statement envisioning a "new" Poland and intimating plans to ignore the existing Polish government-in-exile once Poland was liberated. Janusz L. Stamirowski, director of the Polish Information Service, proclaimed that patriotic Poles would recognize no new government except the government-in-exile in London. As the Red Army pushed the German Wehrmacht back across the pre-1939 Polish border, Polish American demands for reassurances of that border increased. In February, nearly two hundred delegates of the Polish American Council No. 20, representing nearly fifty thousand Polish Americans, met at the Polish Alma Mater Hall on Milwaukee Avenue and insisted that the USSR recognize the old border and the authority of the Polish London government.[33]

The Warsaw uprising in August 1944 saw the Soviet Army camp across the Vistula River as the Nazis destroyed the Polish capital. In turn, the Soviets supported a pro-Communist regime, the Lublin Committee, as the legitimate government of a liberated Poland. The Polish London government-in-exile saw itself as the lawful representative of the Polish people. Chicago's Polish leadership proved very wary of the Lublin Poles and urged the U.S. government not to recognize the pro-Soviet regime. These events made it obvious that Polonia needed an organization to lobby for the Polish cause. The strained relationship with the Soviet Union over Poland's borders and the fear that the country would fall under Communist domination necessitated the creation of a powerful umbrella organization that could unite Polish American efforts on behalf of the homeland.[34]

Again, Chicago's Polonia, as home to the headquarters of the major Polish American institutions, took the lead. On March 4, 1944, the executive committees of the largest Polish American fraternal organizations met at the headquarters of the Polish Women's Alliance. Roughly fifty people attended a meeting that lasted from 10:30 in the morning until 9:00 at night. Charles

Rozmarek gave the keynote address. Peter Yolles, a Polish Jewish journalist, and Frank Januszewski presented the goals of the new organization, eventually called the Polish American Congress (PAC), to collect $100,000 ($1,391,790 in 2017) for Polish American activities. They hoped to gather five million signatures on a petition to President Roosevelt as well as to send letters to senators and congressmen pleading Polish interests. Organizers decided on Buffalo, New York, for the first convention of the group as it had a large Polish American population and provided a compromise between Chicago and New York, the two traditional centers of Polonia power. The meeting also decreed that only organizations and not individuals could join. As a result, PAC became an umbrella group and not a competitor to the various fraternals who would each be represented by a deputy. Delegates elected Rozmarek, of the Polish National Alliance, as president of the new organization and on March 17, PAC Headquarters opened in the PNA building.[35]

On May 29, the Buffalo convention attracted over twenty-two hundred representatives from over a thousand Polish American organizations. More than eight hundred came from Polish parishes, including the Polish National Catholic Church, while the rest represented cultural and educational institutions, religious orders, trade organizations, industrial enterprises, and roughly two hundred distinguished Polonia activists. According to some counts more than three thousand attended in all, the largest meeting of Polonia leaders in the history of the diaspora. The Buffalo convention established the institutional basis for the new organization. The Polish American Congress decided to have an office in Washington, DC, as well as in Chicago. The Washington office was necessary if PAC hoped to have influence on the federal government's foreign policy. By early 1945, Charles Burke took charge in Washington and quickly became a recognized Polish figure in the capital.[36]

Events transpired rapidly, and in December 1944, a special meeting of the directors in Chicago voted to call into session an

extraordinary session of the PAC Supreme Council in Washington, DC, on January 11 and 12, 1945, to condemn the endorsement
by Great Britain of the annexation of Poland's eastern territories
into the Soviet Union. After President Roosevelt's postelection
declaration on December 19 that the United States would have no
objections to the new boundaries, President Rozmarek called on
six million Polish Americans to flood the White House, the State
Department, and Congress with letters and telegrams protesting
the USSR's land grab. The pro-Communist Lublin government
recognized the border shift and the compensation of Poland with
German territory to the west. The Polish American Congress saw
these agreements, secretly ironed out between Stalin, Roosevelt,
and Churchill, as a betrayal to both Poland and Polonia. Rozmarek
had supported the election of Roosevelt to a fourth term in 1944
after assurances that Poland's borders and rights would be pre-
served, and 90 percent of Polish Americans voted for the Democratic ticket that November.[37]

On New Year's Day, 1945, Rozmarek declared that Poles under
Soviet occupation were not free to choose their government. Six
days later, Chicago's Polish Americans organized PAC's Illinois
Division. The new group asserted that it spoke for eight hundred
thousand Polish Americans in Illinois and adopted a resolution
denouncing the Lublin government. Those at the meeting elected
Judge Thaddeus Adesko as its first president. The February 1945
Yalta Conference formalized agreements made at Teheran in 1943
and set postwar boundaries. The Allies confirmed the status of
the Curzon Line at Poland's eastern border and the shifting of
Poland's borders westward as the Allies compensated the country
with German lands in the west. The Western powers recognized
the Communist Lublin government and the new Provisional Government of National Unity, which promised to hold free elections.
Rozmarek and PAC, as well as a group of Polish American congressmen, immediately condemned these actions. Leftist union
organizer Leo Krzycki, of the American Slav Congress and the
American Polish Labor Council, generally considered as Commu-

nist front organizations, supported Roosevelt and called for the president to reject the opinions of other Polish American leaders.[38]

Rallies and meetings continued throughout the year, condemning Allied acquiescence to the Soviet territorial grab. A gathering of representatives from Polish-language newspapers across the United States met in Chicago in February and warned that America had planted the seeds of another world war by agreeing to the Yalta terms. It sent a resolution to President Roosevelt, the State Department, Congress, and the U.S. representatives at the United Nations Conference in San Francisco urging that the Yalta agreements be annulled. The following April, Chicago's archbishop Samuel Stritch addressed the Illinois Division of PAC to acquaint the public with the facts about Soviet claims to Poland's eastern territories. In July 1945 both the United States and the United Kingdom withdrew their recognition of the Polish government-in-exile (London government). By this time, Roosevelt had died and Harry Truman had become president. Despite hopes that he would take a firmer stand on the Polish question, the July Potsdam Conference only reaffirmed previous agreements.[39]

Meanwhile, as the war came to a conclusion in Europe, Polish war relief activities continued. In February, the Legion of Young Polish Women held their annual ball and again donated all proceeds to Polish relief. The following month saw twenty-nine women and four men graduating from a Loyola University School of Social Work program that trained them to serve as case and medical aids in Poland. The bishop's committee for Polish relief and the Catholic League selected these volunteers. A new class of forty students was due to take the classes shortly after Easter. On September 7, the RPA shipped twenty tons of food from Chicago for Poland. The truckloads contained clothing, canned goods, and other food supplies. The RPA had sent nine shipments since the Nazi surrender on May 8.[40]

The RPA committed itself to postwar aid to Poland. In 1945, it put forth a comprehensive review and a budget to help the Polish

Boxes being loaded in Chicago for Polish relief at the end of World War Two in front of the old Polish National Alliance building near Noble and Division Streets. The Polish American Council continued its aid to Poland and to Polish refugees long after the fighting ended. (Author's collection.)

populace once fighting ended. The report called for the mobilization of American Polonia to send aid to the ravaged homeland and to assist in the repatriation of displaced persons. It planned to send American personnel to postwar Poland to distribute goods and provide medical services. Polish American volunteers already being trained in American colleges and universities would provide the services. Foremost among the goals of the RPA was the need to feed and shelter the Polish population, as well as to provide for the aged and disabled.[41]

The RPA began its relief mission in December 1945 with an agreement between the RPA and the Lublin regime. The new Polish government gave RPA complete freedom of operation and control of the distribution of aid. The agreement also called for material to be marked as a gift of the American people and to be distributed to those in most need without discrimination as to ethnicity, creed, or political beliefs. Chicagoan Henry Osinski kept these supplies out of the hands of government officials, and in 1946 about $7,500,000 ($94,148,462 in 2017) worth of clothing and other supplies helped nearly five hundred thousand persons, mainly children, the ill, and the aged. The 1948 budget that had been requested included $2,000,000 ($25,106,256) for food and $1,345,000 ($16,883,719) for clothing and shoes. Medical and school supply budgets tallied at $1,000,000 ($12,553, 128) each, as the RPA hoped to raise $12,500,000 ($156,914,103) to continue its programs.[42]

In May 1946, Rozmarek invited General Tadeusz Bór-Komorowski, one of the leaders of the 1944 Warsaw Uprising, to Chicago. The general arrived at Chicago's Municipal Airport (now Midway Airport) where four hundred Polish Americans greeted him. He gave a talk stating that Poland was not yet free and gave a dark picture of a future under Soviet occupation. He told the crowd that all the Poles could do is look toward America for hope. Bór-Komorowski spoke at the annual Polish Constitution commemoration attended by some two hundred thousand Polish Chicagoans. The usual parade preceded the event, which included various denunciations of Yalta and the United States' role in the agreements. The Polish American Congress kept up its support for the Polish London government and continuously called for the rejection of the various wartime agreements concerning Poland and Eastern Europe.[43]

The Polish American Congress found it impossible to influence American, British, or Allied attitudes toward the Polish question. Military realities on the ground in Eastern Europe and the American desire to have the Soviets join in the final push against Japan mattered more to real politics than aspirations for justice. Also, America's war weariness presented a factor. Nevertheless, other matters soon arose. The displaced persons question became a pressing issue for Chicago's Polonia. Historian Anna Jaroszyńska-Kirchmann has pointed out that European cities and towns had been destroyed and millions of people were on the move, with no homes to return to. Hunger and sickness haunted the continent. As the Allies liberated slave labor, prisoner of war, and concentration camps, the magnitude of the disaster that had befallen Europe became apparent. Polish refugees represented the unfulfilled promises of the Allied victory. Their numbers stood at nearly 1.9 million in Germany, of which over 90 percent had been slave laborers. The rest included concentration camp survivors, prisoners of war, and Poles once slated for Germanization. In addition, roughly sixteen thousand members of the Polish armed forces also now occupied Germany. The ranks of Polish refugees in the American and British zones soon swelled with those who escaped from both the Soviet Zone of occupation and from Poland itself. Most Polish displaced persons (DPs) initially lived in assembly centers or camps created by the United Nations Relief and Rehabilitation Administration (UNRRA). Allied officials encouraged them to resettle in their original homelands, but many refused to return to Soviet-controlled areas. By June 1947, UNRRA repatriated some 562,000 Polish DPs to Poland from camps in Germany, Austria, and Italy. At that time, the UN Relief and Rehabilitation Administration completed its mission and a new organization, the International Refugee Organization, began operations and completed its charge by December 1951. After that, the United Nations High Commission for Refugees handled the affairs of displaced persons.[44]

Throughout this period, Chicagoans raised more money for those dislocated by war. During the same interval, reports of poor conditions in Europe continued. Letters received both from the displaced persons camps and Poland appeared in Polish American newspapers. These told of mistreatment not only by the Germans but by the Soviets and other allies as well. Some reported mistreatment by British or American troops. The victorious Allies hoped to repatriate most of the displaced persons and often did not understand the reluctance of DPs to return home. Nevertheless, the forced migration of millions of individuals during wartime proved impossible to reverse. In June 1946, Świetlik traveled to Europe to assess the needs of Polish refugees and reported on the number and conditions of those across Europe. He stressed poor living conditions and outlined a plan to help those in camps in Germany, France, and Switzerland. Charles Rozmarek took up the cause and petitioned Congress, asking for an investigation into the conditions and treatment of Polish displaced persons. He also claimed they were being forced to repatriate to Poland, a country now under Soviet domination.[45]

Rozmarek arrived in Europe in September 1946 as part of a four-man delegation on both a fact-finding mission regarding Polish refugees and to appeal for Polish freedom at the Paris Peace Conference. By October, Rozmarek charged that Moscow dominated UNRRA. He claimed that, instead of confining itself to feeding and housing displaced Poles, UNRRA policy made life in the camps unbearable in order to compel them to return to Poland. Rozmarek protested that UNRRA camps housed Polish refugees in poor and crowded conditions, transferred them frequently, forced them to abandon what few belongings they had, closed Polish schools, and suspended Polish refugee newspapers unsympathetic to the pro-Soviet Warsaw regime. He reported that families had been broken up. He asked that 150,000 Poles be admitted to the Alaskan territory. Rozmarek further claimed that British officials treated Polish exiles better than did the Americans. He claimed that "much chicanery and pressure" had been put on Polish DPs by UNRRA and the U.S. Army, which recognized the Communist-led regime. Reports from Poland that spoke of the uncertainties, misgivings, and crushed dreams of returnees continued to reach Chicago.

Rozmarek told an audience of roughly eight thousand Polish Chicagoans gathered in the Ashland Boulevard Auditorium that UNRRA forced the repatriation of Poles from across the wartime diaspora. He stated that he left Germany deeply shocked, because

Polish refugee boys on their way from Santa Rosa Mexico, to Alliance College in 1947.
The Polish National Alliance and Polish American Council president, Charles Rozmarek, is in
the center along with Joseph Kotch of Polish National Alliance Lodge 128 in Bremond, Texas.
(Courtesy of *Zgoda*.)

Polish DPs were treated worse than cattle. He spoke of poorly housed, clothed, and fed refugees and pointed out that Polish DPs had a diet of 1,250 calories a day while Germans in the occupied zones received 1,550 calories and American soldiers 4,000 calories per diem. By December, Rozmarek began a call to amend the immigration laws in order to allow refugees into the United States.[46]

In January 1947, Rozmarek asked for a congressional investigation and demanded that Polish displaced persons be treated humanely, as the Yalta agreement deprived them of the protection of a legal government and free homeland. That February, Rozmarek greeted seventy Polish orphans of high school age. Removed by Soviet authorities from their homes in Poland in 1940, they left the Soviet Union in 1942. Their trek took them out of Siberia to Iran, India, and finally Mexico. The boys enrolled in the PNA's Alliance College in Cambridge Springs, Pennsylvania. The girls attended Resurrection Academy in Chicago as well as Correopolis Academy in Pittsburgh.[47]

On May 3, the Polish consulate in Chicago celebrated Polish

Constitution Day, but Rozmarek refused to attend the event. Chicago's Polish organizations held their own celebration on May 4 in Humboldt Park. Ceremonies began with Mass at Holy Trinity Church and were followed by a parade of ten thousand Polish Americans. Arthur Bliss Lane, who had recently resigned the post of ambassador to Warsaw in protest after the Polish election in January, addressed the crowd. Lane condemned the USSR and warned that the Soviets would try to expand into Western Europe. He urged the crowd to oppose appeasement of the Soviet Union. Rozmarek denounced Joseph Winiewicz, Poland's ambassador to the United States, and called him "Stalin's representative."[48]

Rozmarek kept up his activities on behalf of the Polish displaced persons. The PAC leader held the United States responsible for the resettlement of DPs as a result of Washington's betrayal of Poland at Yalta. He testified in support of the Stratton Bill proposed by Republican Illinois Congressman and future governor William Stratton to admit four hundred thousand DPs into the United States over a four-year period. Rozmarek urged that the Stratton Bill be amended to embrace Polish soldiers who should be entitled to enter the United States because of their service as America's allies. Considerable opposition to the Stratton proposal arose, led by the *Chicago Tribune*, which editorialized that the DP issue was a European one, caused by Europeans, and so it should be settled by Europeans. The newspaper, which had been a bastion of isolationist sentiment and anti-Roosevelt politics before Pearl Harbor, often continued to take "America first" stands in its editorial pages. When secretary of state, General George C. Marshall, listed legislation that the State Department hoped Congress would pass, he included a modification of the immigration law in order to welcome Europe's displaced persons. The *Tribune* immediately questioned the wisdom of the project and pointed to the housing shortage in the United States. It asked how refugees could be sheltered and encouraged European nations to accept the exiles and Britain, in particular, to allow Jews to emigrate to Palestine. The editorial claimed that "the British are counting on

America to solve their problems at America's expense." In June 1947, Texas Democratic representative Ed Gossett and Kentucky Republican John M. Robison assailed Stratton's proposal, claiming it was a move to allow "crackpots, Communists, and troublemakers" into the country. The pair instead called for the strengthening of immigration laws. In November, the *Tribune* suggested that DPs be resettled in Australia, Argentina, Brazil, Africa, or some other country that "lacked" population.[49]

While all of that was going on, efforts to help the Polish nation continued. Again, the Legion of Young Polish Women and the Polish Women's Alliance raised funds for Polish Relief Aid. At the end of 1947, the war relief services of the National Catholic Welfare Council sent seven hundred thousand pounds of canned food to aid Poland. The shipment was the first of forty million pounds of such food collected in eighteen thousand Catholic parishes by the War Relief Services Thanksgiving Campaign. Chicago's Rev. Aloysius Wycisło promised that the food would reach the children for whom it was intended. Four American war relief service workers supervised the distribution of food in Poland.[50]

Other efforts concerning Polonia issues, especially the education of Polish American students, continued. Chicago's Polish organizations established various scholarship funds for local youth in the immediate postwar period, as education grew in importance in the still primarily working-class community. In March, Professor Robert Strozier, the dean of students and a member of the Faculty Bureau of Scholarships at the University of Chicago, addressed the Polish Arts Club, and guests from Chicago area student Polish clubs, about scholarship opportunities. The Polish Council of University Clubs soon established a scholarship fund for Polonia students. In turn, the Polish Women's Civic Club established a fund to include the awarding of five full-tuition scholarships to local university students. This signaled a fundamental shift in the attitudes of the majority of Polish Chicago families.[51]

Meanwhile, Chicago Republicans hoped to return to power

over the Yalta issue. Predictions abounded that Polish Americans would flock to the GOP as a result of the Democratic president's betrayal. Politicians looking toward the 1947 aldermanic elections remarked on an upsurge of Republican strength in fourteen Northwest Side wards where Polish Americans made up a large part of the population. Only one Republican alderman, John B. Brandt of the Thirty-Third Ward, represented that part of the city. In almost every ward, Republicans put up a party-endorsed candidate in an attempt to break the Democratic machine. Stanley R. Pulaski, the Republican candidate for city treasurer, called the January elections in Poland a "saddening fiasco" and a result of Yalta, Tehran, and Potsdam. Pulaski, opposed by Democrat John T. Baran, also a Polish American, won the endorsement of the Polish National Alliance Civic League District 13, which had twenty-five thousand members. Frank L. Wozniak, a prominent Polish American Democrat, broke with the party to support Republican Russel M. Root for mayor against Democrat Martin Kennelly. Nevertheless, the Democratic Party held on, and Kennelly won the mayoralty. Four largely Polish wards did see a larger Republican turnout, one that hinted at a permanent shift to the party. The real test for GOP aspirations among Polish Americans would come in the national elections of 1948. National GOP leaders called for an end to New Deal programs and hoped to rescind those policies once they controlled the presidency. Rozmarek broke with the Democrats and supported Republican Thomas Dewey for president. Many felt that Polonia, disgusted with the way Poland had been treated, would follow his lead. Polonia, still very much a part of the working class, nevertheless voted heavily for President Harry Truman. The preservation of New Deal gains by organized labor and the Republican refusal to back immigration laws that allowed displaced persons to enter the United States, meant more to Polish American voters.[52]

Rozmarek kept up political pressure to pass legislation allowing displaced people to enter the country. Finally, in June 1948, President Truman signed a law allowing 205,000 DPs to be

Charles and Wanda Rozmarek greet the first group of Polish displaced persons to enter the United States. Wanda Rozmarek became known as the "Mother of Displaced Persons," many of whom she welcomed into her own Chicago home. (Courtesy of *Zgoda*.)

admitted between July 1, 1948, and June 30, 1950. As soon as the law went into effect, PAC lobbied for its extension and liberalization. In 1950, Congress amended and extended the entire program until July 1, 1951. Furthermore, it raised the number of persons admitted to 341,000, including Polish veterans from Great Britain. The new provisions extended the cutoff date for DPs to have entered the Western Zone of Occupied Germany (the future West Germany) from December 22, 1946, to January 1, 1949. During the four-year period, more than 337,000 displaced persons entered the United States. Three major Polish American organizations helped resettle Polish DPs, including the American Relief for Poland (Rada Polonii) and the Polish Immigration Committee, which were both affiliated with the National Catholic Welfare Conference, and also the American Committee for the Resettlement of Polish DPs, an outgrowth of PAC.

Polish Chicagoans sponsored a great number of DPs, and Polonia delegations greeted them. In 1949, representatives traveled with the refugees on the last leg of their journey to prepare them for their arrival in the city. The Polish National Alliance set up a provisional office, informed immigrants about sponsors, distributed welcoming gifts, and handed out five-dollar bills and the *Dziennik Związkowy*. Leaders from both PAC and PNA presented information about their organizations and urged the new arrivals to join as soon as possible. The Illinois Division of PAC purchased a house in the city that could temporarily accommodate families. In 1951, it added another building to briefly accommodate DP families. In addition, many DPs found themselves guests in the home of Charles and Wanda Rozmarek. Mrs. Rozmarek served as head of the PAC Illinois Division's Displaced Persons Department from the inception of the DP law until it expired. She met refugees at train stations at all times of day and night and drove them to their sponsors' homes, cooked for them, ran errands, and helped them find employment. The Rozmarek house accepted roughly four hundred DP families over time. Wanda Rozmarek covered all expenses herself and, along with her husband, donated $2,000 ($20,314 in 2017) to DP funds. She also championed Polish immigrants who had settled and were poorly treated in the American South and brought them to Chicago.[53]

The wartime experience of Polish Chicago brought Poland to the forefront of attention. As the world entered the long Cold War, Polonia kept its eyes on foreign affairs. The Polish community began to change under the impact of both the new immigration and the wartime experience. The years after 1950 saw a vast transformation across Polish Chicago, resulting from not only demographic change but also the impact of technology, acculturation, and economic trends. These would alter Polonia and again raise the question of what exactly *Polskość* meant, if anything, for yet another generation.

The Long Struggle

Chicago's Polonia, Communist Poland, and a Changing City

My people are so jubilant they don't know what to do.

—ALOYSIUS MAZEWSKI, president of the PNA and PAC, on the election of Pope John Paul II[1]

The tragedy of war shaped the response of the community toward Poland and to the ongoing saga of the displaced persons. Polonia's institutions worked to absorb the new immigration. In addition, the postwar reality included the return of Polonia's sons and daughters, changed by their wartime experience. Many in Polonia turned away from their working-class roots and aspired toward middle-class status. Residents slowly abandoned old neighborhoods for suburbs. Higher educational opportunities further transformed Polonia and shifted political and cultural attitudes.

Chicago's Polish foreign-born population continued to decline, as more and more of the old economic immigration known as *Za Chlebem* (for bread) died. The 1950 federal census counted 315,504 Polish-born Chicago residents, down more than sixty-eight thousand since the previous tally, and nearly eighty-six thousand fewer than 1930. Despite these losses, Chicago's Polonia still seemed large and potentially powerful both economically and politically. Of course, these numbers do not include those Chicagoans who were born of American parents even if they still considered themselves Poles, or at least had some personal attachment to the community. The arrival of displaced persons also complicated matters as the question of what *Polskość* meant returned.[2]

While the Soviet Union dominated Eastern Europe, Chicago's Polonia turned again toward political agitation on behalf of the homeland. The Polish American Congress's initial response to the Polish People's Republic was one of hostility and it called for free elections, a return of the eastern territories ceded to the USSR, and continued support of the Polish London government. The Polish American Congress also remained involved with the plight of refugees (DPs). The organization represented victims of Nazi terror to receive reparations from the West German government for losses during the war and acted on behalf of Polish veterans to get benefits and aid from the U.S. government. The congress established a million dollar fund to promote both freedom in Poland and Polish American culture. Over time, its hostility to the Polish Communist regime, while it did not end, lessened, and PAC opened negotiations for cultural transfers and better relations. This occurred after Stalin's death and Polish reforms in 1956. This opening of the cultural door led to an opportunity for Polish and American scholars, artists, and others to exchange ideas and concerns. The congress supported various liberalization efforts in Poland and eventually welcomed a Polish pope to Chicago and supported the Solidarity movement.[3]

While international events seemed to dominate PAC and its membership in the postwar era, basic structural changes also took place in Polonia. Chicago's Polish community continued to assimilate and the children, grandchildren, and great grandchildren of many of the *Za Chlebem* immigrants moved out of West Town, Pilsen, Bridgeport, Back of the Yards, South Chicago, and Hegewisch. These younger families saw their ties to the old

Women from Chicago's Polish National Alliance District 13 prepare packages for the needy in Poland, ca. 1950. The Polish National Alliance and other Polish American organizations continued aid to the poor in Poland after the war. (Courtesy of *Zgoda*.)

working-class parishes and fraternal organizations erode. Larger contingents of Polish Americans attended Chicago-area colleges and professional schools. In 1980, 932,996 Illinois residents answered the census question on ancestry as Polish, of these only 301,551 lived within the city limits.[4]

Polonia and Communism: The Postwar Years

The community remained largely intact after 1945 and greeted its returning sons and daughters as heroes. Some fears did haunt the city, as memories of the post–World War One era and the Great Depression resurfaced. The Taft-Hartley Bill survived a presidential veto and unions felt under attack. Polonia remained largely working-class in character, and despite labor's gains during the New Deal and the war, Polish neighborhoods remained unsure about the immediate postwar years. Race relations stood on edge as the Great Migration of African Americans entered its second and more massive phase. Politically, despite some Republican gains, Polonia remained firmly in the Democratic camp, because the memory of the New Deal overshadowed Yalta and Poland's postwar tragedy, at least for the time being.

Polonia had given relief to the Polish nation during the war. It had sent its sons and daughters into battle as Americans and helped build the arsenal of democracy at home. Now Poland again struggled under the Soviet yoke, and PAC never missed a chance to bring Poland's plight to the public's attention. During the annual PNA-organized Polish Constitution Day celebration in Humboldt Park on May 4, 1952, a hundred fifty thousand Polish Americans cheered the demand that the United States withdraw diplomatic recognition of the USSR. The crowd warmed to William G. Stratton, the Republican nominee for Illinois governor, who as a congressman had introduced the bill that allowed displaced persons into the United States. Rozmarek expressed the gratitude of the crowd to Stratton. He commended Congress for investigating the Katyn massacre and called for an investigation of the Yalta conference. Rozmarek remained staunch in his opposition to the Warsaw regime. Democratic vice president Alben W. Barkley spoke of a sense of frustration that Poland remained a Soviet satellite and expressed confidence that Poland would regain its freedom.

At the opening of the annual national meeting of the PAC in Atlantic City later that month, Rozmarek again called for the severance of all ties with the Soviet Union and its satellites and urged the cancellation of the Yalta agreement, the elimination of Communist-dominated governments from the United Nations, the use of Chinese nationalist troops in the Korean conflict, and caution in the foreign aid program in order to prevent American bankruptcy. He blamed the plight of Poland on American foreign policy and claimed it had been molded by Communist sympathizers in the U.S. government. The following year, Rozmarek even advocated the use of H-bombs in French Indochina and claimed that nuclear weapons would save not only the "unconquered" nations of the world but Poland and other satellites as well. He charged that pro-Soviet diplomats in the U.S. State Department caused the fall of both Poland and China to Communism. The PNA-led rally endorsed Senator Joseph McCarthy's investigation into Communist activities and condemned his opponents. Rozmarek, like many Americans, dove headlong into Red Scare and Cold War attitudes. President Dwight D. Eisenhower's Republican administration did little to please Chicago's Polonia. In March 1953, Polish American leaders decried the new president's refusal to repudiate Yalta. General Kazimierz Sosnowski, president-designate of the London government, visited Chicago and voiced a "deep discouragement and disappointment" in Eisenhower. Sosnowski then called for American recognition of the Polish government-in-exile. The annual Constitution Day celebrations in Humboldt Park consistently voiced opposition to the Warsaw regime.[5]

All the while, Polish Chicago's social life continued, now often with anti-Communist themes. The Polonia Day picnic sponsored by PAC's Illinois Division on July 12, 1953, at Elm Tree Grove on Irving Park Road featured hundreds of helium-filled balloons bearing the inscription "Free Poland Will Rise Again" that were set free by children at the climax of a ceremony condemning Communism. Previous picnics had raised $75,000 to help settle displaced persons in the Chicago area, but since DP immigration had basically ceased, funds now went to aid Polish veterans abroad. In September 1955, Polish Chicagoans gathered in Humboldt Park to celebrate the thirty-fifth anniversary of the "Miracle of the Vistula," when Polish troops defeated the Red Army in 1920, and to pray for another miracle that would again liberate Poland. Chicago's Samuel Cardinal Stritch predicted that their prayers would be answered.[6]

Polish Chicago celebrated two Polish pilots who had escaped to Denmark in 1953 with their MiG-15 fighter planes. On March 5, Lt. Franciszek Jarewski, a twenty-one-year-old pilot, landed his plane on Denmark's Bornholm Island, sixty miles from the Polish coast.

Forty members of the PNA headed by Rozmarek greeted the pilot in Chicago on May 1 as a hero. The young pilot, now a political refugee, spoke at the Polish Constitution Day ceremonies. The American Legion feted him and presented him with their distinguished award citation. On May 20, another Pole, Lt. Zdzisław Jaźwiński, crash landed a different MiG-15 on Bornholm Island. The two pilots met each other in New York City in July. Jaźwiński visited Chicago that September and addressed three thousand people at a PAC Illinois Division assembly to mark the fourteenth anniversary of the beginning of World War Two. Such events rallied the Polish community and provided support for the Polish struggle. Historian Anna Jaroszyńska-Kirchmann has called this the "exile mission," a mission that Chicago's Polonia embraced from its beginning. The Chicago-based Polish American Congress embodied this mission during the Cold War.[7]

The arrival of thousands of refugees did not proceed without some conflict. Many post-1945 Polish immigrants came from a different social class than those who had arrived more than thirty years earlier. They had different childhood experiences and had spent their adult years in an independent Poland. The children of the *Za Chlebem* migration, who now led most of the Polish American organizations, identified culturally with Poland but not so much politically as their parents had. Of course, class also influenced these people; the earlier immigration was primarily peasant in nature, while the later immigration came from various classes but with a large number of former military officers, intellectuals, and upper-class Poles who had refused to return to Communist Poland. These new arrivals imagined that, as in interwar Poland, they would take leadership positions in Polonia. The working-class nature of Polish Chicago often shocked and discouraged them. These initial contacts between the two immigration cohorts proved a bitter disappointment for the new immigrants. Highly politicized, they expected the entire community to be more militant in the struggle for Polish freedom.

Initially, the old Polonia reacted with aid. Soon, however, they resented what they sensed as the old upper-class elitist attitudes of the Polish *Szlachta* (gentry/noble classes). When DPs came to Chicago, Polish Chicagoans expected them to work alongside them in factories, packinghouses, and steel mills. The newcomers often took these positions but saw themselves as more middle and upper class. Many refused to live in the old Polish ghettoes and moved out as soon as possible. Chicago's Polish community thus became somewhat bifurcated. This proved to be a common experience across Polonia centers. The two immigrant cohorts had a hard time understanding each other despite a common claim to *Polskość*.[8]

Sociologist Mary Patrice Erdmans has pointed out the various migration waves and explained that the differences revolved around the realities of the Poland the immigrants had left and the cause for migration. The Nazi attack and the imposition of a Communist government on Poland after the war made displaced persons fiercely nationalistic and their leadership highly politicized. Polish Americans, in contrast, increasingly saw themselves as a cultural rather than a political group. The newer immigrants spoke a higher, more refined Polish. Polish Americans, when they spoke Polish, spoke a patois of Polish words mixed with English that often had a Polish ending attached. This resulted from the fact that when the economic immigrants left Poland, words designating certain objects simply did not exist, or peasants were unaware of them. In America, they adopted the English word. In other cases, the English word was simpler and was used or better understood by their children or older, more settled inhabitants. These words and phrases usually appeared only in the spoken language and not in print. Chicagoans often referred to this "language" as *po Chicagosku*, or the Chicago dialect. The newer immigrants found this watering down of the Polish language reprehensible. Polish American accents also differed from proper Polish ones. American pronunciation had an impact on Polish Americans speaking their ancestral tongue. The new immigrants believed that if Chicago really was "Poland elsewhere," then Polish had to be the language of its residents. This caused problems not only on the streets of the city but at fraternal meetings as well. Nevertheless, as Erdmans has suggested, the distaste for Communism provided a unifying factor between Polish Americans and newer immigrants.[9]

The newcomers both joined Polish American organizations and created their own. They referred to themselves as the *Nowa Emigracja* or New Emigration in contrast to *Stara Polonia* (Old Polonia). In 1949, Chicago's immigrants created the Samopomoc Nowej Emigracji (Mutual Aid Association of the New Polish Emigration), which focused on services such as housing, document translation, sponsorships, applications for war reparations, and financial aid. It also presented a cultural program that included lectures on a wide variety of topics, the creation of a library, and a community center for the newcomers. Samopomoc joined PAC and cooperated with various old and new Polonia organizations. New immigrants also organized theater groups, including Teatr Dramatyczny (The Dramatic Theater), Teatr Aktora (Actor's Theater), Radio Teatr Wyobraźni (Radio Theater of the Imagination), and Teatr Ref-Rena (Ref-Ren's Theater), among others. These cultural groups played largely to the postwar immigrant community, although some older Polish Chicagoans could be found in the audiences as well.

Immigrant youth and *Polskość* became an issue for the *Nowa Emigracja*. Polish American parochial schools educated some, but the quality of education, especially concerning Polish history and literature, and the rapid decline of the teaching of the Polish language in the years after the Depression and World War Two, disturbed immigrant parents. They came to support Polish Saturday schools and the Polish scouting movement. Leaders saw both of these as not only preserving Polishness but also preparing the younger generation to return to a non-Communist Poland. While most did not know it, these organizations actually reflected the same concerns of Polonia's leadership in the years before 1914.

Polish Army veterans arrived in large numbers, and tensions between them and Polonia veterans' organizations broke out. In 1952, the Association of Veterans of the Polish Army (Stowarzyszenia Weteranów Armii Polskiej), which represented World War One Blue Army veterans, held its convention in Utica, New York. At the meeting, members adopted a new rule requiring candidates for office to be American, Canadian, or Cuban citizens and members of the organization for five years. All members were to wear the blue uniform of Haller's Army. Leaders of the Stowarzyszenia Weteranów Armii Polskiej feared that the arrival of massive numbers of new Polish Army veterans would take over the organization. Indeed, some exile politicians did want to do just that, wishing to establish themselves as "commanders" of American Polonia. A rival organization then appeared called the Association of Polish Combatants (Stowarczstwo Poliskich Kombatantów). Due to the anti-Communist orientation of both the Stowarczstwo Poliskich Kombatantów and the Polish American Congress, the two groups cooperated with one another. Other veteran organizations also appeared, reflecting various Polish wartime experiences.[10]

Polish Chicago: The Postwar Era

Polish Chicago had always been defined as working class in character, but in reality, Polonia had a rather complex class structure. While the peasantry predominated in the *Za Chlebem* migration, Polish intellectuals, businessmen, politicians, and clerics had long served Chicago's Polish community. Some of them came from Poland, others were American born and raised. The post–World War Two migration brought yet more social class diversity. As the children and grandchildren of the original migration came to dominate Polonia, education and upward mobility, too, became factors. The postwar years saw the community go through a social transformation. The GI Bill after World War Two provided educational opportunities for many veterans who had seen no such path to success before the war. Polish American participation in higher education in Chicago grew in the 1950s and even more so in the 1960s and 1970s.

While the pre-1940 years witnessed the growth of the professional class, the majority in Polonia remained in the working class. This explained the continued allegiance of Polish Americans to organized labor and the Democratic Party. Juvenile delinquency also still haunted many Polonia neighborhoods. Gangs prevailed in the working-class quarters of the city, regardless of race or ethnicity. The most notorious of these gangs, perhaps, came to the attention of the public in the late 1950s in the Back of the Yards neighborhood. Despite the efforts of the Back of the Yards Neighborhood Council, the area still harbored groups such as the Rebels, a largely Polish American gang. Back of the Yards sat in the shadow of Chicago's most famous industry, with massive meatpacking plants and the Union Stock Yard to the north and east. Three Polish parishes served its dominant ethnic community. Eleven other ethnic Catholic parishes also operated within the district's boundaries. Concurrently, just to the south and east, African Americans moved into the Englewood community. Racial conflict often flared up, and the neighborhood had a long-standing reputation for its anti-black attitude.

On the night of March 11, 1957, a seventeen-year-old African American student, Alvin Palmer, waited for the bus on the corner of Fifty-Ninth Street and Kedzie Avenue in Chicago Lawn, just southwest of Back of the Yards. White teenagers in two cars, all members of the Rebels, drove up, and one of them, Joe Schwartz, beat Palmer with a ball-peen hammer. Palmer died shortly thereafter. The Rebels quickly returned to their candy store hangout and bragged about what happened. The randomness of the attack and the involvement of youth gangs stunned the city. The Rebels, who had long terrorized neighborhood residences and businesses, emerged as a symbol of juvenile delinquency across Chicago and the nation. In 1957 the killing of Palmer brought forth the possibility of another massive race riot, as black and white gangs stared each other down across racial boundaries.

The state indicted fifteen boys for the Palmer murder; eleven of these had identifiable Polish names. Five came from Sacred Heart, a Polish American parish just west of the stockyards. Police brought in the gang members on murder charges. That June, Joe Schwartz received a five-year prison sentence. Benjamin Adamowski, the newly elected Republican state's attorney of Cook County, declared that all the Rebels should be hung. Mayor Richard J. Daley called Palmer's death merely "an unfortunate incident," fearing more racial conflict. He hoped that police presence would reach a point where such incidents could not happen. The reality of the city's racial history and politics made that highly unlikely, however.[11]

Both Polish immigrants and Polish Americans dominated many of these gangs. Some of these same gangs would later be dominated by Mexicans or Puerto Ricans as ethnic change occurred in the 1970s and 1980s.[12] Gangs were a product of poverty and also of a rapidly changing demography. Many Polish Americans, despite increased wages and some upward mobility, still lived in economically disadvantaged parts of the city and feared that they could lose their longtime neighborhoods to the growing African American and Hispanic communities. Some of this was a protective communal response, but it also showed assimilation as Polonia became more and more entrenched in the racist attitudes of the United States: white flight and racism were hardly restricted to Polonia.

Violence between Polish Americans and other ethnic and racial groups broke out regularly on the city's streets. Both ethnic and neighborhood leaders attempted to deal with a problem that eventually diminished as Polonia entered the middle class and moved to residential suburbs. Poles and African Americans competed for housing in Chicago's poorer parts of the city in the period after World War Two. Polish investment in parishes, schools, fraternal headquarters, and business made them reluctant to leave those areas. Job competition also provided the basis for conflict between the two groups. Polish neighborhoods, however, actually faced transition because of other factors as well, especially the phenomenal growth of the Hispanic population after 1965. Hispanics, principally Mexicans and Puerto Ricans, moved into largely Slavic neighborhoods as the 1960s and 1970s progressed. By the 1980s, many Catholic churches offered Mass in Spanish as well as in Polish and English. Ethnic walls crumbled as the 1960s and 1970s progressed.[13]

Polish Downtown, South Chicago, and Back of the Yards all witnessed ethnic and racial transformations after World War Two. The neighborhood that Ed Marciniak referred to in his study as East Humboldt Park (Stanisławowo-Trójcowo, Polish Downtown or West Town), which lies northwest of the Loop, witnessed massive change during this period. Prior to 1960, this traditionally Polish American neighborhood housed the major Polish institutions in the city along with its largely Polish population. Younger Polish American families sought better housing opportunities, and many moved to the suburbs. African American, Puerto Rican, and Mexican newcomers entered the district in large numbers. The neighborhood, which had never been wealthy and had been considered among the worst of the late nineteenth- and early twentieth-century slums, reverted to that profile. Many Polish American businesses remained and tried to adjust but ultimately closed or moved as customers now needed Spanish-speaking salespeople and what white ethnic merchants considered "exotic" ethnic goods. Saint Stanislaus Kostka, Holy Trinity, and St. Boniface Parishes all saw their traditional memberships decline. Sunday attendance shrunk, as did the size of weekly collections. Saint Boniface ran a trilingual kindergarten, with a teacher that spoke English, Spanish, and Polish. Local politicians hoped that the population shift could be stopped or reversed but remained thankful that the new residents also supported the Democratic Party.

In the late 1950s, the city presented plans for the Northwest Expressway (now called the Kennedy Expressway) and urban renewal. In East Humboldt Park, some four hundred families saw the city take their homes in order to build the highway. Most of these belonged to St. Stanislaus Kostka and St. Boniface Parishes. The original plan for the expressway went right through St. Stanislaus Kostka Church. Residents protested, and Polish American politicians intervened to save Polonia's mother church. Under pressure from the neighborhood and their politicians, the city's Department of Public Works finally moved the expressway slightly to the east. Nevertheless, the road passed just under the parish rectory's windows. But this reconfiguring of the expressway resulted from a still politically potent Polish community.[14]

The neighborhood's ethnic makeover continued, as demographic change, once begun, is nearly impossible to stop. West Town's residents would learn that over and over again as the twentieth century progressed. The expansion of educational and financial opportunities, as well as further assimilation, provided the key to this change. This all occurred within the framework of vast technological and economic shifts in the poorer parts of the city and within the American working class. The neighborhood system that seemed to stand so solidly in the 1950s had a long history stretching back to the nineteenth century. Industrialization provided the foundation for it and tied Chicago to the developing Atlantic economy. Steamship lines, railroads, factories, steel mills, packinghouses, and the like provided a transportation system and economic base that attracted vast numbers of immigrants. Poles and others lured to industrial centers brought their rural communal cultures to create a protective sense of community in the new American industrial environment.

During the years after World War Two, technological change and the increased buying power of working-class whites in particular began to again alter the system. Polonia's communalism created not only parishes and schools, whether Roman Catholic or Polish National Catholic, but also influenced the establishment of labor unions, neighborhood organizations, and political machines. This neighborhood system had its roots in the communal peasant past of its residents. That peasant experience receded quickly in the decades after World War Two. New Polish immigrants had long ago left their rural village past behind, while members of the American-born generation saw their lives transformed by educational opportunities and upper mobility during his period. The Polish immigrant ghetto walls crumbled before the onslaught of various demographic, social, economic, and technological factors.

Suburbanization, the automobile, automation, and education changed the structure of Chicago's Polonia. Polish Americans had long been moving away from the original settlements. On the North Side, they followed Milwaukee Avenue to the city limits and beyond. In Pilsen and the West Side, they shadowed Czechs down Blue Island Avenue and Cermak Road (Twenty-Second Street) toward Cicero, Berwyn, and the western suburbs. From Back of the Yards and Bridgeport, Polish families traveled southwest along Archer Avenue and Forty-Seventh Street. The Southeast Side Polonia left South Chicago and Hegewisch for neighborhoods and suburbs like Lansing to the south and, eventually, those in Indiana.

The Great Depression and the Second World War halted, and in many cases reversed, this outward movement, but the years following the war saw it restarted. Veterans returning from the fighting wanted a new life. Most returned to the working class, but the prosperity of the postwar years changed working-class living patterns. The automobile proved to be a key to residential mobility. The car allowed workers to live farther away from the industries that employed them, often in outlying residential neighborhoods and suburbs. In turn, the truck, as it came to replace, in part, the railroad system, especially in the meatpacking industry, changed the industrial structure of the city.[15]

Chicago's Old Polonia: The Last Hurrah

Poland celebrated a thousand years of nationhood in 1966. Poles all over the world marked the event with celebrations, both religious and secular, as well as with political proclamations. On April 16, official observances took place in Poland, with organ

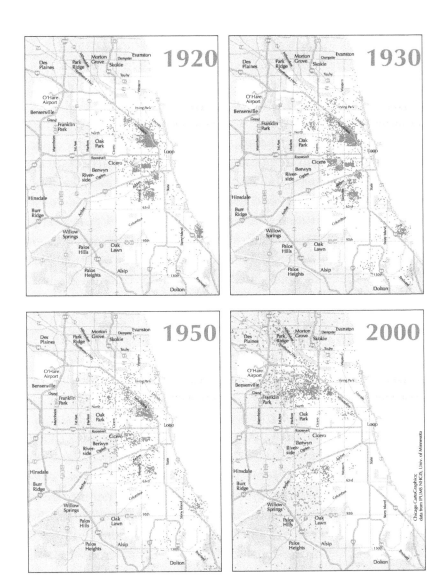

Maps showing outward movement of Polonia across the cityscape, 1920–2000. Each dot represents fifty persons. (Courtesy of Chicago CartoGraphics.)

music, blaring bands, speeches, and military parades. In Gniezno, Poland's ancient capital, both the Communist state and the Catholic Church marked the occasion. The church and state agreed to have separate observances, one ending before the other began in the city. The Catholic Church's jubilee celebration centered on the conversion of Poland's ruler Mieszko I with a liturgy. Later, a military parade took place that bypassed the cathedral district. The Polish Army marked the crossing of the Oder River in pursuit pf the retreating German Army in 1945.

Despite the temporary truce, the Polish Communist regime and the Catholic Church continued to struggle with each other. Władysław Gomulka, the head of the Communist Party, barred a proposed trip by Pope Paul VI to Poland to take part in the celebration of a thousand years of Christianity in Poland. He cited Polish Primate Stefan Cardinal Wyszyński's "harmful" policy toward the state as a reason. Polish bishops had invited the pope and bishops from fifty-six countries to come to the shrine in Częstochowa on May 3, the traditional date for recollecting Poland's groundbreaking eighteenth-century democratic constitution. Obviously, allowing such a visit would have been a great propaganda victory for the Roman Catholic Church. Warsaw also refused to issue a passport for Wyszyński to visit either Rome or Chicago, where he had been invited him to take part in a celebration planned at Soldier Field. The Polish government then prohibited American diplomats from attending the May 3 services.

Some Chicagoans did make their way to Poland. The official Chicago pilgrimage departed on April 28 for Copenhagen on Scandinavian Airlines. Tourists who obtained Polish visas continued to Warsaw, while those who hadn't visited other European cities. Those in Warsaw planned to rejoin the group in Rome. The Communist government liberalized its travel policies for the celebrations. Orbis, the Polish travel office, cooperated with visa applications, hotel, reservations, sightseeing, and other arrangements.[16]

While celebrations of the Polish Millennium occurred across Polish Chicago and the suburbs, the main event took place on August 28, 1966, in Soldier Field on the city's lakefront. Although some spectators came as early as 11 a.m., stadium gates only opened at 4 p.m., two hours before the festivities began. More than seventy-five thousand attended the four-hour-long celebration, which climaxed with a Mass performed by Chicago's John Cardinal Cody, Cardinal Wyszyński's representative, Bishop Władysław Rubin, and twenty-three other clerics. Soldier Field was decked out in traditional Polish colors. A red carpet led from the south entrance to a huge altar in the center of the stadium. A vacant throne stood near the altar to symbolize the absence of Wyszyński. The commemoration began with a parade of twenty-five hundred people dressed in traditional national costumes. Chicagoans of Polish, Czech, Slovak, Lithuanian, Ukrainian, Serbian, and Latvian descent took part in the procession around the field's track. The crowd joined in singing Polish hymns. Cardinal Cody sang the liturgy in Polish. He had been studying the language for the past year in preparation for the celebratory Mass. Clergymen, nuns, and special guests, in seats situated near the altar, bowed their heads and knelt in prayer. A tableau dramatized the highlights of Polish history for the crowd as a twelve hundred–voice choir sang. Following the Mass, they processed to a large painting of Our Lady of Częstochowa at the north end of the stadium.

Bishop Rubin read a message from Wyszyński, who wrote that, despite the fact that Poland had suffered much, "the people are strong in spirit and God will fill their hearts with joy." Cody lauded Polonia for remaining steadfast in its faith. In turn, Governor Otto Kerner, himself of Czech descent, and Mayor Richard J. Daley gave brief greetings to the crowd. Meanwhile, in Poland, Cardinal Wyszyński kept up pressure on the Polish Communists by charging that the government treated Catholics as second-class citizens.

The replica of the original painting of Our Lady of Częstochowa, a gift of St. Joseph's Parish in Back of the Yards, was the work of two South Chicagoans, Richard Sendzik and Jerome Krauski. It consisted of twenty panels and stood at thirty-two feet by twenty feet. Afterward, it was to be moved to the grounds of the Our Lady of Victory motherhouse of the Franciscan Sisters of Blessed Kunegunda in Lemont, Illinois. Reverend Alfred Abramowicz, chairman of the Chicagoland Observance of Poland's Mil-

The children of Chicago's St. James Parochial School celebrate the Millennium of Polish Christianity, 1966. In Chicago, Polonia's network of parishes, parochial schools, and institutions celebrated a Christian idea of Poland and *Polskość* in 1966. (Courtesy of *Zgoda*.)

lennium of Christianity Committee, said the painting would be moved to the site and visitors could enter the grounds and pray to the virgin. Abramowicz said: "It is really a striking painting and many of us did not want to see it simply stored away."[17] In many ways, the move of the painting of Our Lady of Częstochowa to Lemont was symbolic. Before the war, such a work of art would have been placed in an urban location, but Chicago had changed and so had Polonia. The 1966 celebration of Poland's millennium was the last gasp of a generation that would soon see vast changes in Polonia and in Poland as well.

On to Suburbia

The *Chicago Sun-Times* claimed that four hundred thousand Polish Americans had left the city for the suburbs by 1968. The median income for Chicago's Polish Americans stood at $12,100. Suburban Polish Americans had a median income of $13,600. Both remained higher than the median income for either the city or suburbs. Many Polish Chicagoans toiled as operators and laborers (32 percent), mostly in good union-protected jobs. Another 28 percent worked as sales and clerical workers, while only 14 percent held professional or managerial positions. A greater percentage of Polish Americans worked as skilled craftsmen (16 percent) than did the general population (13 percent).

Chicago provided a home for roughly 8 percent of the nation's Polish foreign-stock population or 191,955 Chicago Poles, which included both those born abroad or the child of one or more immigrant parents. Despite a decrease of 66,702 since 1960, Poles accounted for 6 percent of the city's population. The census counted 108,793 foreign-stock Poles in the suburbs. The census, of course, treated the American born of American-born Polish simply as native-born whites. A 1975 survey indicated that some 250,000 Chicagoans and 190,000 suburbanites considered themselves Polish Americans. Other sources claimed a million Poles in the city and suburbs. Whatever the exact number, it was evident that as late as 1970 Polish Americans still made up a large part of Chicago's population. A spot map from a 1970 study by Chicago's Department of Development and Planning showed a heavy concentration of foreign-stock Poles still living in the original industrial neighborhoods and in those districts just beyond their borders, such as Brighton Park, Gage Park, Jefferson Park, and Avondale. While slightly more than 44 percent of Chicago's foreign-stock Poles arrived before 1924, nearly 66 percent had arrived after 1945. Chicago's Polish population in 1970 was an aging one, with a median age of 53.3 years as compared to 29.6 years for the city's population overall. Suburban Poles were only slightly younger, with a median age of 50.3 years, compared to 27 years for all suburbanites. The city continued to attract new arrivals. As late as 1985, the Northwestern University Settlement in Stanisławowo-Trójcowo reported a still sizable Polish population. Staff attributed this to a yet more recent wave of Polish immigrants in a neighborhood increasingly dominated by Hispanics.

Home ownership was also a factor in 1970. Both the Polish foreign stock and those born in the United States tended to heavily invest in real estate. In 1976, 62 percent of the city's Polish families owned their own homes, as compared to 35 percent of all Chicago households. Polish Chicagoans tended to stay in place. Only 27 percent of Polish families moved between 1965 and 1970, as compared to 55 percent of all Chicagoans. Some Polonia residents spoke of their attachment of to their institutions and neighborhoods. The various waves of migration that replenished the populations of these neighborhoods provided another explanation. Still, by the Vietnam War era and beyond, Polish Americans increasingly followed their neighbors and relatives to the suburbs. Third and fourth generation Polish Americans were among the most likely to move.[18]

Given the large number of industrial suburbs of Chicago, suburbanization did not necessarily mean upward mobility. Still, various trends indicated economic advances beyond the working class. A study of Chicago area medical, dental, and law schools in the mid-1970s by the Polish American Congress Charitable Foundation showed increased participation by students with identifiably Polish names. Loyola University Medical School and the Chicago College of Osteopathic Medicine had the highest Polish American participation. Loyola University, a Catholic institution, not surprisingly attracted Polish Americans, and osteopathic hospitals tended to serve the Midwest, particularly Michigan, with large Polish American populations. In addition, three Polish Americans served on the College of Osteopathic Medicine board of trustees. A survey made of area dental and law schools also showed increased Polish American participation, even though the report pointed out that Polish Americans remained underrepresented.[19]

An earlier Polish American Congress Charitable Foundation report found that much of the poverty in Polonia centered on the aging community left behind by upwardly mobile Polish ethnics. By the 1980s, the old Polish neighborhood known as Stanisławowo-Trójcowo held a very diverse population of older Polish residents, other white ethnics, Hispanics, blacks, and a growing number of young urban professionals. In short, there remained a large impoverished minority population of African Americans and Hispanics along with a concentration of impoverished Polish senior citizens in the area. In the report, these elderly Polish Americans spoke of a general feeling of abandonment and betrayal. They felt deserted not only by the government but also by ethnic leaders and the Catholic Church.

As early as 1949, Weber High School (originally St. Stanislaus College), founded in 1890, relocated several miles to the northwest. Lenard's Restaurant, a neighborhood Polish institution, soon followed up Milwaukee Avenue and eventually closed in the 1960s. By the end of the 1970s, two of the larger fraternal organizations, the Polish Women's Alliance and the Polish National Alliance, also left the neighborhood. The Illinois Division of the Polish American Congress also moved from the old Polonia core. In 1974, the May Third Polish Constitution Day Parade, an annual show of Polish American pride, abandoned its traditional march down Division Street to Humboldt Park, choosing, instead, a parade route through the city's downtown. Even the statue of Kosciuszko was removed from Humboldt Park to the drive leading to the planetarium in Grant Park on the city's lakefront. Polonia seemed to be abandoning its home.[20]

The 1973 PAC Charitable Foundation report revealed a profound feeling of alienation among Polish Americans. Language difficulties provided a major obstacle, primarily for Polish women who had been in the United States for a long time but who had never learned English because of their continued residence in neighborhoods served by Polish churches, businesses, and fraternals. Those who did not work outside the home had no need to learn English. Now, as senior citizens left behind in neighborhoods that were increasingly African American or Hispanic, or

The Polish Constitution Day Parade in the Loop remains a positive symbol of Chicago's Polonia. It is also a way to tie Polish American families and especially children to the idea of *Polskość*. Pictured here is the float for Polish National Alliance District 12 of Chicago in 1992. (Photograph by the author.)

that had an increasingly young urban professional residential structure, they found themselves alone. To these elderly residents the new ethnic ghetto walls of poverty and abandonment seemed greater than any that had existed before.

The deindustrialization of much of Chicago's manufacturing base hit Polonia hard. Large meat packers left the city between 1952 and 1961 and, the Chicago Union Stockyards closed its gates in 1971, depleting the economic vitality of several neighborhoods across the South Side. Industries left the river wards in droves between 1950 and 1980, many going to the suburbs and the American South and West, as well as overseas or simply out of business. The garment industry was long gone, and the steel industry soon followed. Even the massive Western Electric plant, which employed many Polish Chicagoans, closed its doors in the 1980s. The transformation of capitalist Chicago in the last years of the twentieth century and into the twenty-first meant that the old industrial order and the neighborhood system it had maintained simply vanished.[21]

The Ethnic Reaction

The 1970s witnessed a short-lived white ethnic revival. Many observers saw this "new" ethnicity as a reaction to, and imitation of, the black civil rights movement of the 1950s and 1960s. Michael Novak's 1972 book *The Rise of the Unmeltable Ethnics* proclaimed the resurrection of ethnicity, especially among ethnics from eastern and southern Europe, as a political force to be reckoned with by establishment powers. Novak said that these "PIGS" (Poles, Italians, Greeks, and Slavs) would emerge as a potent force in the political restructuring of the United States after the convulsions of the Vietnam War era. Novak, a conservative, predicted the rise of the Reagan Democrats in the 1980s.[22]

In Chicago, this movement presented itself in various ways. Congressman Roman C. Pucinski, of the city's Northwest Side, introduced a bill in 1970 in the House of Representatives to fund ethnic heritage studies centers. He declared: "I find the whole doctrine of the melting pot repugnant. I don't want to be melted down." Pucinski and other ethnic leaders rejected complete assimilation and called for their communities to rally around cultural traditions and for Congress to affirm American pluralism. Congress passed the Ethnic Heritage Studies Act in 1972 and designated $15,000,000 for the first year of the program. The late historian Arthur Mann pointed out that in the wake of the 1960s this led to the further fragmentation of American society. Ethnic leaders, many of them third-generation intellectuals, called for college and secondary school classes in ethnic languages, literature, and history. Chicago's Polonia benefited from this program, and in 1976, a $38,000 grant established the Archives of Chicago Polonia, housed at the Chicago History Museum.[23]

The 1970s saw an explosion of ethnic studies programs. Intellectuals such as Novak, Andrew Greeley, and Norman Podhoretz celebrated the "new" ethnics. Polish Chicago appeared more militant as the 1970s unfolded. Chicago's Polonia, in the midst of a vast demographic and economic transformation, attempted to find its way. For years, ethnic leaders felt that they had been put down by the dominant society. Now, in the 1970s, they sensed that elites looked past them to the African American community. While Chicago's Polonia still struggled with its immigrant ghetto past, and many of its members abandoned traditional neighborhoods, an inferiority complex powerfully presented itself. Aloysius Mazewski, elected president of the Polish National Alliance in 1967 and, later, president of the Polish American Congress, promised that PAC would conduct a relentless campaign against Polish jokes, which he and most members of the community felt demeaned the ethnic group. Chicago's Polonia leader remarked, "American Poles are now fighting back against their detractors and defamers. The Congress is demanding, with considerable success, that the communications media present a true image of the Polish community." Jan Krawiec, a postwar émigré journalist and social worker, called the jokes "thoughtless, savage, and uncouth." Polish American professionals joined the campaign and claimed reverse discrimination. The jokes and the lack of representation of Polish Americans in the media and corporate offices seemed part of the same plot. Mazewski complained to the ABC television network about comedian Bob Einstein's August 10, 1972, skit on a show hosted by Steve Allen. Allen apologized for himself, the network, and Einstein.[24] This was a largely middle-class response to a negative stereotype perpetrated by comedians and elites against Polonia. Polish Chicago in particular became a center for these protests as Polish Americans climbed corporate, media, and academic ladders.

Still other activists became involved in what they considered the neglect of their traditional neighborhoods. On the Northwest Side, this could be seen with Polish participation in the Northwest Community Organization and its Community 21/East Humboldt Park offshoot. On the Near West Side, St. Adalbert's Parish in Pilsen witnessed a demographic transformation: Matilda Jakubowski led a campaign in 1974 to save the parish, the mother church of the Southwest and West Side Polonia. By the 1970s,

Wojciechowo had seen the same changes that had affected the Stanisławowo-Trójcowo area. The homes around the church, once occupied by a largely Polish population, now housed Mexican and black families. Jakubowski admonished the Archdiocese of Chicago, saying, "The blacks and Spanish people who have moved in are still here. They have souls too."[25]

Chicago's Polish Americans who had hoped to climb the ladder of upward mobility also felt an unexpected drop in social status. Their traditional rivalry with African Americans, Mexicans, and Puerto Ricans had revolved around neighborhoods and jobs. The issue of Polish jokes and, at times, unfounded charges of racism against Poles brought deep psychic hurt to Polonia, as it still felt insecure in American society. This was especially true of the Polish American professional class, which attempted to leave Polonia's working-class past behind. Polish American solidarity seemed to be a reaction by the new ethnic upper-middle class against the insecurities of a rapidly changing Chicago.

In the 1970s, Mitchell P. Kobelinski began a movement to create a new Polish cultural center named after the famous Polish astronomer Nicholas Copernicus. On May 21, 1972, the Copernicus Foundation held a successful Founder's Day event and unveiled the project. The group hired a professional fund-raiser and announced the erection of a replica of the famous Warsaw Copernicus Monument in front of the Adler Planetarium. In addition, the Museum of Science and Industry scheduled a Copernican exhibit for July 1973. The organization's ultimate goal was the construction of a $5,000,000 community center. The foundation organized the first general membership meeting at the Polish Women's Alliance Hall on January 28, 1973. Showing its middle-class roots, only persons and organizations who had pledged at least $500 and donated at least $100 to the fund in fulfillment of their promise could vote at the meeting. In the early 1980s, the opening of the Copernicus Cultural Center in the old Gateway Theater near the intersection of Milwaukee and Lawrence Avenues created a new center for Chicago's Polonia. Ted Swigon, then president of the Polish Museum, questioned the claim that it would threaten his older traditional Polonia institution still situated in the Polish Downtown. Later, another social and cultural center opened to house the Illinois Division of the Polish American Congress not far from the Copernicus Center. Milwaukee Avenue near the Copernicus Center had sixty-four brightly colored signs erected depicting the coat of arms of Polish provinces to give the shopping district a more distinctly Polish identity.[26]

At the same time, change continued on both the main and side streets of Polonia. The 1970s and 1980s saw more and more outmigration. For the Polish American working class, it seemed that the rules had changed, as stable union manufacturing jobs were disappearing. Northwest Side industries moved, and the same was true for the good-paying jobs on the heavily industrial Southeast Side. In 1980, Wisconsin Steel closed its doors. Four years later, U.S. Steel announced the closing of most of its operations at the South Works, located near St. Michael's Catholic Parish. In 1992, the plant closed forever. Within a few years, only a small skeleton crew worked Chicago's steel industry, once one of the largest employers in the Midwest. In 2017, the archdiocese announced the closing of St. Michael's parochial school as student enrollment continued to decline.[27]

Chicago's Polonia had suffered the unexpected changes brought about by deindustrialization. Polish neighborhoods witnessed demographic shifts, and residents searched out "better" neighborhoods. One Polish American who grew up speaking Polish at home, attended Holy Trinity High School on Division Street, and had lived in the Stanisławowo-Trójcowo neighborhood remarked, "It was a good place to grow up." She now worked as a computer programmer and lived in a high-rise with a view of Lake Michigan, far from Milwaukee Avenue. While most of Polonia did not live in lakefront high-rises, the American-born generation expected upward mobility, if not for them, then for their children. A job with the police or fire department meant good wages and a secure job. It also meant an ongoing tie with the Democratic machine. Others found themselves in the professions. Many Polish Americans moved into Chicago's outlying Bungalow Belt and beyond, leaving old neighborhoods behind.[28]

A Polish Pope

In August 1976, Karol Cardinal Wojtyła of Kraków and fifteen Polish bishops on a six-week tour of the United States arrived in Chicago for a four-day visit. Wojtyła had visited Chicago previously, in 1969. Mayor Richard J. Daley accompanied the Polish churchman on a tour of St. Mary of Nazareth Hospital on Division Street, an institution founded by Polish nuns. Hospital workers lined the balconies, and children in traditional Polish costumes greeted him. Chicago's Polonia opened its heart and its homes to the cardinal, who represented the struggle of the church against Communist authorities in Poland. Little did anyone imagine that Wojtyła would soon become Pope John Paul II and, later, a Catholic saint.[29]

On October 16, 1978, the College of Cardinals elected fifty-eight-year-old Karol Cardinal Wojtyła as the first non-Italian pope since 1523. The announcement came after two full days of balloting by 111 cardinals and shocked the world. The crowd of two hundred thousand gathered in St. Peter's Square greeted the announcement with a loud moan mixed with some applause and cheering. Most expected another Italian; the election of John Paul II, a Pole, was a complete surprise. The new pope spoke to the crowd in accented Italian. He said, "The most eminent cardinals have called a new bishop of Rome. They have called him from a far-away country." At that point, the crowd broke out in applause and shouts of "Viva Il Papa." Then, showing both his humility and political wisdom, John Paul II asked the crowd to help him with his Italian. Observers knew he sided with workers in his native Poland in their demands for better working conditions and wages. Wojtyła was a staunch supporter of Cardinal Wyszyński in his struggle with the Warsaw regime. During the Second Vatican

Karol Cardinal Wojtyła of Kraków visits with Polish American Congress president Aloysius Mazewski in 1976, two years before the College of Cardinals elected Wojtyła pope. (Courtesy of *Zgoda*.)

Council, the new pope sided with conservatives on doctrinal questions but with progressives on several issues involving reforms in the church and modernization. Born in the town of Wadowice of working-class parents, he worked in his youth in a chemical factory. Ordained a priest in 1946, Wojtyła taught at the Catholic University of Lublin and at the Jagiellonian University in Kraków. Known both for his intellectual rigor and his love of ordinary people, he also was known to write poetry in a café once favored by such famed artists as Frederic Chopin, Stanisław Wyspiański, and Kazimierz Tetmajer, the Café Zakopianka, located on the Planty, parkland surrounding the center of Kraków.

Chicago's Polish Americans were jubilant about his election. Abramowicz, now the auxiliary bishop of Chicago, described the new pope as pastoral and recalled his visits to Chicago. He pointed out that the new pope wanted to see the economically disadvantaged parts of the city, understand the city's problems, know what Chicagoans rights were, and what they did to protect them. Other Chicago Catholics also had warm memories of Wojtyła. Sister Stella Louise Slomka, an administrator at St. Mary of Nazareth Hospital, recalled the new pope as a "tremendously warm person, outgoing, and deeply spiritual." Joseph Drobot, president of the PRCUA, called his election "a proud moment for us." The PNA's Mazewski said: "I was struck by his humility. He is a very modest man, also very intellectual. We all feel a high regard for him because of his firm convictions."[30]

Chicago's Polonia naturally felt a surge of pride. The city's English-language newspapers sought out comments from local business, fraternal, and church leaders. Ironically, the move of Chicago's Polonia to the suburbs could clearly be seen in these interviews. Reverend Donald Bilinski of the Polish Museum of America shared the hope that "the selection of a Polish pope could unify the Polish people remaining in the old neighborhood here, and could bring some who have moved away back for cultural activities." Bilinski shared the wistful thought that, if the pope had been elected a few years earlier, it might have stemmed the tide of demographic change that took place. Al Mazewski remarked that the PNA and PAC had moved two years previously and had followed his own move from the area. Businesses such as the White Eagle Restaurant, owned by Ted Przybyło, also left the area, moving to Niles, Illinois, where he joined an already sizable Polish community. When visitors to the museum asked where Chicago's legendary Polish community is, Bilinski would tell them "it is gone." Still, many of the older residents continued to stay on in the neighborhoods they had known all their lives.[31]

On Thursday evening, October 4, 1979, Pope John Paul II arrived at O'Hare Airport for his third visit to Chicago and first as head of the Roman Catholic Church. He flew in on a TWA 727 airliner that had been dubbed "Shepard One." He was the first Pope to visit what was then the largest Catholic archdiocese in North America. John Paul II had scheduled more time in the historic capital of the Polish diaspora than in any other of the six cities on his tour. He visited Quigley Preparatory Seminary South, Providence of God Parish in Pilsen, and Five Holy Martyrs Church in Brighton Park, where he offered Mass in Polish. On Friday afternoon, the pope concelebrated Mass with more than 350 Catholic bishops in Grant Park. He left Chicago early Saturday morning, October 6.[32]

The election of John Paul II as supreme pontiff of the Roman Catholic Church marked both a change in the perception of Chicago's Polonia and the decline of that community in the city. Despite the attention surrounding the election and the papal visit, Polish Americans continued to leave the city for the suburbs. While Bilinski was only half right in his 1978 declaration that Polonia was no more, its numbers had, without doubt, dwindled. Polish institutions left the central city that had been their home for nearly a century. Businesses on the North Side, in South Chicago and Back of the Yards, once displayed notices that stated "Mowiemy po Polsku" (we speak Polish), and Old Style beer signs announced that bars served "Zimno Piwo" (cold beer). Those placards were being joined by those that read "Hablamos Español" and "Cerveza Fria." Soon, the Polish words simply disappeared, as Mexican and Puerto Rican businesses replaced Polish ones on Milwaukee and Commercial Avenues and along Forty-Seventh Street. This change eventually took place in outlying Polish neighborhoods as well, such as Brighton Park, Garfield Ridge, and Jefferson Park. The old Polonia seemed to slowly but surely disappear into the suburban haze.

A New Polonia

Now there is a need for brain power in Poland, and this brain power
can come not only from Poland, but from outside Poland.
—LECH WAŁĘSA, Chicago, November 18, 1978[1]

For Immigrants, America is Best
—SEWERYN WOJCIECH, Polish demonstrator, Immigrant Rights March,
Chicago, May 1, 2006[2]

The election of Karol Wojtyła to the throne of St. Peter had rever-
berations well beyond the Vatican. John Paul II's papacy emerged
as part of a new dynamic that brought change not only to Poland
and Eastern Europe but to the entire world as well. Chicago's
Polonia watched this transformation and gave what aid it could,
as it helped bring about the end of the Soviet empire. Lech Wałęsa,
a heretofore unknown electrician in Gdańsk (prewar Danzig),
emerged as an international figure who led the struggle of Polish workers and started a rebellion against Communism that had
been long in the making. John Paul II would be his happy ally in

that revolutionary moment. Again, Poland would be at the fore-front of conflict and change in the twentieth century.

The End of Communism and Chicago's Polonia

John Paul II's election and his visit to Poland in 1979 marked a new era in the country's history. During his return tour of the country, hundreds of thousands of Polish Catholics and dissidents attended his Papal Masses, which gave hope to a country reeling from economic mismanagement and Communist Party corruption. The vast Lenin Shipyards in Gdańsk, long a symbol of the Polish socialist economy, became in the 1980s a sign of Poland's struggle to regain its independence and freedom. When the shipyard strikes began on August 14, 1980, a decade-long struggle ensued that eventually saw the Independent Self-Governing Labor Union "Solidarity" (Niezależny Samorządny Związek Zawodowy "Solidarność"), commonly referred to as Solidarity or in Polish "Solidarność," bring down the regime and reinstate democracy to the nation. Lech Wałęsa, who had been dismissed from the shipyard in 1976, climbed over the facility's fence and emerged as the leader of the struggle. Earlier, a group of intellectuals led by Antoni Macierewicz and Piotr Naimski formed the Komitet Obrony Robotników, or Workers' Defense Committee, the first anti-Communist civic group in the Soviet Bloc. The Komitet Obrony Robotników joined Solidarity in its struggle and published an underground newspaper, *Robotnik* (The worker), which recalled Józef Piłsudski's underground paper of the same name. *Robotnik* and other underground publications told the story of Solidarity's struggle to the nation.

On August 18, the Szczecin Shipyard joined the strike. Soon, work stoppages spread along the coast, closing ports and crippling the Polish economy. By the time three days had passed, most of Poland had joined the movement. On September 3, the unions and the government signed an agreement guaranteeing workers' rights, especially the right to strike. Known as the September or Gdańsk Agreement, it was the first in a series of events that eventually led to the dissolution of the Soviet Union. Wałęsa emerged as a worldwide symbol of the struggle against totalitarian regimes. The following years saw martial law and more struggle, but Solidarność proved to be on the right side of history. In February 1989, the Round Table Talks took place, which radically changed the Polish governing structure. On April 17, Solidarity was legalized and became a potent political force that then defeated the Communist government in free elections. Solidarity's overwhelming victory saw Tadeusz Mazowiecki elected as the first non-Communist Polish prime minister since World War Two. More political struggle followed, but Poland finally reached its great desire, to break out of the Soviet orbit and join the West.[3]

The Polish American Congress and the fraternals threw their support behind Wałęsa and Solidarność, helping in any way they could. As early as 1981, leaders of Chicago's Polonia invited Wałęsa to visit. He intended to come to Chicago on November 20, after a visit to Washington, DC. Organizers planned a huge rally in the International Amphitheater. The American Federation of Labor and Congress of Industrial Organizations prepared to sponsor the trip as an act of solidarity between labor unions. Alderman Pucinski claimed the rally would be the largest ever held in the United States. Wałęsa had canceled previous trips due to conditions in Poland, and this tour, unfortunately, was no exception.

In December, Communist authorities arrested the union leader and held him until November 1982. The Nobel Committee, the following October, awarded Wałęsa its peace prize. The hero's cousin, Robert Wałęsa of suburban Park Ridge, Illinois, sent a telegram of congratulations and offered to travel to Sweden to accept the prize for him if the Polish government would not let him travel. Lech Wałęsa, afraid that he might not be allowed to return to the country, instead had his wife Danuta accept the prize in his place. On New Year's Eve, Pucinski made a call to Wałęsa's home at about 11:00 p.m., Gdańsk time, to see if restrictions on him had been somewhat eased. To his surprise, the Solidarity leader

Containers being loaded with medical and hospital supplies, as well as food and clothing for Poland during the Solidarity crisis. Al Mazewski, president of both the Polish National Alliance and Polish American Congress, is pictured *second from right.* (Courtesy of *Zgoda.*)

answered the phone. He wished Chicago's Polonia a Happy New Year and promised to visit when he could be guaranteed that he could return to Poland. Wałęsa also said he appreciated the food and medicine sent to the Polish people from Chicago.[4]

Wałęsa finally visited Chicago in 1989, seeking investment for Poland. He flew into Midway Airport on Friday, November 17. That Saturday, he had several private meetings with Polonia leaders and Chicago politicians. At noon, the Chicago Council on Foreign Relations, the Chicago Federation of Labor, the City of Chicago, and other civic groups honored Wałęsa at a luncheon at the Chicago Hilton and Towers. Proceeds from the $100-a-plate lunch went directly to Solidarity. At about 2 p.m., Wałęsa arrived for a rally at Daley Plaza where more than fifteen thousand Chicagoans greeted him. Wałęsa proclaimed that "no government force can stop the march of history." During his visit, the Polish leader emphasized that Poland, ready for democratic change, required America's economic help. He told Chicago's Polish American leaders that "our homeland is again in need and it is you that should be ambassadors of the Polish cause." Wałęsa invoked the traditional immigrant exile mission. He begged forgiveness for asking for money, "But it comes from the fact that we do not have much time." Some in the crowd wore buttons that said "Make the Check to Lech." At the Daley Plaza rally, he stated that his country needed American entrepreneurs.[5]

Chicago's Polonia had reservations about investing in Poland. Perhaps some remembered, or had been told stories, of those who returned to the newly independent homeland after the First World War and lost their money. Many may have been hesitant to open their life savings to a republic that could easily be erased by Soviet tanks. Polish Chicagoans told reporters that, while Wałęsa energized them, they were wary to invest in a bankrupt Poland. Peter Lybulski, a Polish immigrant who owned a construction company, stated, "I have been thinking about investing in Poland for the last two years. There will have to be a lot more dramatic changes before I do." Edward Moskal, now president of the PNA, said that there had to be more evidence of fundamental economic changes. The PNA promised to launch a nationwide campaign to explain to American businesses that investing in Poland could be profitable. Pucinski claimed that Wałęsa's visit marked a turning point for Poland's economy in that Congress had approved $846.5 million in aid and Illinois and Michigan had pledged to purchase $35,000,000 of Poland's "Freedom Bonds."[6]

Wałęsa returned two years later, this time as president of Poland, again looking for investors. He hoped to meet with politicians and business executives who could help promote obtaining much-needed funds for the struggling Polish economy. In Washington, DC, Wałęsa spoke with President George H. W. Bush, congressional leaders, business executives, and Polish survivors of the Holocaust. He flew to Los Angeles and had lunch with former president Ronald Reagan. Finally, he returned to Chicago for a three-day visit to meet with government, business, and Polish Americans leaders. Wałęsa pointed to the failing Soviet economy and said there was no plan, no concept of how to solve their problems. He also called for the withdrawal of fifty thousand Soviet troops from Poland.

The Polish leader and his wife attended Palm Sunday Mass at St. Hyacinth Church, where supporters greeted him with welcoming banners. Loudspeakers broadcast the ninety-minute liturgy to the overflow crowd. Later, Mayor Richard M. Daley and Governor Jim Edgar joined Wałęsa at the State of Illinois Building. The second visit proved to be more businesslike than the first one, which was met with Polonia's joy over Solidarity's success. By 1991, Poland was experiencing difficult times as it transformed itself from a socialist to a capitalist economy. This second visit of Wałęsa's incorporated an even greater plea to transform Poland's economy with American investment. Falling living standards and growing inflation had made Wałęsa less popular in Poland. Previous to his Chicago visit, Polish American leaders announced the establishment of a U.S.-Poland Chamber of Commerce to promote bilateral trade, investment, and practical assistance to businesses interested in investing in Poland. This was in stark contrast to the charitable investments made during and after World War Two.[7]

The Solidarity and Post-Solidarity Immigration

The upheavals in Poland led to increased emigration as Poles fled, first from the crackdown on Solidarity in the early 1980s and, then, from the post-Communist economic readjustment. Chicago again became a destination for many of these people, who in many ways mirrored the old economic migration of the nineteenth and early twentieth centuries. As Mary Patrice Erdmans has pointed out in her groundbreaking study of this immigration, modern-day Communist Poland shaped the new Polish immigrants' thinking and their immigrant status shaped their social identity. This new immigration rejected old definitions of what it meant to be a Pole in America and introduced new symbols and traditions. While they shared social space in Chicago with older generations of Polish Americans, and held common beliefs rooted in the struggle for Polish independence, the different generations again disagreed over the idea of *Polskość*. The question of who exactly a Pole was emerged time and time again. Solidarity immigrants claimed the right to be the political voice of Poland in exile. They spoke a more modern version of the Polish language and had very different political and social experiences from those who had preceded them, and they questioned the legitimacy of those who had maintained the exile mission over the years. Within Polonia a feeling of "us" and "them" appeared. While this had happened after World War Two, between the older immigration and those displaced by war, the divide after 1980 seemed much greater. The three main groups consisted of native-born Polish Americans, World War Two émigrés, and the Solidarity-era immigrants. Polonia remained, as always, divided internally.[8]

The Polish American Congress supported Poland's struggle for independence and the DP generation heartily reinforced this effort, but Polish Americans were primarily concerned with their position in American society. When Mazewski succeeded Rozmarek for the presidency of the Polish National Alliance and thus the PAC, Polish American concerns became more important than concerns about Poland. Never, however, were Poland and Polish affairs wholly abandoned. The new group of Solidarity immigrants further complicated matters. They naturally focused more on the homeland, especially after the declaration of martial law and the arrest of Wałęsa before the eventual victory of Solidarność. Congress passed the Refugee Act of 1980, and when the Polish government lifted martial law, an influx of Polish immigrants who had been activists and spent time in prison or hiding arrived in the United States. In the 1980s, over thirty-three thousand Poles reached America as political refugees. Almost a thousand of these settled in Chicago. A secondary migration to the city of those who had originally settled elsewhere in the country followed. In addition, a large number of *wakacjusze* (vacationers) also came, one-third of whom overstayed their visas. Somewhere between fifty and a hundred thousand *wakacjusze* made Chicago their home. Many blended into Chicago's large Polonia, found labor as construction workers, painters, and domestic help, and simply lived their lives. One such "vacationer" in 2016 remarked that he had been in America on "vacation" for more than twenty-five years, worked hard, bought a home, raised children, and had a good life. The Chicago connection remained a magnet for Solidarity-era immigrants as it had for the generations before. These sojourners at first rejuvenated Chicago's Polonia. This was especially true in St. Hyacinth's Parish in Avondale, known as Jackowo among its Polish residents. By 1987, recent immigrants made up more than half of the parishioners. According to Erdmans, most of the Poles living in the neighborhood were so-called vacationers. The upheavals in Polish society led to a vast diaspora.[9]

The Polish American Congress spent a great deal of effort in supporting the Solidarity movement. The congress organized drives to supply Poles with food, medicine, clothing, and money. Before the election of John Paul II and the rise of the free labor movement in Poland, the Polish American Congress Charitable Foundation had focused on Polish American concerns, but the profile of the foundation changed in 1981 once the Solidarity movement took off. That year, the Charitable Commission of the Polish Episcopate received, with aid from the foundation, some $2,800,000 ($7,597,980 in 2017) in food assistance. In addition, the foundation provided funds to Project Hope to provide medical aid in Poland. Martial law complicated matters in 1981, but the next year, aid flowed again to Poland. By 1988, the worth of medical supplies delivered to Poland totaled close to $80,000,000 ($165,535,757 in 2017). Once more, Chicago led American Polonia in fulfilling the exile mission. These efforts on behalf of Solidarity and organizations set up by Polish exiles attracted the attention of the Polish Intelligence Services, which attempted to follow their efforts outside of the country.[10]

Despite Polonia's exertions on behalf of the struggle in Poland, clashes continued between the Solidarity-era immigrants and old Polonia. The hatred of Communists had long been nurtured in Polonia, and this fear aroused suspicions of the new arrivals. Having been raised in Communist Poland, educated in Communist schools, and employed by Communist bosses, how could their attitudes toward democratic and capitalist America not have been affected? Some Polish Americans refused to help Solidarity immigrants because they might be Communists. Some feared that Communist-reared individuals would have a difficult time adjusting to American life.[11]

The Loss of Polish Chicago's Clout

Change happens on various levels in the demographic, cultural, and political life of a city. Polish Chicago had long been a player in Chicago politics, exhibiting considerable influence in both the Democratic and Republican Parties. As the twentieth century counted down, Polonia's political power declined: it had, in short, lost its clout. Nowhere can this be seen more startlingly than on the city's Northwest Side. Once the home of powerful Polish American politicians like Dan Rostenkowski, that clout quickly faded as demographic shifts brought a very different Chicago into being.

Polish ward bosses understood that the Chicago Democratic machine remained based on ethnicity, social class, and political spoils. The Polish Catholic parish system provided an institutional base that supported political as well as economic power. Polish politicians with legendary names such as Rostenkowski, Pucinski, and Kluczynski led a citywide Polish political bloc that won influence in the Irish-led Democratic Party. Former Democratic renegade Benjamin Adamowski and GOP stalwarts Edmund J. Kucharski and Edward Derwinski even held sway in the local Republican Party. Dan Rostenkowski's father, tavern owner and alderman Joseph "Rosty" Rostenkowski, came out of the rough-and-tumble ward politics of Stanisławowo-Trójcowo. He understood his constituents and their desires and appreciated how they chafed under the image of the dumb working-class "Polack." Years later in 1989, his son, the powerful Congressman Dan Rostenkowski, would come to tears recalling his feelings of Polish inferiority when listening to an address by Lech Wałęsa.[12]

A scandal in 1996 resulted in Dan Rostenkowski receiving a seventeen-month jail sentence and brought immediate change to the Fifth Congressional District of Illinois. The powerful chairman of the House Ways and Means Committee pleaded guilty to mail fraud, ending his career. The election to replace Rostenkowski in Congress ended with Rod Blagojevich, son-in-law of Alderman Richard Mell, defeating Nancy Kaszak, a popular local candidate who had served in the state legislature and had a long record in Springfield. Blagojevich's eventual decision to run for governor set the stage for another crucial political race in 2002. Nancy Kaszak again ran for the congressional seat.[13]

Kazszak was the favorite to win the Democratic primary, but Rahm Emanuel, who had served in the Clinton White House, returned to Chicago to challenge her. *Chicago Sun-Times'* political columnist Steve Neal claimed that Kaszak was the most progressive candidate in the race for the Fifth Congressional District. He derided Emanuel as a representative of big business and wrote that Emanuel had assisted a corporate merger that resulted in the layoff of 3,350 workers. Neal claimed that Emanuel would spend up to $3,000,000 to "purchase" the nomination, but that Kaszak had the support of the Northwest Side's workers. For his part, Emanuel said that Kaszak was soft on crime, an approach taken by Blagojevich in 1996 when he asserted that Kaszak had flip-flopped on the death penalty. Emanuel had no such legislative record on which to be criticized, even though he had worked with Mayor Daley's younger brother, Bill Daley, to pass the North American Free Trade Agreement during the first Clinton administration, a treaty that remained anathema to the labor movement.

In the Kings Hall of the Copernicus Center, Nancy Kaszak, a Polish American, announced her intention to run. Framed by portraits of the kings of Poland, Kaszak cited her gender and ethnic background as well as her community activism as reasons for Northwest Side Democrats to support her. She promised to protect Social Security, vote for some form of prescription drug coverage for seniors, and increase the number of teachers and their salaries.[14]

Just before Christmas 2001, Polish American political leaders held a rally of three thousand supporters of Kaszak at the White Eagle Banquet Hall in Niles. They called for the reinvigoration of Polish political power in Chicago and across northeastern Illinois. Feeling increasingly politically impotent, the city's Polish Americans charged that they had been gerrymandered out of power. Alderman Michael Wojcik saw his Thirtieth Ward boundaries shift. As a result, Wojcik decided to run for a state senate seat in 2002. Mayor Richard M. Daley supported Iris Martinez in the primary instead of Wojcik, even though six years earlier, Daley had supported Wojcik in his successful run against Ted Lechowicz for the powerful position of Thirty-Fifth Ward Democratic Committeeman. Lechowicz was running for Cook County Commissioner in 2002, and both he and Wojcik faced off against Daley allies Forrest Claypool and Martinez. Daley took advantage of the demographic changes as Polonia continued to move to the suburbs. As Polish voting power waned in the city, new groups, especially Hispanics and young professionals, had to be reckoned with and demanded their own clout.[15]

According to a telephone survey in February 2002, 33 percent of eight hundred likely Democratic voters favored Kaszak compared to Rahm Emanuel's 18 percent, while former U.S. transportation secretary Peter Dagher would receive only 2 percent of the projected vote. Kaszak led Emanuel among key Democratic demographics such as blue-collar men, pro-choice voters, and senior citizens. Still, 45 percent of voters remained undecided. Issues that favored Kaszak and her legislative record interested Fifth District voters the most. More than a fourth of the district's voters listed jobs as the most important issue facing the country. As a member of the Illinois House, Kaszak had passed legislation that favored small businesses. Her pro-labor voting record also brought her to the attention to Northwest Side voters. In contrast, Emanuel had lobbied for the North American Free Trade Agreement, which some claimed had cost Illinois ten thousand jobs. Health care and Social Security issues also tended to favor female candidates and played in Kaszak's favor. She led Emanuel four to one among women voters under the age of forty-five and by a two-to-one margin among working women in February 2002. Kaszak seemed to be gaining momentum in the Polish community, which also pointed to a win over Emanuel.[16]

At the end of February, however, the Kaszak campaign found itself in an embarrassing position. Fliers appeared in largely Polish American Jefferson Park linking Rahm Emanuel to Osama bin Laden. At the top of the handout, capital letters screamed out the question, "Is Congressional Candidate Linked to Terrorist?" Beneath the headline appeared Emanuel's name, also in capital letters, with an arrow pointing to a photograph of a young man in a turban sitting next to the organizer of the September 11 attack. Becky Carroll, Emanuel's press secretary, and Greg Goldner, his campaign manager, both mentioned a "whispering campaign" against their candidate. Goldner did not blame any of the other candidates but said, "That's the kind of politics (some) people are trying to fuel the race towards."[17] The ridiculousness of the claims obviously embarrassed Kaszak as the front-runner and brought up the specter of Polish anti-Semitism.

A defining moment in the election occurred in early March. After Mazewski's death in 1988, Edward Moskal was elected as president of both the Polish National Alliance and of the Polish American Congress. He became involved in the Kaszak-Emanuel race. On Monday, March 4, Moskal addressed a crowded Pulaski Day celebration attended by a string of candidates in the March 19, 2002, primary election, during which he called Emanuel "the carpetbagger" and claimed Emanuel knew "nothing about our values, our causes, our expectations, or our heritage." He claimed that Emanuel was a citizen of "another country" (Israel) and had served in its armed forces for two years. He further ranted that certain elements to which Emanuel gave his allegiance defiled the Polish homeland and continued to hurl insults at the Polish people. He told the crowd, "Sadly, there are those among us who will accept thirty pieces of silver to betray Polonia." Kaszak quickly distanced herself from Moskal's obviously anti-Semitic comments as the PNA leader told the press, "My remarks as far as Mr. Emanuel don't warrant any kind of apology. Not one bit." Polish anti-Semitism quickly presented itself as a campaign issue in the race for the Fifth Congressional District. Moskal's remarks drew national attention as the National Jewish Democratic Council condemned them on March 7. To make matters worse, T. Ron Jasinski-Herbert, a spokesperson for the Polish National Alliance, told the *Chicago Tribune* that Moskal's comments were not hateful but, rather, were "born of frustration with Jews." He said that "Mr. Moskal could have said 'la-di-da' and Emanuel would have said it was anti-Semitic."[18]

Charges of anti-Semitism had haunted Moskal for some time. In 1996, he had complained about Jews trying to denigrate Poles worldwide. Four years later, he had invited controversial Polish Catholic priest Rev. Henryk Jankowski to address the annual Polish Constitution Day gathering in Chicago. Jankowski had openly offended Jews in the past by comparing the Star of David to the Nazi swastika and to the Communist hammer and sickle. Professor Stanley Blejwas, a distinguished expert on Polish and Polish American history, led a national protest and published a letter signed by a wide variety of Polish American leaders and opinion makers in academia, politics, journalism, and other fields condemning Moskal's invitation of Jankowski.[19]

During the 2002 primary, when Kaszak was trying to distance herself from Moskal, she condemned Moskal's statement and handed back the endorsement of the Polish American Congress. She promised to accept no further support from Moskal and said the she objected to the PAC leader's statements "just as fully as Mr. Emanuel does." Despite these actions, the damage had already been done. Polls showed her and Emanuel now in a virtual tie for the Democratic nomination. Kaszak found herself in a difficult position. Christine Mather, Kaszak's campaign manager, said that while Kaszak was morally correct in cutting ties with Moskal, "We probably alienated ourselves from an important part of Nancy's support," though at least some Polish American voters responded negatively to Moskal. George Majewski, a seventy-seven-year-old retired postal worker remarked, "Can you believe what that fellow said about that Clinton guy, Rahm? My feeling is this guy Rahm was born in America and he's American like the rest of us." Sophie Bielikowicz, a Polish immigrant who had arrived in the United States in the 1950s, said, "I think what he said was rude, just terrible." Most importantly, on Saturday, March 9, Mayor Richard M. Daley, who rarely involved himself publicly in Democratic primaries, openly threw his support behind Emanuel.[20]

Daley's support for Emanuel was both payback for perceived earlier slights and response to changing demographics. Some pointed to a long-running North Side–South Side Democratic feud that traced itself to Daley's failed mayoral election in 1983, which split the white vote and resulted in North Sider Jane Byrne losing to Harold Washington, the city's first African American mayor. Indeed, once Richard M. Daley became mayor in 1989, he attempted to oust certain North Side politicians. In the years after Daley's election, South Siders replaced North Siders in the crucial political posts of Cook County board president, Cook County sheriff, and clerk of the circuit court.[21]

Daley threw his support behind Emanuel for several reasons besides the obvious political connection and personal friendship between the two men. Though his father, Richard J. Daley, would not have moved against the strong Polish Northwest Side bloc to support a non-Pole in the Democratic primary—Polish Americans having made up too strong a voting bloc at the time and having been an important part of the Democratic machine until Dan Rostenkowski's fall—the demographics of the city were changing. By 2000, Polish Chicagoans, like other white voters before them, were leaving for the suburbs in droves and largely being replaced in important wards by Hispanics. Although Chicagoans claiming Polish ancestry in 2000 still made up 7.5 percent of the population, their numbers dropped rapidly. Of the 933,000 persons of Polish ancestry in Illinois, some 65 percent lived in Chicago's suburbs, only 23 percent resided in the city, and 12 percent downstate. That is, about 70,000 of 139,000 Polish immigrants in the Chicago area called the city home. Of these, approximately only 40 percent were citizens. The foreign-stock and ancestry data for Chicago showed a dramatic shift over the seventy-year period after 1930. That year, roughly 80 percent of Polish immigrants in the area lived in the city, but by 2000, only about a quarter of persons of Polish ancestry lived in Chicago. Hispanics, in particular the Mexican population, saw tremendous population growth, and their numbers surged to more than 753,000 at the time of the 2002 election. Furthermore, they played an increasingly important part in the Democratic machine, gaining a good deal of clout.[22]

While President Bill Clinton and Mayor Daley supported Rahm Emanuel, an impressive array of supporters were still gathered behind Nancy Kaszak, including Ed Kelly, the longtime Democratic leader of the North Side's Forty-Seventh Ward, former mayor Jane Byrne, feminist Gloria Steinem, National Organization of Women president Kim Gandy, and Chicago philanthropist Susan Pritzker. Emily's List, a donor network that assisted pro-choice Democratic women, also backed the Polish American candidate. Kaszak also garnered the sponsorship of the Polish American Police Association.[23] Despite this support, Rahm Emanuel handily beat Nancy Kaszak on Tuesday March 19, 2002, in the Democratic primary and went on to victory in the November election. Daley's and Clinton's support of Emanuel, a massive fundraising campaign for him, and Moskal's anti-Semitic comments during the election helped Emanuel turn the tide. David Axelrod, Emanuel's longtime friend and a campaign consultant, said that Moskal's remarks cost Kaszak heavily along the lakefront, a traditional bastion of liberal Democrats. His comments also helped sway undecided voters to Emanuel, who got 50 percent of the vote to Kaszak's 39 percent, crushing her by a larger margin than Blagojevich had in 1996. In addition, Emanuel put together a large coalition that Kaszak could not match. Candidates spent well over $2,000,000 on the race. Emanuel expended $1,600,000 on the campaign, while Kaszak raised and spent some $850,000.

The election proved very satisfying for the mayor as well. He had defeated his foes in the Democratic primary and maintained a solid grasp on the levers of power in the city. All the candidates he openly supported had won, including Rahm Emanuel, Lisa Madigan, Luis Gutierrez, Forrest Claypool, and Iris Martinez. In the wake of the campaign, Polish American Democratic stalwarts Wojcik and Lechowicz stood among the losers.[24]

The question remains, why was the large Polish American community on the North Side unable to help Nancy Kaszak win the Democratic nomination? As a matter of fact, why did three Northwest Side Polish candidates go down in defeat in 2002? Soon the Polish contingent also lost control over the city clerk's office, long considered a Polish office. Southwest Side resident James Laski won the office in 1996. Ten years later, during the Hired Truck scandal, Laski was convicted of taking bribes. The office then went to a Hispanic Democrat with Daley's support. What had once been regarded as a Polish American office had now become a Hispanic one.[25]

In 1958, Polish Chicagoans elected four members to the U.S. House of Representatives. They made up a part of a contingent of twelve Polish American congressmen nationwide. In addition, Edmund Muskie (originally Marciszewski) went to the Senate from Maine that year as the first Polish American Senator. By the time the twentieth century ended, however, political and demographic realities had changed. The old urban ethnic neighborhoods broke up, and like other white ethnics, Polish Americans moved to the suburbs, diluting their once powerful political base. Many Polish Americans intermarried and no longer identified primarily with their ethnic group. Others had become Reagan

Democrats and would not support progressive candidates such as Nancy Kaszak. Furthermore, there had always been a divide between the North Side and South Side Polish communities. South Side Poles tended to follow the lead of Daley's regular democratic organization, which seemed intent on cleaning house of North Side politicians they did not trust after Jane Byrne's term in office.[26]

Emanuel eventually returned to the White House staff before coming back again to Chicago to succeed his longtime political ally, Richard M. Daley, as the city's first Jewish mayor. In 2011, several Polish American activists, including Daniel Pogorzelski, Mark Dobrzycki, and Robert Groszek attempted to influence the drawing of Chicago's ward boundaries to create a largely Polish Northwest Side ward. While the attempt to create a Polish super ward failed, the group did get some of its demands met, and Polish Americans comprised about 30 percent of voters in the new Thirtieth Ward. Once a political powerhouse that never reached its full potential, by 2002 Chicago's Polonia, due to internal divisions, a lack of coalition building, increased assimilation, and ongoing suburbanization, had become less and less important to Chicago's political structure. Polish Chicago had finally lost its clout.[27]

Polonia Resurrexeit

By the twenty-first century, Polonia had gone through yet another transformation. Originally, most of those who had joined the city's industrial workforce came primarily from peasant backgrounds, but Polonia had slowly moved into the lower-middle class and, over the generations, into the solid middle and upper-middle classes. This is not to say that everyone had undergone this change or that slippage had not also occurred. Certainly, many Polish Americans remained in the working class. But attitudes had shifted in tandem with the experiences of both World War Two and postwar prosperity.

While signs of demographic transformation and gentrification could be seen in the 1960s and 1970s across Polonia, by the twenty-first century, these changes were unstoppable. In 2002, owners listed a refurbished single-family building that was once a red-brick two-flat on the 800 block of North Hermitage Avenue for $529,000! This building stood near the heart of the old Polonia in an area that real estate developers now christened Village East. The one-time two-flat boasted three bedrooms, two bathrooms, a fire-place, a backyard deck, a large garden, and a two-car garage. The following year, the *Chicago Tribune* ran a story about the changing nature of Milwaukee Avenue, but a part of Milwaukee Avenue far from Stanisławowo-Trójcowo. Instead of the businesses near the intersection of Division Street and Milwaukee and Ashland Avenues, it featured those to the northwest, in St. Hyacinth's Parish in the Avondale neighborhood. The newspaper interviewed Barbara Kuta, the owner of the Calisia Gift Shop on the 3000 block of North Milwaukee Avenue, who stated that "before, it was Polish. Strictly Polish." The change had begun some five years earlier, and while the city gave the area the sobriquet "Polish Village," it was less and less Polish as the years went by. One Polish business owner remarked, "It's changed. It's Polish, Mexican, lots of people from Russia, from Ukraine, from Romania, from Bulgaria—it's a mix. But that's life." At nearby St. Hyacinth's Church, priests cele-brated three Sunday masses in English and four in Polish, but the parochial school's student body included many Latin American names. In 2003, Francis Cardinal George proclaimed St. Hyacinth Church the third basilica in the city, giving it certain papal privi-leges. On weekends, many Poles who had left the neighborhood returned to shop, and the commercial strip was becoming more of a shopping destination than a neighborhood center.

Migration to the United States and the West in general is part of a long-standing Polish habit. Economic and political factors may increase this migratory movement, but cultural and social factors explain its continuation. Some people dream of coming to Chicago, a legendary second home for Polish immigrants. As Erd-mans has concluded, the Immigration Act of 1990 further stim-

Spot map showing major Polish American population concentrations in the suburbs, 2012–16 (Courtesy of Chicago CartoGraphics.)

ulated the movement. Slots set aside for "diversity immigrants," defined as those adversely effected by the 1965 Immigration Act, included Poles. Between 1992 and 1996, more than fifty thousand Poles entered the United States under this program. The 1990 act also expanded categories and ceilings for nonimmigrants arriving for cultural exchange, business, employment, and tourism. These policies brought into the United States a larger group of immigrants willing to work. Many of the new Polish immigrants labored in unskilled positions in hospitals, construction, and domestic help. For many this meant downward mobility, but they chose to come because of political and economic uncertainties in Poland. In general, the Polish immigrant population was more likely to work in semi- and low-skilled positions despite their educational and life experiences. Various reasons existed for this, including the lack of permanent status (a green card), family obligations that required them to take any job offered, and language barriers. By the 1990s, some fifty-two thousand Poles were being admitted into the United States annually. In addition, Erdmans's study showed that, by the mid-1980s, some ninety-five thousand Poles were living and working in the country illegally. About eighteen thousand Poles and their dependents received amnesty through the 1986 Immigration Reform and Control Act. Ten years later, the estimate of illegal Polish immigrants stood at about seventy thousand nationally. Chicago attracted the largest share of these. One third of all Polish immigrants lived in Illinois, largely in the Chicago area. During the early 1990s, roughly eleven thousand new Polish immigrants resettled in the city.[28]

Meanwhile, the exodus to outlying neighborhoods and the suburbs continued. Even as more and more Polish immigrants arrived in the Chicago area, the city continued to see Polonia moving out and, for many, up the economic ladder. By 2003, the number of Polish immigrants in the area had jumped to 138,000 approaching the historic high of 165,000 in 1930. About seventy thousand of these newcomers lived in the city proper. Despite suburbanization, Poles still made up the largest European ethnic group in Chicago, second only to Mexicans in numbers. Nearly half of Polish immigrants had been in the United States less than ten years. When newcomers arrived, they tended to first locate in Chicago—probably because of Polish institutions and family connections—but they soon moved out. The Polish American Association (formerly the Polish Welfare Association) continued its work in helping immigrants with various problems. Its staff of ninety-five full-time and eighty-five part-time employees helped immigrants with alcohol addiction, landlord-tenant disputes, and a host of other problems.[29]

In 2003, the Portage Park neighborhood on the far Northwest Side contained the largest number of residents of Polish origin. On the Southwest Side, Archer Heights became more and more intensely a Polish neighborhood. In central parts of the city, longtime Polish restaurants such as the Patria and the Busy Bee in Wicker Park disappeared. New Polish businesses sprouted up in suburbs such as Niles and even Naperville. In 2005, the Wood Dale Historical Society and the City of Wood Dale presented Polish Heritage Day at Yesterday's Farm Museum in DuPage County, where the Lajkonik Polish Folk Ensemble performed and an exhibit from the Polish Museum of America was featured. The Polish Genealogical Society of America, Polish Scouts, and Polish School Singers also participated. In suburban Lombard, hundreds of Polish immigrants and their children, members of the Divine Mercy Polish Mission, arrived every Sunday to celebrate Mass in their native language in the auditorium of Montini Catholic High School. An overflow of worshippers knelt in the cafeteria and in the school's hallways, where the priest's intonation of the Mass could be heard over loudspeakers. Parishioners hoped to build a Polish church in unincorporated DuPage County. Churchgoers came from Addison, Villa Park, and across the suburbs.

The next year, the *Chicago Tribune* told its readers to enjoy the old-school Polish charm of Jefferson Park while they still could. Meanwhile, the original Polish neighborhood centered on the intersection of Milwaukee Avenue with Division Street and Ashland Avenue had changed forever. A three-sided park named the Polish Triangle at the intersection was just big enough to hold some benches, a bus shelter, some trees, a fountain, and a stairway down to the Blue Line subway station. In 1998, the city dedicated the small fountain in the Polish Triangle to the first National Book Award winner, the writer Nelson Algren. This caused some consternation, as Algren, not of Polish descent, was seen by some Polish Chicagoans as someone who had long denigrated their community. The neighborhood was no longer primarily Polish, but it still held several Polish American institutions and many memories for Polonia. Now largely Hispanic, it soon saw rapid gentrification. The Division Street of which Algren had written in such works as *Never Come Morning* had changed and would see even more change over the next ten years, as wine bars, hip coffee shops, and expensive restaurants opened were once working-class Polish and Puerto Rican bars had predominated. Algren's and Polonia's commercial strip rapidly disappeared.[30]

Nonetheless, Chicago's Polonia continued to celebrate Polish culture, whether in the city or suburbs. In 1989, Christopher Kamyszew and a few colleagues came up with the idea of showcasing Polish cinema in the city as a way of promoting Polish culture. The festival started with twelve titles and drew about three thousand people. Today, it remains as a citywide film festival. Moreover, in 2001, the Great Polish Books Group met in suburban Park Ridge. The group, sponsored by the Polish Women's Alliance, expanded and, by 2004, also held meetings in the village of Westmont in DuPage County. That same year, the Legion of Young Polish Women held their sixty-fifth annual Red and White Ball, which originally procured funds for Polish War Relief and now raised funds for charity. In 2005, the Chicago Park District announced it would accept one hundred nine-foot-tall cast iron sculptures by the Polish artist Magdalena Abakanowicz in honor of Chicago's sister city relationship with Warsaw. Christened *Agora*, the large sculptures blended human and natural form and was erected in the south end of Grant Park.[31]

Chicago's Polonia was saddened when Pope John Paul II died on April 2, 2005. On the day of his funeral in Rome, thousands of Polish Chicagoans marched solemnly up Milwaukee Avenue. Led by a police car and altar boys carrying a crucifix, the procession made its way from Holy Trinity Polish Mission (formerly parish) to St. Hyacinth Basilica. For many, the day began as early as 3:00 a.m., the same time as the funeral in the Vatican. Predawn services began at St. Constance Church on the Northwest Side, where some fifteen hundred parishioners gathered to pray for the deceased bishop of Rome. A Polish-language telecast of the funeral lasted two and a half hours. A similar gathering occurred at Five Holy Martyrs Church on the Southwest Side, where the pope had celebrated Mass in 1979. At noon, bells tolled across the Archdiocese of Chicago. That evening, a Mass was held at Holy Name Cathedral for representatives of all of the archdiocesan parishes.[32]

In August of 2006, another sign of change occurred, Li'l Wally Jagiello, the Polka King, a Polonia icon and the creator of the polka world's Chicago sound died in his Florida home. Walter Jagiello, known as Mały Władziu to his Polish American fans, was born and raised in Chicago. He began playing and singing polka music at the age of eight and started his career on Division Street in those same bars that Algren wrote about, places like the Gold Star, the Midnight Inn, Phyllis's, Zosia's, Al's Village Inn, the Orange Lantern, and the Lucky Stop. Roughly sixty taverns lined Division Street in Polonia, and most offered live music. A consummate performer, Li'l Wally performed nearly nonstop his entire career. His 1956 hit "I Wish I Was Single Again" was on the top 40 charts, a rarity for a polka recording. Jagiello was one of the first inductees into the Polka Hall of Fame. While Polish American elites and non-Poles may have dismissed Jagiello and his music, he, Eddie Zima, Marion Lush, Eddie Blazończyk, and many others made Polish Chicago sing and dance. In 1959, Jagiello cowrote the Chicago White Sox anthem "Let's Go, Go-Go White Sox" to honor the team's American League championship drive. He married a young

Li'l Wally Jagiello, the Polka King, pictured in the 1970s. (Chicago Public Library, Special Collections, Heise Chicago Photographs-Bio., box 62, folder 47, image 002.)

South Side woman known to Polish American radio audiences as "Polka Jeanette." Jeanette Kozak was raised in Sacred Heart Parish in Back of the Yards of immigrant parents.

In the 1950s, Li'l Wally emerged as the greatest representative of Chicago-style polka, which featured a slower beat, clarinet, trumpet, and a driving concertina. The style was improvisational and had an urgency of expression that communicated with its audience. It derived from Polish village music that had become popular in Chicago in the 1920s and always stayed true to its roots. Jagiello's records sold astonishingly well given the fact that at first local radio shows shunned the recordings. Li'l Wally eventually took his band on the road throughout what some called the Polka Belt of the Midwest and East Coast. He created his own record label, Jay-Jay Records, and continued his success. The Chicago style kept evolving, absorbing new influences and reaching the heights of polka popularity in the early 1960s. If anyone can be credited with writing, playing, and promoting the music that made Chicago's Polonia dance, it was Mały Władziu and his wife and business partner, Polka Jeanette.

Chicago's Polonia lost another icon that year, Zbigniew "Bob" Lewandowski, who died at the age of eighty-six. Trained as an actor and singer in Poland, he began his career as a broadcaster for Radio Free Europe, eventually making his way to Chicago in 1953, where he was a local radio and television personality for some forty years. He hosted *The Bob Lewandowski Show* on WCIU-TV for nearly thirty years. Lewandowski remained active in the theater, and in 1974, he directed a run of the play *The Odd Couple* in Poland. Long known as a philanthropist, he helped raise money for Polish orphans, for medicine for Poland, and for the construction of the Copernicus monument. After leaving the airways in 1996, he continued to write a newspaper column for the *Dziennik Związkowy*. With the passing of the Li'l Wally and Bob Lewandowski, an era had come to an end.[33]

As the twentieth century progressed, immigration again became a major social issue in the United States, and many immigrant communities came under attack. On May 1, 2006, Polish and other immigrant groups marched in Chicago's Loop for immigrant rights. They made up the largest non-Hispanic group and walked alongside Mexicans, Guatemalans, Irish, Arabs, Koreans, and others. Official estimates claimed four hundred thousand marched, but organizers put the number closer to seven hundred thousand. An earlier demonstration in March had also brought a hundred thousand to the Loop. The May Day march was one of the largest peaceful demonstrations in the city's history. Police made no arrests. Some Polish demonstrators wrapped themselves in Polish flags and wore "We Are Not Terrorists" t-shirts. A man carrying a Mexican flag yelled "Viva Polonia." Poles shouted back,

"Viva Mexico." After several speeches, Chicago's Francis Cardinal George led the crowd in prayers in Polish, Spanish, and English. The rally closed at 5 p.m.[34]

The different immigrations that took place during the 1980s reshaped Polonia. So did the fact that the descendants of nineteenth- and early twentieth-century economic immigration had simply become American. Polish American weddings still celebrated certain traditions, but by the 1990s, rock and roll largely replaced polkas as wedding music, although some of the traditional melodies might still be played for older guests. The idea that ethnicity consisted of famous people, food, and music also faded. New immigrants preferred jazz and popular songs to polkas and mazurkas. Polish restaurants, while still serving traditional items such as kielbasa (Polish sausage), *kapusta* (sauerkraut) *gołumbki* (cabbage rolls), pierogi (filled dumplings), and *czarnina* (duck's blood soup), often served more American dishes, as well as what might seem as strange adaptations of Polish favorites such as jalapeño-stuffed pierogi. The closing of Bobak's Deli on the Southwest Side proved to be another blow to Polonia. Founded in 1967, it opened the Archer Avenue location in 1989 as Back of the Yards became mostly Hispanic and African American. Then, in 2015, it closed the shop near Midway Airport. Polonia had indeed changed.[35]

Americans have long accepted income inequality due to perceived high levels of social mobility, which underpinned the American dream. Hope for the future centered traditionally on the *pursuit* of economic opportunity. In turn, this quest attracted generations of immigrants, including Poles. Yet by the twenty-first century, the opportunity to live the American dream seemed less widely shared than just a few decades earlier. While 90 percent of the children born in 1940 ended up in higher ranks of the income distribution than their parents had been in, only 40 percent of those born in 1980 have done so. During the financial crisis that began in 2008, white working-class and lower-middle-class Americans especially developed a negative attitude toward

Polish Constitution Day Parade in Chicago's Loop, May 2, 2015. The banner reads,
in English, "Two homelands, one heart," expressing the dual nature of Polonia.
(Photograph by the author.)

the future prospects for themselves and their children. Observers have pointed out that the economic collapse heightened these feelings of loss. The impact of deindustrialization, globalization, and an aging population had a profound impact on American society. This change in attitude could not but effect Chicago's Polonia, and when tied to the growing Polish economy, it had an impact on immigration as well.[36]

In 2004, Poland joined the European Union, a move that gave Poles the right to work legally anywhere in Europe: they no longer had to cross the ocean to find economic opportunity. "Vacationers" did not have to disappear into the Polonia underground in order to find employment. Working in other European countries allowed an easier return to visit family in Poland for the holidays or on vacations. Daily buses, not to mention trains and airplanes, tied Poland to the rest of the European Union. Four years later, Poland was the only European Union economy not to suffer from the recession. While the U.S. economy sank, Poland's continued to grow and soon became the fastest growing in Europe. By 2017, the Polish economy, once near the bottom of European economies, was the eighth largest in the European Union. Since 1991, its economy has grown at an average annual rate of 4 percent and has not suffered a single year of negative growth. During that period, Poland's average income rose from $2,300 to nearly $13,000.[37]

Suddenly, the economic forces that had brought Polish immigrants to Chicago reversed themselves, and Polish Chicagoans began to return to Europe. The U.S. Census Bureau reported that, from 2000 to 2010, the number of foreign-born Poles in Chicago dropped by twenty-three thousand. In 2013, the English as a second language classes offered by the Polish American Association stood nearly empty. Over a five-year period, from 2008 to 2013, some thousand students left the Saturday Polish Language Schools. The 2008 Great Recession brought hardship to Polonia, and many returned to a new democratic and capitalist Poland. At least sixty thousand Poles left for Poland in the first year of the recession. Poland's youth were now more likely to emigrate to England, Ireland, Norway, and Italy. By 2011, the number of Polish immigrants obtaining permanent status in the United States dropped to the lowest level in at least twenty years. The great Polish migration to Chicago had ended.[38]

By 2017, traditional Polish neighborhoods had changed, with signs in Spanish now dotting stores. Then along came Starbucks, wine bars, fancy restaurants, and other signs of gentrification. Both New York City and London attracted more Polish immigrants than Chicago in 2017. Immigrants who left Poland now saw themselves as modern, educated, and, if they stayed in the United States, they expected to be part of a growing elite. The quaint Polish stores and restaurants that served working-class Polish Chicagoans on Milwaukee and Archer Avenues closed.

In turn, Poland, now a member of both the European Union and the North Atlantic Treaty Organization, operated in a way that peasants who were part of the nineteenth- and early twentieth-century migration could not even have dreamed of. The displaced persons of the postwar period might have had such dreams, but they disappeared under Communism. Solidarity immigrants also saw such a future, but it still seemed unreachable. The "exile mission," so eloquently portrayed by historian Anna Jaroszyńska-Kirchmann in her book of that name, had largely been fulfilled. The future may bring more tests, but Poland is now a full-fledged member of the West.[39]

Chicago's Polonia lives on, not simply in memory but as a vibrant Polish American community in both the city and suburbs. It has become more middle class, more American in its attitudes. Festivals are still marked. The Polish Constitution Day Parade is still held and is supposedly the largest Polish parade in the world. Newspapers in the Podhale region of Poland still run ads for Chicago businesses, and immigrants still arrive here from Poland.[40] The Polish Film Festival celebrates Poland's rich cinematic tradition across the Chicago area even in the heavily Irish and African American neighborhood of Beverly. The Polish Chicago connection remains and will remain for a long time. The neighborhoods are now more mixed or have changed ethnicity completely, but the city still holds onto its immigrant tradition. Chicago's Polonia has been yet again resurrected anew.

ACKNOWLEDGMENTS

Polish Chicago has a long and fascinating history. I have been lucky enough to have been born and to have lived my entire life in this vibrant community. Early on in my career, I came under the influence of a man who molded much of the Polish Chicago experience from 1967 until his death twenty-one years later at the age of seventy-two. Aloysius A. Mazewski was a giant among those in Chicago's Polonia. As president of the Polish National Alliance and the Polish American Congress, Mazewski wielded a tremendous amount of influence. In 1971, he was the founder of and driving force behind the Polish American Congress Charitable Foundation. Two years later, Mazewski brought me onboard through the foundation as a researcher to look into Polish American poverty. The position was paid for by a grant from the Nixon White House. While our politics did not match up—he was a staunch Republican and I a left-leaning Democrat—he never failed to support my goal of obtaining a PhD in history. Over the years, Mazewski referred to me as his "house" radical and found various research jobs to help keep me financially afloat during my graduate school years. This study owes much to him and his good nature. I will always remember him fondly and with a great deal of gratitude.

Other leaders of Polonia have also helped and influenced me during those years, especially Jerzy Przyłuski and Kazimierz Lukomski. Three good friends from graduate school at the University of Illinois at Chicago, Philip Kozlowski, Adam Rogulski, and Arnold Hirsch, all now unfortunately deceased, spent hours with me discussing Polish America, Polish history, and Chicago history. They are missed. So is Professor Edward C. Thaden, who helped to form me as a historian and shared his wealth of knowledge about Russia and the Soviet Union and Eastern Europe. He touched us all with his wit and dry sense of humor. Thaden introduced me to the man who became my mentor and long-time adviser and confidant, Leo Schelbert. Schelbert has proven to be a friend and supporter ever since. Perry Duis familiarized me with the history of Chicago and has always encouraged my work. Professors Richard Fried, John Kulczycki, the late Robert Remini, Daniel Scott Smith, Richard Millman, Bentley Gilbert, and Stanley Mellon all gave me encouragement and expanded my knowledge of history. Keely Stauter-Halsted, who holds the Hejna Chair of Polish History at the University of Illinois at Chicago, has proven her friendship and provided encouragement for this project.

Over the years, the late Raymond Gadke, the manager of the Reading Room at the Regenstein Library of the University of Chicago, offered help and provided incredible insights into the history of Chicago's neighborhoods. I owe much to him and the staff of the Regenstein Library. Janet C. Olson, Jason Krause, and Kevin Leonard of the Special Collections Department at Northwestern University helped me access the papers of the Northwestern University Settlement. Małgorzata Kot and Julita Siegel of the Polish Museum of America provided access to the wonderful photograph collection of the museum. Daniel Necas and the staff of the

Immigration History Research Center at the University of Minnesota helped my research in many ways. The staff of the Chicago History Museum aided my search for Polonia's history. Gregorz Dziedzic of the *Dziennik Związkowy* and Magda Marczewska of WPNA-FM Radio have encouraged me and provided insights into contemporary Polish Chicago. Jacek Niemczyk, the general manager of WPNA-FM Radio, gave me the opportunity to try out some of the ideas in this book in a weekly podcast on the WPNA-FM website from March of 2018 to March 2019. Ewa Malcher, also of the *Dziennik Związkowy*, provided help with illustrations, as did Alicja Kuklińska of *Zgoda*.

Columbia College deans Steve Corey and Jan Chindlund, Provost Stan Wearden, former acting chair of the Humanities, History, and Social Science Department Erin McCarthy, and Edzen Lebita of the college library provided support and, above all, encouragement for this project. Columbia College also awarded a Faculty Development Grant to this project. My good friends and fellow Polish American Historical Association members, James Pula, M. B. B. Biskupski, Anna Jaroszyńska-Kirchman, Mary Erdmans, Dorota Praszałowicz, and Adam Walaszek gave advice, encouragement, and what only friendship can provide. At the University of Chicago Press, Tim Mennel edited the manuscript and provided suggestions for its improvement, as did Bill Savage of Northwestern University. So, too, did two anonymous peer reviewers whose insights helped tremendously. Rachel Kelly Unger assisted the project in innumerable ways. Yvonne Zipter did her usual fine job of copyediting the book. Mark Reschke played an essential role in the preparation of the final manuscript. Dennis McClendon of Chicago CartoGraphics created the maps in his usual expert manner. Many in Polonia offered advice, and I wish to thank them all.

My spouse, Kathleen Alaimo, herself a busy academic, gave me great emotional support throughout the entire project. I could not have written this book without her. Our two daughters, Johanna and Beatrice, have lived with stories of Polonia their entire lives.

This book is dedicated to Beatrice in recognition of her sense of *Polskość*.

Of course, I have both heeded advice and ignored it, and in the end, I am solely responsible for the mistakes and shortcomings of this book.

NOTES

Introduction

1. Quoted in Keely Stauter-Halsted, *The Nation in the Village: The Genesis of Peasant National Identity in Austrian Poland, 1848-1914* (Ithaca, NY, 2001), 107.

2. Stefan Kieniewicz, *The Emancipation of the Polish Peasantry* (Chicago, 1969).

3. *Zgoda*, January 2, 1896.

4. Stauter-Halsted, *Nation in the Village*, 8, 97, 137–40; Dominic A. Pacyga, "Czechs and Poles in Chicago: Pan-Slavism and the Origins of the Cermak Democratic Machine, 1860–1931," *Studya Migracyjne — Przegląd Polonynich* (Krakow) 4 (2015): 55–68.

5. For the exploration of a definition of ethnicity, see Kathleen Neils Conzen, David A. Gerber, Ewa Morawska, George E. Pozzetta, and Rudolph J. Vecoli, "The Invention of Ethnicity: A Perspective from the U.S.A.," *Journal of American Ethnic History* 12, no. 1 (Fall 1992): 3–41; Lawrence H. Fuchs, David A. Gerber, Ewa Morawska, and George E. Pozzetta, "The Invention of Ethnicity: The Amen Corner," *Journal of American Ethnic History* 12, no. 1 (Fall 1992): 53–63; Herbert J. Gans, "Comment: Ethnic Invention and Acculturation, a Bumpy-Line Approach," *Journal of American Ethnic History* 12, no. 1 (Fall 1992): 42–52. For a Polish American view of ethnicity, see Helena Znaniecka Lopata, *Polish Americans* (New Brunswick, NJ, 1994), 170–75.

6. William I. Thomas and Florian Znaniecki, *The Polish Peasant in Europe and America*, 5 vols. (Chicago, 1919–20); Edward R. Kantowicz, *Polish-American Politics in Chicago, 1888–1940* (Chicago, 1975); Victor Greene, *For God and Country: The Rise of Polish and Lithuanian Ethnic Consciousness in America, 1860–1910* (Madison, WI, 1975); Joseph John Parot, *Polish Catholics in Chicago, 1850–1920: A Religious History* (DeKalb, IL, 1981); Dominic A. Pacyga, *Polish Immigrants and Industrial Chicago: Workers on the South Side, 1880–1922* (Chicago, 2003); Mary Patrice Erdmans, *Opposite Poles: Immigrants and Ethnics in Polish Chicago, 1976–1990* (University Park, PA, 1998).

Chapter One

1. *Chicago Tribune* (hereafter *CT*), October 8, 1893.

2. For a detailed and interesting examination of Polish, Irish, and Italian celebrations and their impact on ethnic identity, see Megan Elizabeth Geigner, "Staging Chicago's Immigrants: Immigrant Discourse, Civic Performance, and Hyphenated Identity, 1890–1920" (PhD diss., Northwestern University, 2016).

3. *CT*, October 8, 1893; *Dziennik Chicagoski* (hereafter *DzC*), October 10, 1893; *Chicago Daily News*, October 7, 1893; *CT*, October 8, 1893; Stanisław Osadę, *Historia Związku Nardówego Polskiego*, vol. 1, *1880–1905* (Chicago, 1957), 373–81.

4. *DzC*, April 4, 1893, April 15, 1893, August 26, August 28, August 31, 1893; *CT*, October 6, 1893.

5. Arthur Loesser, *Men, Women, and Pianos: A Social History* (New York, 1990), 559–60; World's Columbian Exposition, *Music Hall Series Programme*, no. 2 (Chicago, May 2, 1893); *CT*, April 30, 1893, May 3, 1893.

6. *DzC*, August 5, 1893; Jane J. Palczynska, "Chicago Poles Share in City Art History," in *Poles of Chicago, 1837–1937: A History of One Century of Polish Contribution to the City of Chicago*, ed. Leon Thaddeus Zglenicki (Chicago, 1937), 46–47.

7. *DzC*, January 5, 1893; Patrice Dabrowski, *Commemorations and the Shaping of Modern Poland* (Bloomington, 2004), 19–20; Dr. Emil Habdank Dunikowski, *Wśrod Polonii w Ameryce* (Lwów, 1893).

8. Dabrowski, *Commemorations*, 13–16, 127–28; for the quote from Dunikowski, see *DzC*, January 5, 1893.

9. Charles Morley, ed. and trans., *Portrait of America: Letters of Henryk Sienkiewicz* (New York, 1959), 278, 288–90.

10. Mieczyslaw Haiman, *Zjednoczenie Polskie Rzymsko-Katolickie w Ameryce, 1873–1948* (Chicago, 1948), 124–26; Dunikowski, *Wśrod Polonii w Ameryce*, 61.

11. *DzC*, September 26, 1892, September 30, 1892.

12. *DzC*, January 12, 1893.

13. *DzC*, February 27, 1893.

14. *DzC*, August 23, 1893.

15. *DzC*, August 19, 1893.

16. *DzC*, September 6, 7, and 10, 1893.

17. *DzC*, February 27, 1893, January 2, 1894.

18. *DzC*, October 20, 21, and 25, 1893.

19. *DzC*, November 3, 1893, December 1, 1893, November 30, 1894, December 17, 1894.

20. *DzC*, March 19 and 21, 1894

21. Jacek Purchla, "W Stulecie Powszechniej Wystawy Krajowey," *Cracovia/Leopolis Kwartalnik*, no. 2 (1995), 6–7; Jurij Brijulow, "Chodząc po Wystawie," *Cracovia/Leopolis Kwartalnik*, no. 2 (1995), 8–12; Markian Prokopovych, *Hapsburg Lemberg: Architecture, Public Space, and Politics in the Galician Capital, 1772–1914* (West Lafayette, IN, 2009) 247–452; Larry Wolff, *The Idea of Galicia: History and Fantasy in Hapsburg Political Culture* (Stanford, CA, 2010), 282–94; Edyta Barucka, "Redefining Polishness: The Revival of Crafts in Galicia around 1900," *Acta Slavica Iaponica*, no. 28 (2010), 72–77.

22. *DzC*, July 10, 1894; Osadę, *Historia Związku Naródowego Polskiego*, 1:382–86.

23. *DzC*, March 29, 1892, April 7 and 28, 1892, May 13, 1892, December 17 and 21, 1892, April 17, 1893.

24. *DzC*, February 6, 1892, October 10, 1892, December 14, 1892, January 10, 1893; *CT*, November 26, 1893.

25. Dabrowski, *Commemorations*, 134–35.

26. *DzC*, February 27, 1895; *Zgoda*, June 17, 1897, March 16, 1899; *Naród Polski*, March 15, 1899, April 19, 1899; Palczynska, "Chicago Poles Share in City Art History," 47–48.

27. *Zgoda*, November 22, 1900, December 6, 1900.

28. *Naród Polski*, September 14, 1904; *DzC*, June 22, 1904, September 12, 1904; *CT*, September 11 and 12, 1904.

29. Susan G. Davis, *Parades and Power: Street Theatre in Nineteenth-Century Philadelphia* (Philadelphia, 1986); Mary Ryan, "The American Parade: Representations of the Nineteenth-Century Social Order," in *The Making of Urban America*, ed. Raymond A. Mohl, 2nd ed. (Lanham, MD, 1997), 73–89.

30. *CT*, September 13, 1883, November 30, 1886, April 29, 1894, December 2, 1894; Anna D. Jaroszyńska-Kirchmann, "'Memories of Greatness': American Polonia and the Rituals of National Commemorations before World War I," *Polish American Studies* (hereafter *PAS*) 74, no. 1 (April 2017): 28.

31. For a discussion of the rivalry between these two parishes, see Joseph Parot, *Polish Catholics in Chicago, 1850–1920: A Religious History* (DeKalb, IL, 1981).

32. The literature on this process of nationalizing the peasantry in France is among the most extensive. See Eugen Weber, *Peasants into Frenchmen: The Modernization of Rural France, 1870–1914* (Stanford, CA, 1976); Roberta Pollack Seid, *The Dissolution of Traditional Rural Culture in Nineteenth Century France: A Study of the Bethmale Costume* (New York, 1987); Stephen L. Harp, *Learning to Be Loyal: Primary Schooling as Nation Building in Alsace and Lorraine, 1850–1940* (DeKalb, IL, 1998); François Furet and Jacques Ozouf, *Reading and Writing: Literacy in France from Calvin to Jules Ferry* (Cambridge, 1982) For Poland, see especially Dabrowski, *Commemorations*.

33. For the importance of literacy, print, and a national language on the growth of nationalism, see Benedict Anderson, *Imagined Communities: Reflections on the Origin and Spread of Nationalism* (London, 1995), 44–46, 71–80.

34. Patrice Dabrowski, "Folk, Faith, and Fatherland: Defining the Polish Nation in 1883," *Nationalities Papers* 28, no. 3 (2010): 397–416. For this process in the Podhale region, see Adrianna Dominika Sznapik, *Tartrzańska Arkadia: Zakopane Jako Ośrodek Artysyczno-Intelektualny od około 1880 do 1914 Roku* (Warsaw 2009); Timothy J. Cooley, *Making Music in the Polish Tatras: Tourists, Ethnographers, and Mountain Musicians* (Bloomington, 2005), is an interesting study of Polish highlander music and its appreciation.

35. Keely Stauter-Halsted, *The Nation in the Village: The Genesis of Peasant National Identity in Austrian Poland, 1848–1914* (Ithaca, NY, 2001), see esp. the introduction.

Chapter Two

1. Quoted in John Radziłowski, *The Eagle and the Cross: A History of the Polish Roman Catholic Union of America* (Boulder, CO, 2003), 41.

2. Joseph John Parot, *Polish Catholics in Chicago, 1850–1920: A Religious History* (DeKalb, IL, 1981), 19–24; Edward R. Kantowicz, *Polish Politics in Chicago, 1888–1940* (Chicago, 1975), 14; Wacław Kruszka, *A History of the Poles in America to 1908*, pt. 2, *The Poles in Illinois*, ed. James S. Pula, trans. Krystyna Jankowski (Washington, DC, 1994), 16–17; Victor Greene, *For God and Country: The Rise of Polish and Lithuanian Ethnic Consciousness in America, 1860–1910* (Madison, WI, 1975), 59–60; James S. Pula, "Schermann, Antoni," in *Polish American Encyclopedia*, ed. James S. Pula (Jefferson, NC, 2011), 474.

3. *Naród Polski*, May 2, 1917; Kruszka, *A History of the Poles in America*, 16–35, Parot, *Polish Catholics in Chicago*, 27–46.

4. For an explanation of the changing nature of who was a Pole, see Piotr S. Wandycz, *The United States and Poland* (Cambridge, 1980), 59.

5. Anticlerical groups often attempted to set up rival centers to parishes for communal activities. See W. I. Thomas and Florian Znaniecki, *The Polish Peasant in Europe and America*, vol. 3, *Organization and Disorganization in America* (Boston, 1920), 46.

6. Helen Busyn, "Peter Kiolbassa—Maker of Polish America," *PAS* 8, nos. 3–4 (July–December 1951): 75–76; Parot, *Polish Catholics in Chicago*, 50–57. For a comprehensive look at Rev. Barzyński, see Michael J. Dziallo, "Reverend Vincent (Wincenty) Barzyński, C.R.: A Nineteenth Century Transformative Leader for Chicago Polonia" (PhD diss., Lewis University, 2013); Thomas and Znaniecki *The Polish Peasant*, 3:46–47.

7. Parot, *Polish Catholics in Chicago*, 59–61; M. Ardea, "The Societies of St. Stanislaus Kostka Parish, Chicago," *PAS* 9, nos. 1–2 (January–June 1952): 27–37; Radziłowski, *The Eagle and the Cross*, 43–51, 89–90; Donald E. Pienkos, *PNA: A Centennial History of the Polish National Alliance of the United States of North America* (Boulder, CO, 1984), 51–63; Constance Krasowska, "The Polish National Alliance and the Liberation of Poland," *PAS* 12, nos. 1–2 (January–June 1955), 11–18.

8. Parot, *Polish Catholics in Chicago*, 100–101; *Zgoda*, June 7, 1893, Pienkos, *PNA*, 75.

9. Parot, *Polish Catholics in Chicago*, 105–6, Donald E. Pienkos, "Brother against Brother: Conflict in the Polish National Alliance, 1900–1940," *Polish Review* 3 (2012): 51–53.

10. Kantowicz, *Polish Politics in Chicago*, 53–56; James S. Pula, "Piotr Kiołbassa," in *Polish American Encyclopedia*, ed. Pula, 227.

11. Dorota Praszałowicz, "Polish American Sisterhoods: The Americanization Process," *U.S. Catholic Historian* 27, no. 3 (Summer 2009): 45–48; Anthony Kuzniewski, "Boot Straps and Book Learning: Reflections on the Education of Polish Americans," *PAS* 32, no. 2 (Autumn 1975): 6–10; Thaddeus C. Radzialowski, "Reflections on the History of the Felicians in America," *PAS* 32, no. 1 (Spring 1975): 19–24; Anne Marie Knawa, "Jane Addams and Josephine Dudzik: Social Service Pioneers," *PAS* 35, nos. 1–2 (Spring–Autumn 1978): 13–14. For a general history of the Felician sisters, see Sister Ellen Marie Ryba, CSSS, ed., *Response: The Felician Sisters Centennial in America, 1874–1974* (Ponca City, OK, 1974). For the Franciscan Sisters of Blessed Kunegunda (now Franciscan Sisters of Chicago), see Sister Anne Marie Knawa, OSF, *As God Shall Ordain: A History of the Franciscan Sisters of Chicago, 1894–1987* (Lemont, IL, 1989). Also see Rev. Henry M. Malak, *Therese of Chicago* (Lemont, IL, 1975).

12. Maria Anna Knothe, "Recent Arrivals: Polish Immigrant Women's Response to the City," in *Peasant Maids—City Women: From the European Countryside to Urban America*, ed. Christine Harzig (Ithaca, NY, 1997), 299–338; Pien Versteegh, "A League of Their Own: Strategic Networks of Polish

Women as a Female Response to Male Dominated Networks," in *Irish and Polish Migration in Comparative Perspective*, ed. John Belcham and Klaus Tenfelde (Essen, Germany, 2003), 212;

13. *Zgoda*, June 7, 1893; Pienkos, *PNA*, 49, and "Brother against Brother, 53.

14. Rev. Msgr. Harry C. Koenig, STD, *A History of the Parishes of the Archdiocese of Chicago*, 2 vols. (Chicago, 1980), 1:17.

15. For the 1876 strike, see *Chicago Inter Ocean*, May 9, 1876; A. T. Andreas, *History of Chicago; From the Earliest Period to the Present Time*, vol. 3, *From the Fire of 1871 until 1885* (Chicago, 1886), 108–9; For the interethnic makeup of the strikers and their supporters, see Philip S. Foner, *The Great Uprising of 1877* (New York, 1877), 153–54; CT, July 27, 1877, August 5, 1877, November 10, 1878, December 31, 1881.

16. CT, June 18, 1887; *Chicago Inter Ocean*, June 19, 1887; Patrice Dabrowski, *Commemorations and the Shaping of Modern Poland* (Bloomington, 2004), 32–35, 48; Anna D. Jaroszyńska-Kirchmann, "'Memories of Greatness': American Polonia and the Rituals of National Commemorations before World War I," *PAS* 74, no. 1 (April 2017), 35.

17. *Chicago Inter Ocean*, January 9, 1890, March 9, 1890.

18. Thomas and Znaniecki, *The Polish Peasant*, 3:65.

19. CT, March 16, 1895, June 13 and 17, 1895; *Chicago Inter Ocean*, November 11, 1895. See also "History of All Saints Cathedral, PNCC, Chicago, Illinois," *(Was a) Deacon's Blog*, accessed on September 13, 2015, http://konicki.com/blog2/pncc-documents/history-of-all-saints-cathedral-pncc-chicago-illinois/.

20. Parot, *Polish Catholics in Chicago*, chap. 5, contains a more thorough discussion of the issues surrounding the creation of All Saints and the growth of the independent movement.

21. Daniel S. Buczek, "Polish Americans and the Catholic Church," *Polish Studies* 21, no. 3 (1976): 39–61, 53–54; Parot, *Polish Catholics in Chicago*, 99–100, 155–58.

22. Parot, *Polish Catholics in Chicago*, 126–27.

23. Koenig, *A History of the Parishes of the Archdiocese of Chicago*, 1:643–44, 1:781–83; DzC, December 30, 1895, May 4, 1896, June 5, 1896.

24. Parot, *Polish Catholics in Chicago*, 134, 142–58. Parot goes into much more detail concerning these events than I can here.

25. CT, July 30, 1908; DzC, July 30, 1908.

26. Edward R. Kantowicz, *Corporation Sole: Cardinal Mundelein and Chicago Catholicism* (Notre Dame, 1983), 75–83.

27. My discussion of social space owes much to conversations with both Perry Duis and Kathleen Alaimo. For a more complete discussion of social

space in Chicago's Polonia, see Dominic A. Pacyga, "Progressive Era Reform, Public Space, and Chicago's Working-Class Polonia, 1865–1930, in *Ethnicity, Culture, City*, ed. Thomas Gladsky, Adam Walaszek, and Magorzata M. Wawrykiewicz (Warsaw, 1998), 221–37.

28. Natalie Kunka, "The Amateur Theater Among the Poles," in *Poles of Chicago, 1837–1937: A History of One Century of Polish Contribution to the City of Chicago*, ed. Leon Thaddeus Zglenicki (Chicago, 1937), 68; *DzZ*, March 16, 1908.

29. *Zgoda*, November 10, 1889, April 30, 1890, *CT*, January 2, 1893.

30. *CT*, July 13, 1896, November 22, 1896; *Zgoda*, November 26, 1896.

31. For a complete list of Chicago's Polish newspapers and their publishers, see Edward R. Kantowicz, *Polish American Politics in Chicago, 1880–1940* (Chicago, 1975), 36. For the importance of the ethnic press in creating a public sphere, particularly in Polonia, see Anna Jaroszyńska-Kirchmann, *The Polish Hearst: Amerika-Echo and the Public Role of the Immigrant Press* (Urbana, IL, 2015).

32. Craig Calhoun, "Introduction: Habermas and the Public Sphere," in *Habermas and the Public Sphere*, ed. Craig Calhoun (Cambridge, 1992), 1–7.

33. Donald E. Pienkos, "Dyniewiccz, Władysław" in Pula, ed., *Polish American Encyclopedia*, 87; S. M. Ancilla, FSSJ, "Catholic Book Publishing in U.S., 1871–1900," *PAS* 16, nos. 1–2 (January–June 1959): 1–11; Helen Chrzanowska, "Polish Book Publishing in Chicago," *PAS* 4, nos. 1–2 (January–June 1947): 37–39. See also Bernard Pacyniak, "An Historical Outline of the Polish Press in America," in *Poles in America: Bicentennial Essays*, ed. Frank Mocha (Stevens Point, WI, 1978), 509–30.

34. *CT*, May 29, 2000; Anna D. Jaroszyńska-Kirchmann, "Introduction," in *Letters from Readers in the Polish American Press, 1902–1969*, ed. Anna D. Jaroszyńska-Kirchmann (Lanham, MD, 2014). See Pula, ed., *Polish American Encyclopedia*, 87–90, for histories of various Chicago Polonia newspapers.

Chapter Three

1. Brian McCook, *The Border of Integration: Polish Migrants in Germany and the United States, 1870–1914* (Columbus, OH, 2011), 20–21; Victor Greene, *The Slavic Community on Strike: Immigrant Labor in Pennsylvania Anthracite* (South Bend, IN, 1968), 15–16. See also Andrzej Brożek, "Ruchy migracyjne z ziem polskich pod panowaniem pruskim w latach 1850–1918," in *Emigracja z ziem polskich w czasach nowożytnych I najnowszych (XVIII-XXw)*, ed. Andrzeja Pilcha (Warsaw, 1984), 141–95.

2. Ewa Morawska, "Labor Migrations of Poles in the Atlantic World Economy, 1880–1914," *Comparative Studies in Society and History* 31, no. 2 (April 1989): 237–72.

3. W. I. Thomas and Florian Znaniecki, *The Polish Peasant in Europe and America*, vol. 3, *Organization and Disorganization in America* (Boston, 1920), 46, 71.

4. Sister M. Inviolata, SSJ, "Noble Street in Chicago," *PAS* 11, nos. 1–2 (January–June, 1954), 1–3.

5. All information taken from *CT*, Mach 14, 1886. For the importance of Polish parochial schools, see Thomas and Znaniecki, *The Polish Peasant*, 3:50–51

6. *CT*, March 24, 1895.

7. Maria Anna Knothe, "Recent Arrivals: Polish Immigrant Women's Response to the City," in *Peasant Maids — City Women: From the European Countryside to Urban America*, ed. Christine Harzig (Ithaca, NY, 1997), 311; Pien Versteegh, "A League of Their Own: Strategic Networks of Polish Women as a Female Response to Male Dominated Networks," in *Irish and Polish Migration in Comparative Perspective*, ed. John Belcham and Klaus Tenfelde (Essen, Germany, 2003), 202–4; Thaddeus C. Radzilowski, "Family, Women, and Gender: The Polish Experience," in *Polish Americans and Their History: Community, Culture, and Politics*, ed. John J. Bukowczyk (Pittsburgh, 1996), 61–62, 70; Dorothee Schneider, "Polish Peasants into Americans: U.S. Citizenship and Americanization among Polish Immigrants in the Inter-War Era," *Polish Sociological Review*, no. 158, (2007), 164.

8. Radzilowski "Family, Women, and Gender," 61, 75; James S. Pula, "Polish American Women," in James S. Pula ed. *Polish American Encyclopedia* (North Carolina and London, 2011), 548. For an explanation of the important connection between family members and neighbors or *rodacy*, see Thomas and Znaniecki, *The Polish Peasant*, 3:32.

9. *CT*, July 26, 1903; Casimir J. B. Wronski, "Early Days of Sport among Polish Americans of Chicagoland," in *Poles of Chicago, 1837–1937: A History of One Century of Polish Contribution to the City of Chicago*, ed. Leon Thaddeus Zglenicki (Chicago, 1937), 145.

10. Robert Hunter, *Report by the Investigating Committee of the City Homes Association* (Chicago, 1901), 14, 28–31, 41, 54–64, 90, 92, 104, 109, 114, 118, 126, 133, 141, 187, 188, 190, 193, 198, 201.

11. Sophonisba P. Breckinridge and Edith Abbott, "Chicago Housing Conditions," pt. 4, "The West Side Revisited," *American Journal of Sociology* 17, no. 1 (July 1911): 7, 12, 18, 23, 31.

12. Sophonisba P. Breckinridge and Edith Abbott, "Housing Conditions in Chicago," pt. 3, "Back of the Yards," *American Journal of Sociology* 16, no. 4 (January 1911): 433–68; Sophonisba P. Breckinridge and Edith Abbott, "Chicago Housing Conditions," pt. 5, "South Chicago at the Gates of the Steel Mills," *American Journal of Sociology* 17, no. 2 (September 1911): 145–76.

13. Hunter, *Report by the Investigating Committee*, 181–82.

14. Breckinridge and Abbott, "Housing Conditions," pt. 5, 147–52, 158, 162–66, 169, 174.

15. Breckinridge and Abbott, "Housing Conditions," pt. 3, 434–50, 455.

16. Julius John Ozog, "A Study of Polish Home Ownership in Chicago" (MA diss., University of Chicago, 1942), 51–57.

17. Thomas and Znaniecki, *The Polish Peasant*, 3:32.

18. *CT*, May 6, 1894.

19. *CT*, August 4, 1888, April 9, 1911.

20. Breckinridge and Abbott, "Housing Conditions IV," 8. For a look at Polish American relationships with various ethnic groups in Chicago, see Dominic A. Pacyga, "To Live amongst Others: Poles and Their Neighbors in Industrial Chicago, 1865–1930," *Journal of American Ethnic History* 16, no. 1 (Fall 1996): 55–73. For a discussion on Czech Polish relationships, see Dominic A. Pacyga, "Czechs and Poles in Chicago: Pan-Slavism and the Origins of the Cermak Democratic Machine, 1860–1931." *Studya Migracyjne—Przegląd Polonynich* (Krakow) 4 (2015): 55–68.

21. *CT*, April 19, 1865, January 24, 1873, September 24, 1871, February 28, 1876; *Chicago Inter Ocean*, June 17, 1878.

22. *CT*, May 25, 1883; *Svornost*, March 27, 1883, *Chicago Foreign Language Press Survey*, https://flps.newberry.org/.

23. *CT*, August 26, 1893, September 14, 1893.

24. For the growth of socialism among the Czechs, see Thomas Čapek, *The Čechs (Bohemians) in America; A Study of Their National, Cultural, Political, Social, Economic, and Religious Life* (Boston, 1920), chap. 12; *CT*, December 21, 1896.

25. *Svornost*, March 8, 1884, July 24, 1890, *Chicago Foreign Language Press Survey*; Jeffrey Mirel, *Patriotic Pluralism: Americanization, Education, and European Immigrants* (Cambridge, 2010), 109.

26. *CT*, May 5, 1902, August 2, 1908. For the earlier conflict at St. Boniface, see Rev. Msgr. Harry C. Koenig, STD, ed. *A History of the Parishes of the Archdiocese of Chicago*, 2 vols. (Chicago, 1980), 1:136–37.

27. Immaculate Conception BVM Parish, *Diamond Jubilee: Immaculate Conception B.V.M. Parish, 1882–1957* (Chicago, 1957), 26; *Dziennik Związkowy*, November 26, 1910, December 10, 1910, February 1, 1908; *DzC*, September 22, 1892, March 30, 1895.

28. Victor Greene, *For God and Country: The Rise of Polish and Lithuanian National Consciousness in America, 1860–1910* (Madison, WI, 1975), 144; Caroline Hill, ed., *Mary McDowell and Municipal Housekeeping: A Symposium* (Chicago, 1938), 27;

29. *Lietuva*, May 30, 1896, June 5, 1903, September 11, 1908, April 23,

1909, October 19, 1917, *Chicago Foreign Language Press Survey*; *Naujienos* June 3,1914, *Chicago Foreign Language Press Survey*.

30. *Dziennik Związkowy*, May 27, 1918.

31. *CT*, Mach 14, 1886, March 24, 1895; Helena Znaniecka Lopata, *Polish Americans* (New Brunswick, NJ, 1994), 134–37.

32. Ewa Morawska, "Polish-Jewish Relations in America, 1880–1940: Old Elements, New Configurations," in *Polish Jewish Relations in North America*, ed. Mieczysław B. Biskupski and Antony Polonsky, Polin: Studies in Polish Jewry, vol. 19 (Oxford, 2007), 73–77.

33. *Zgoda*, October 31, 1888; *Daily Calumet* (Chicago), February 22, 1896; *Dziennik Ludowy* (hereafter *DzL*), May 7, 1907.

34. *DzC*, August 10, 1896.

35. *Dziennik Związkowy*, August 30, 1911

36. Andrzej Kapiszewski, "The Polish-Jewish Conflicts in the United States at the Beginning of World War I," *PAS* 48, no. 1 (Spring 1991): 63–78.

37. On Irish and Polish street gangs and race relations, see Dominic A. Pacyga, "Chicago's 1919 Race Riot: Ethnicity, Class, and Urban Violence," in *The Making of Urban America*, ed. Raymond Mohl, 2nd ed. (Wilmington, DE, 1997), 187–207. See also Andrew Diamond, *Mean Streets: Chicago Youths and the Everyday Struggle for Empowerment in the Multiracial City, 1908–1969* (Oakland, CA, 2009).

Chapter Four

1. Translated by Dorothea Prall Radin, in *Poems by Adam Mickiewicz*, ed. George Rapall Noyes (New York, 1944), 414–15.

2. *DzC*, January 26 and 30, 1896; *Zgoda*, June 2, 1910, December 5, 1912, February 6 and 13, 1913.

3. Norman Davies, *God's Playground: A History of Poland*, vol. 2, *1795 to the Present* (New York, 1982), chaps. 17 and 18; M. B. Biskupski, *The United States and the Rebirth of Poland, 1914–1918* (Dordrecht, Netherlands, 2012), 1–6, 19. Biskupski's work is the best look at events both in Europe and the United States during this period.

4. *DzZ*, August 4, 1914; *CT*, August 4, 1914.

5. *DzZ*, August 10, 1914.

6. *DzZ*, August 1 and 14, 1914.

7. *DzZ*, August 20, 1914.

8. Biskupski, *The United States and the Rebirth of Poland*, 44–45; *CT*, August 16 and 17, 1914; *DzZ*, September 14, 1914, October 5, 1914.

9. Stanislaus Blejwas, "American Polonia and the School Strike in Września," *PAS* 59, no. 1(Spring 2002): 9–59. Also see John Kulczycki, *School*

Strikes in Prussian Poland, 1901–1907: The Struggle over Bilingual Education (Boulder, CO, 1981).

10. *DzZ*, October 23, 1914; Biskupski, *The United States and the Rebirth of Poland*, 223–27.

11. *DzZ*, November 18, 1914

12. *DzZ*, January 8, 1915.

13. *DzZ*, January 12 and 21, 1915, Donald E. Pienkos, *PNA: A Centennial History of the Polish National Alliance of the United States of North America* (Boulder, CO, 1984), 107–8.

14. Biskupski, *The United States and the Rebirth of Poland*, 54–56, 58–63.

15. *DzZ*, March 13, 1915.

16. *DzZ*, March 15, 1915; *Naród Polski*, May 19, 1915; Pienkos, *PNA*, 108.

17. *CT*, May 22 and 29, 1915; Biskupski, *The United States and the Rebirth of Poland*, 133, 157; see also M. B. Biskupski, "Paderewski as Leader of American Polonia, 1914–1918," *PAS*, 43, no. 1 (Spring 1986): 37–56.

18. Biskupski, *The United States and the Rebirth of Poland*, chap. 5.

19. *DzZ*, February 26, 1916; *Naród Polski*, March 22, 1918, June 7, 1916; Biskupski, *The United States and the Rebirth of Poland*, 139; Pienkos, *PNA*, 108.

20. *Naród Polski*, January 5, 1916, July 19, 1916; *DzZ*, December 4 and 9, 1916.

21. For a complete understanding of the various political moves and intrigues both in the United States and in Europe regarding the various Polish political factions, see Biskupski, *The United States and the Rebirth of Poland*, chap. 6.

22. Pienkos, *PNA*, 111; *DzZ*, April 7, 1917.

23. *DzZ*, June 4, 1917.

24. http://archivescanada.accesstomemory.org/turczynowicz-laura-de -1878-1953 accessed on January 19, 2016; *DzZ*, July 10, 1917.

25. *DzZ*, August 6, 1917.

26. *DzZ*, October 26, 1917.

27. *DzZ*, October 10 and 16, 1917; Pienkos, *PNA*, 112–13; Paul S. Valasek, *Haller's Polish Army in France* (Chicago, 2006), 156.

28. *DzZ*, September 10, 1917; *Chicago Tribune*, September 10, 1917. For the complex issues revolving around recruitment for the Polish Army, see Joseph T. Hapak, "Selective Service and Polish Army Recruitment during World War I," *Journal of American Ethnic History* 10, no. 4 (Summer 1991): 38–60.

29. Valasek, *Haller's Polish Army in France*, 37; *Dziennik Związkowy*, October 15, 1917; *Naród Polski*, October 24, 1917; *CT*, October 15, 1917.

30. *DzZ*, March 11, 13, 15, 16, 18, and 28, 1918; *CT*, January 8, 1916, April 5, 1918. For the Polish White cross, see Magdalena Grassman and

Eva Niklinska, "The Polish White Cross—Birthed on American Soil to Support Polish Soldiers Abroad," *Hektoen International: A Journal of Medical Humanities* (Winter 2018), http://hekint.org/2018/02/20/polish-white-cross -birthed-american-soil-support-polish-soldiers-abroad/.

31. *DzZ*, April 10, 11, 23, 24, and 25, 1917, May 2 and 28, 1917, September 13, 1918; *Naród Polski*, April 25, 1917; *Polonia*, June 20, 1918; Hapak, "Selective Service and Polish Army Recruitment," 55, Miecislaus Haiman, "The Poles in Chicago," *Poles of Chicago, 1837–1937: A History of One Century of Polish Contribution to the City of Chicago*, ed. Leon Thaddeus Zglenicki (Chicago, 1937), 7.

32. Pienkos, *PNA*, 111–12; *DzZ*, June 14, 1917, April 11 and 16, 1918, September 27, 1918; *Polonia*, January 3 and 31, 1918.

33. Program of the Loyalty March July 4, 1918, IHRC2032, box 1, folder 1, Ludwik Panek Papers, Immigration History Research Center Archives, University of Minnesota Libraries, Minneapolis (hereafter referred to as IHRC).

34. *Denni Hlasatel*, November 11, 1914, March 10, 1915, February 2, 1921 (Chicago Foreign Language Press Survey). Chicago's Czech community donated some $100,000 ($1,569,649 in 2015) for war relief and aid to the Czechoslovak independence movement. Čapek, *The Čechs (Bohemians) in America*, 269.

35. This discussion of World War One is largely based on the essay by Melvin G. Holli, "The Great War Sinks German *Kultur*," in *Ethnic Chicago*, ed. Melvin G. Holli and Peter d'A Jones (Grand Rapids, MI, 1984), 460. For the argument over the Bismarck name and bust and the textbooks, see *Denni Hlasatel*, April 20, 1917, July 25, 1917, August 6, 1917, *Chicago Foreign Language Press Survey*; *DzZ*, March 28,1918. For the attempt to change the Kosciuszko School name, see *CT*, July 19, 1917, April 26, 1918. For the Czech and Polish reaction as well as the Czarnecki resolution, see Mirel, *Patriotic Pluralism*, 109–10.

36. *DzZ*, March 15, 1918; *Denni Hlasatel*, March 4, 1918 (Chicago Foreign Language Press Survey); *CT*, March 4, 1918.

37. Robert Szymczak, "An Act of Devotion: The Polish Grey Samaritans and the American Relief Effort in Poland, 1919–1921," *PAS* 43, no. 1 (Spring, 1986): 13–36.

Chapter Five

1. *CT*, August 10, 1934.

2. For a discussion of these industries after the war, see Dominic A. Pacyga, *Polish Immigrants and Industrial Chicago: Workers on the South Side, 1880–1922* (Chicago, 2003), see chap. 6; *CT*, January 9, 1919.

3. Michał Kasprzak, "Buying a New Identity: Polish-Americans and Mass Consumerism in the Interwar Years," *Polish Review* 56, no. 4 (2011): 362.

4. Gary Krist, *City of Scoundrels: The 12 Days of Disaster That Gave Birth to Modern Chicago* (New York, 2012), 1–19.

5. For a discussion of the race riot and Polonia's role in it, see Dominic A. Pacyga, "Chicago's 1919 Race Riot: Ethnicity, Class, and Urban Violence," in *The Making of Urban America*, ed. Raymond Mohl, 2nd ed. (Wilmington, DE, 1997), 187–207.

6. For a discussion of both the 1919 steel strike and the packinghouse strike of 1921–22, see Dominic A. Pacyga, *Polish Immigrants and Industrial Chicago*, chap. 6.

7. Roger Daniels, *Guarding the Golden Door: American immigration Policy and Immigrants since 1882* (New York, 2005), chaps. 1 and 2.

8. *CT*, August 15, 1909; Tristan Almazon and Sarah Coleman, "George Amos Dorsey: A Curator and His Comrades," in *Fieldiania: Anthropology*, ed. Stephen E. Nash and Gary M. Feineman, Publication 1525, September 30, 2003, 87.

9. *CT*, November 14, 1909, March 30, 1910, October 27, 1910,

10. *CT*, November 5, 6, 9, and 14, 1910, December 1 and 10, 1910; George A. Dorsey, "Race and Civilization," in *Wither Mankind: A Panorama of Modern Civilization*, ed. Charles A. Beard (New York, 1928), 229–63. Dorsey went on to a distinguished publishing career, including such popular works as *Why We Behave Like Humans* (New York, 1925), *The Nature of Man* (London, 1927), *Hows and Whys of Human Behavior* (New York, 1929), and *Man's Own Show: Civilization* (New York, 1931).

11. Madison Grant, *The Passing of the Great Race* (New York, 1916); Katherine Benton-Cohen, *Inventing the Immigration Problem: The Dillingham Commission and Its Legacy* (Cambridge, MA, 2018).

12. Alex Gottfried, *Boss Cermak of Chicago: A Study of Political Leadership* (Seattle, 1962), 48–61, 169–204.

13. James S. Pula, "American Immigration and the Dillingham Commission," *PAS* 57, no. 1 (Spring 1980): 5–31; James S. Pula, "The Progressives, the Immigrant, and the Workplace," *PAS* 52, no. 2 (Autumn 1995): 57–69; Dale T. Knobel, *America for Americans: The Nativist Movement in the United States* (New York, 1996), 258–61; Roger Daniels, *Guarding the Golden Door: American Immigration Policy and Immigrants since 1882* (New York, 2004), 47–52.

14. William I. Thomas and Florian Znaniecki, *The Polish Peasant in Europe and America*, 5 vols. (Boston 1919–20).

15. Frederic Thrasher, *The Gang: A Study of 1,313 gangs in Chicago* (Chicago, 1927); Clifford Shaw, *The Jack-Roller* (Chicago, 1930).

16. *CT*, March 6, 7, 8, and 16, 1928, October 27, 1928.

17. *DzC*, May 21, 1895; *CT*, May 3, 1901, September 9, 1908,

18. *CT*, April 27, 1902.

19. *DzL*, June 30, 1908.

20. *CT*, October 21 and 24, 1911. As is often the case with Polish names, various spellings appeared in the newspapers.

21. *DzZ*, December 2, 21, and 22, 1911; *CT*, December 29, 1911, February 14 and 19, 1911.

22. Mabel Carter Rhoades, "A Case Study of Delinquent Boys in the Juvenile Court of Chicago," *American Journal of Sociology* 13, no. 1 (July 1907): 56–78.

23. Case Records 128, 137, 140, 141, 149, 150, 151, 153, and 155, box 2, folder 1, ser. 41/3 Northwestern University Settlement, the Northwestern University Settlement Association Delinquent Boy Case Files, 1929–31, 1938–38, Special Collections/University Archives, Northwestern University. Henceforth referred to as Northwestern University Settlement Collection.

24. Case Record 158, box 2, folder 2, ser. 41/3; Case Record 24, box 1, folder 2, Series 41/3, Northwestern University Settlement Collection.

25. The history of the Polish Welfare Association No. 1 of St. Stanislaus Kostka Parish is well covered in the *DzC*, February 8, 16, and 25, 1892, March 7, 12, and 25, 1892, April 4, 1892, May 4, 1892, July 6, 9, 11, 12, and 22, 1892, September 17, 1892.

26. *Naród Polski*, April 19, 1916.

27. *DzC*, January 10, 1922; *Dziennik Zjednoczenia*, May 2, 1922; *CT*, January 17, 1927; www.polish.org/en/home/our-history visited on May 27, 2016. For problems with the courts, see Evelina Belden, "The Boys' Court of Chicago: A Record of Six Months Work," *American Journal of Sociology* 20, no. 6 (May 1915): 731–44.

28. For a complete discussion of what would become the Russell Square Community and the Chicago Area Project, see Dominic A. Pacyga, "The Russell Square Community Committee: An Ethnic Response to Urban Problems," *Journal of Urban History* 15 (February 1989): 159–84. This section is based on this article.

29. For a history of the Back of the Yards Neighborhood Council, see Robert A. Slayton, *Back of the Yards: The Making of a Local Democracy* (Chicago, 1986); and Thomas J. Jablonsky, *Pride in the Jungle: Community and Everyday Life in Back of the Yards Chicago* (Baltimore, 1992).

30. Leon C. Nyka, "The Polish Day Association—a Force of Good in the Community," in *Poles in America: Their Contribution to a Century of Progress*, ed. Anthony C. Tomczak (Chicago, 1933), 10–11.

31. "The Polish Week of Hospitality: At a Century of Progress International Exposition," in *Poles in America*, ed. Tomczak, 13–15; *CT*, July 9, 13, and 22, 1933.

32. *CT*, August 19 and 26, 1934.

33. *CT*, August 10, 1934, December 2 and 11, 1934; Andrew A. Urbanik

and Joseph O. Baylen, "The Development of Polish Cultural-Educational Policy towards American Polonia, 1918–1935," *PAS* 41, no. 1 (Spring 1984): 5–24.

34. "To the Managing Committee of the Democratic Party of Cook County, Illinois" (December 11, 1931); "Resolution" 1930; Executive Committee of Polish American A. J. Cermak for Mayor Organization; "Executive Committee Democratic Party of Cook County," all in box 1, Polish American Democratic Organization Papers, Chicago History Museum (hereafter referred to as PADO Papers); *CT*, March 23 and 30, 1931; *DzC*, January 12, 1922, January 3, 1928. For Szymczak's biography, see James S, Pula, "Miecislaus Stephen Szymczak," in *Polish American Encyclopedia*, ed. James S. Pula (Jefferson, NC, 2011), 515; and "M. S. Szymczak," Federal Reserve History, accessed March 22, 2017, http://www.federalreservehistory.org/People/DetailView/72.

35. *Dziennik Zjednoczenia*, May 8, 1922, September 9, 1922, October 21, 1922, January 22, 1927, February 1 and 21, 1927, June 3, 1927; *CT*, March 30, 1927, April 1, 1927, October 13, 1928.

36. *CT*, April 28, 1931. For examples of these pleas for help, see various letters in box 1, folder 2, PADO Papers, and especially letter from Agnieszka Kasilewicz to Szymczak, August 9, 1932 in box 1, folder 3, PADO Papers.

37. Sigmund Odalski to M. S. Szymczak, December 13, 1932, M. S. Szymczak to Albert J. Horan, December 7, 1932, M. S. Szymczak to Joseph C. Niec, December 12, 1932—all in box 1, folder 4, PADO Papers.

38. See letters from W. F. Panek and Mathew Wyrzykowski, Polish Singers Alliance, to Mayor Anton J. Cermak, December 13, 1932; Adam F. Soska, Paul Hadamik, and J. S. Kozlowski, Polish Alma Mater, to James D. Farley, Chairman of the Democratic Party, in box 1, folder 4, PADO Papers. For endorsements for mayor, see Klub Parafija Dębica to M. S. Szymczak, Letter of Endorsement of M. S. Szymczak by J. J. Olejniczak, President of the PRCUA, J. Romaszkiewicz, President of the PNA et al., March 11, 1933; and various other letters of endorsement, all in box 2, folder 3, February–March 1933, PADO Papers.

39. Edward R. Kantowicz, *Polish-American Politics in Chicago, 1888–1940* (Chicago, 1975), 193–95.

40. Letter from Frank V. Zintak, Managing Director, and W. F. Walkowiak, Secretary, to the PADO membership, September 21, 1934; Education Hour Script, October 7, 1934; Contributions for Flood Relief in Poland, September 4, 1934—all in box 3, folder, January–November 1934, PADO Papers.

41. Miles Goldberg, Committee on Unjust Discrimination, to M. S. Szymczak, December 22, 1932, in box 1, folder 4, PADO Papers.

Chapter Six

1. *CT*, April 21, 1941.

2. *DzC*, July 1, 1939, August 25, 1939. For an example of a donors list, see *Zgoda*, June 22, 1939, August 3, 1939.

3. For a short history of the RPA, see Florian Piskarski, "Report of the Delegate of the American Polish War Relief (American Relief for Poland) on the Activities of the Delegation from 1941 to 1948" in box 1, folder 2, 2–4, Francis B. Świetlik Papers, Polish National Alliance Collection, Immigration History Research Center, University of Minnesota, Minneapolis.

4. *CT*, August 26, 27, and 30, 1939; *Zgoda*, August 3, 1939; *DzC*, August 28 and 30, 1939.

5. *DzC*, September 1, 1939, *Chicago Daily News*, September 2 and 4, 1939.

6. *CT*, September 4, 5, and 7, 1939; *DzC*, September 2, 4, 5, 6, and 8, 1939; *Zgoda*, August 17, 1939, September 7, 21, and 28, 1939, October 5, 12, and 19, 1939; Bradley E. Fels, "'Whatever Your Heart Dictates and Your Pocket Permits': Polish-American Aid to Polish Refugees during World War II," *Journal of American Ethnic History* 22, no. 2(Winter 2003), 8.

7. *CT*, September 27, 1939, October 5 and 10, 1939.

8. *Zgoda*, September 21 and 28, 1939, October 5, 1939.

9. *CT*, October 2, 1939.

10. *Zgoda*, October 12, 1939; *CT*, October 8 and 9, 1939.

11. *CT*, October 17 and 22, 1939, January 11, 14, 18, 22, 1940; Fels, "Whatever Your Heart Dictates and Your Pocket Permits," 12.

12. *CT*, February 6, 1940, February 10, 1940; *Zgoda*, February 15, 1940; *DzC*, February 5, 1940, February 10, 1940, February 11, 1939; Donald Pienkos, *For Your Freedom through Ours: Polish American Efforts on Poland's Behalf, 1863–1991* (New York, 1991), 84.

13. *CT*, February 21 and 25, 1940, March 6, 11, 17, and 31, 1940; *DzC*, May 5 and 6, 1940; *Zgoda*, May 16, 1940.

14. *Zgoda*, June 9, 1940.

15. *Zgoda*, June 28, 1940, August 11, 1940, October 13, 1940.

16. *CT*, January 26, 1941, February 13 and 23, 1941, March 27, 1941.

17. *CT*, April 11, 16, 17, and 19, 1941, July 19, 1941, September 5, 1941; *Chicago Daily News*, April 19, 1941; *DzC*, April 19 and 21, 1941; Pienkos, *For Your Freedom through Ours*, 77, 84.

18. *CT*, June 30, 1941, July 3, 1941, November 3 and 4, 1941; *Zgoda*, July 6, 1941.

19. In particular, see Joseph A. Wytrwal, *Behold! The Polish Americans* (Detroit, 1977), 355.

20. Rob Paral, *The Polish Community in Metro Chicago: A Community Profile of Strengths and Needs* (Chicago, 2004), 3.

21. *Zgoda*, October 20, 1940.

22. *DzC*, December 8, 1941; *Zgoda*, December 21, 1941.

23. *Zgoda*, December 28, 1941

24. *CT*, February 22, 1942, April 19, 1942.

25. *CT*, April 27, 1942; Pienkos, *For Your Freedom through Ours*, 73–103.

26. *CT*, May 3 and 4, 1942.

27. *CT*, May 31, 1942, June 28, 1942.

28. *CT*, July 18 and 19, 1942, November 17, 1942, December 6, 1942.

29. *CT*, December 17, 18, and 23, 1942; Fels, "Whatever Your Heart Dictates and Your Pocket Permits," 14.

30. *CT*, February 27, 1943, March 13, 1943, April 23, 27, and 30, 1943, July 11, 1943. The massacre of thousands of Polish officers and intelligentsia in the Katyn Forest created a controversy that roiled the alliance. The Soviets claimed that the Germans had committed the atrocity. The Germans claimed that the Russians had killed the Poles. It was later proven that murders were carried out by Soviet authorities.

31. *CT*, January 3, 9, and 26, 1944. April 16 and 27, 1944, May 8, 1944, October 15, 1944.

32. *CT*, January 11, 1944.

33. *CT*, February 6, 7, 8, and 29, 1944,

34. Norman Davies, *Rising '44: The Battle for Warsaw* (London, 2004), is perhaps the best account of the fighting during the Warsaw Uprising against the German occupiers.

35. "Lista Reprezentztów na Konfereancja Zwołana do Domu Zwiazku Polek w Ameryce—Dnia 4go Marca 1944," box 3, folder 15, 6; "Deklaracyja," box 3, folder 15, 2; "Aims and Objectives of the Polish American Congress," box 3, folder 17, 2—all in Polish American Congress (PAC) Papers, IHRC.

36. Joanna Wojdon, *White and Red Umbrella: The Polish American Congress in the Cold War Era, 1944–1988* (Reno, NV, 2015), 15–38. This is the best English-language study of the Polish American Congress.

37. *CT*, December 20, 1944; Anna D. Jaroszyńska-Kirchmann, *The Exile Mission: The Polish Political Diaspora and Polish Americans, 1939–1956* (Athens, OH, 2004), 49. *The Exile Mission* is by far the best study of the postwar Polish diaspora in the United States.

38. *CT*, January 2 and 8, 1945; Jaroszyńska-Kirchmann, *The Exile Mission*, 50.

39. *CT*, February 19, 1945, March 5, 1945; Jaroszyńska-Kirchmann, *The Exile Mission*, 50.

40. *CT*, February 10, 1945, March 15 and 30, 1945, April 30, 1945, September 8, 1945.

41. "Proposed Postwar Relief Work in Poland to be Carried Out by Polish War Relief" (1945), in Francis B. Świetlik Papers, box 1, folder 3, IHRC.

42. "Budget of American Relief for Poland, from American Overseas Aid," 1948, in Francis B. Świetlik Papers, box 1, folder 4, IHRC.

43. *CT*, May 4, 5, and 6, 1945; Wojdon, *White and Red Umbrella*, 81–82.

44. Jaroszyńska-Kirchmann, *The Exile Mission*, 60–61.

45. *CT*, February 3 and 23, 1946; Anna D. Jaroszyńska-Kirchmann, "The Mobilization of American Polonia for the Cause of the Displaced Persons," *PAS* 58, no. 1 (Spring 2001): 31–37.

46. *CT*, August 28, 1946, October 6, 12, and 20, 1946, December 2 and 9, 1946.

47. *CT*, January 8, 1947, February 2 and 3, 1947.

48. *CT*, May 4 and 5, 1947.

49. *CT*, February 8, 1947, June 5 and 14, 1947, November 17, 1947.

50. *CT*, February 2, 1947, April 26, 1947, December 12, 1947.

51. *CT*, March 23, 1947, September 24, 1947, November 5, 1947,

52. *CT*, January 2, 19, and 22, 1947, March 22 and 23, 1947, April 3, 1947; George H. Janczewski, "The Significance of the Polish Vote in the American National Election Campaign of 1948," *Polish Review* 13, no. 4 (Autumn 1968): 101–9.

53. Jaroszyńska-Kirchmann, *The Exile Mission*, 112–21.

Chapter Seven

1. *CT*, October 17, 1978.

2. Rob Paral, *The Polish Community in Metro Chicago: A Community Profile of Strengths and Needs* (Chicago, 2004), 3

3. Wojdon, *White and Red Umbrella*.

4. Paral, *The Polish Community in Metro Chicago*, 3.

5. *CT*, May 5 and 31, 1952, October 31, 1952, May 3 and 23, 1954, April 30, 1954.

6. *CT*, July 5, 1953, September 11 and 12, 1955.

7. *CT*, March 15, 1953, May 2, 3, and 5, 1953, July 12 and 30, 1953, September 14, 1953; Anna D. Jaroszyńska-Kirchmann, *The Exile Mission: The Polish Political Diaspora and Polish Americans, 1939-1956* (Athens, OH, 2004).

8. See Donna Solecka Urbikas, *My Sister's Mother: A Memoir of War, Exile, and Stalin's Siberia* (Madison, WI, 2016), for a look at the Polish DP experience.

9. Stanislaus Blejwas, "Old and New Polonias: Tensions within an Ethnic Community," *PAS* 38, no. 2 (Autumn 1981): 55–83; Mary Patrice Erdmans, *Opposite Poles: Immigrants and Ethnics in Polish Chicago, 1976-1990* (University Park, PA, 1998), 8–10; Eugene E. Obidinski and Helen Stankiewicz Zand, *Polish Folkways in America: Community and Family* (Lanham, MD, 1987), chap. 4.

10. Jaroszyńska-Kirchmann, *The Exile Mission*, 136–41; Blejwas, "Old and New Polonias," 71. For theater groups, see also in Wojciech Białasiewicz, "O twóczości i emigacyjnym Teatrze 'Ref-Rena'" in *W kręgu chicagowskiej polonii: Szkice o czasach minionych I ludziach których przeważnie już nie ma* (Chicago, 2001), 265–74; Białasiewicz, "Teatr w środowiskach polonijnych," in *W kręgu chicagowskiej polonii*, 221–28.

11. For a more complete look at the Palmer murder, see Dominic A. Pacyga, "Assimilation and Its Discontents: The Murder of Alvin Palmer and Chicago's Polonia in the 1950s," *Przegląd Polononych* 4 (2005): 129–40.

12. I grew up in Back of the Yards and was raised in Sacred Heart Parish. I knew many of these gang members. One gang, the Saints, are known today as the Latin Saints.

13. Joseph Parot has made the argument that Polish Americans suffered from terrible housing conditions early in their history and that they feared housing competition from African Americans. See his "Ethnic versus Black Metropolis: The Origins of Polish-Black Housing Tensions in Chicago," *PAS* 29, nos. 1–2 (Spring–Autumn 1972), 5–33. For job competition, see Thaddeus Radzialowski, "The Competition for Jobs and Racial Stereotypes: Poles and Blacks in Chicago," *PAS* 33, no. 2 (Autumn 1976): 5–18. For the growth of the Hispanic population in Polish neighborhoods, see Dominic A. Pacyga, "Polish America in Transition: Social Change and the Chicago Polonia, 1945–1980," *PAS* 44, no. 1 (Spring 1987): 38.

14. Ed Marciniak, *Reviving an Inner City Community* (Chicago, 1977), 17–19.

15. Pacyga, "Polish America in Transition," 37–39, 42–43.

16. *CT*, April 17, 18, and 24, 1966, May 1, 1966.

17. *CT*, August 29, 1966, September 8, 1966; and the souvenir booklet *Poland's Millennium of Christianity: Chicagoland Observance, Soldier Field, August 28, 1966* (Chicago, 1966).

18. *Chicago Sun-Times* (hereafter *CST*), June 28, 1968; *New York Times*, May 26, 1981; Chicago Department of Development and Planning, *Chicago's Polish Population* (Chicago, 1976), 3–6, 9, 14–17, 25–28; *Northwestern University Settlement Annual Program Report, 1983–84* (Chicago, 1984).

19. *CST*, September 2, 1975; Dominic A. Pacyga, "Polish Americans and the Chicago Medical Schools," paper presented to the Polish American Congress Charitable Foundation, September 1976, 2, 18–19, and "Polish Americans and the Chicago Area Dental and Law Schools," paper presented to the Polish American Congress Charitable Foundation, January 1977.

20. Marciniak, *Reviving an Inner City Community*, 49–50; *CT*, May 5, 1974. For the importance of the parade as a symbol of unity and of political power, see Białasiewicz, "W kalejdoskopie polonijnych parad," in *W kręgu chicagowskiej polonii*, 55–62.

21. *CST*, February 12, 1982; Dominic A. Pacyga, "Action—Polish American Congress Report," paper presented to Polish American Charitable Foundation, September 1973. For a more complete look at these demographic trends, see Pacyga, "Polish America in Transition."

22. Michael Novak, *The Rise of the Unmeltable Ethnics: The New Political Force of the Seventies* (New York, 1972).

23. Arthur Mann, *The One and the Many* (Chicago, 1979), 20, 37; Richard Polenberg, *One Nation Divisible: Class, Race, and Ethnicity in the United States since 1938* (New York, 1984), 246; *Chicago Reader*, October 22, 1976.

24. *CT*, October 10, 1971, April 30, 1972; News Release, Polish American Congress, August 12, 1972, in Roznanski Papers, Polish American Congress Collection, IHRC144, box 61, folder 9, IHRC.

25. Marciniak, *Reviving an Inner City Community*, 34–47; *CT*, February 15, 1976.

26. Letter to Members and Donors of the Copernicus Foundation from Mitchell P. Kobelinski, president, January 8, 1972, in Roznanski Papers, Polish American Congress Collection, IHRC144, box 14, folder 2; *CST*, August 14 and 27, 1982, September 2, 1973; *CT*, March 19, 1978.

27. *Daily Calumet* (Chicago), June 30, 1982, August 7 and 19, 1982.

28. Marciniak, *Reviving an Inner City Community*, 55. The Bungalow Belt consisted of some eighty thousand Chicago brick bungalows located on the edge of Chicago and built for the most part between 1915 and 1930. Another twenty thousand were constructed in the first ring of suburbs during the same time period. See Joseph C. Bigott, *From Cottage to Bungalow: Houses and the Working Class in Metropolitan Chicago, 1869–1929* (Chicago, 2001). For a memoir concerning the second and third generation of Polish Americans on Chicago's South Side, see Douglas Bukowski, *Pictures of Home: A Memoir of Family and City* (Chicago, 2004).

29. *CT*, August 21, 1976.

30. *CT*, October 17, 1978.

31. *CT*, October 22, 1978.

32. *CT*, October 1, 1978.

Chapter Eight

1. *CT*, November 19, 1989.

2. *CST*, May 2, 2006.

3. There are many books on the rise of the Solidarity Trade Union. See, esp., Andrzej Paczkowski and Malcolm Byrne, *From Solidarity to Martial Law: The Polish Crisis of 1980–1981: A Documentary History* (Budapest, 2008); Timothy Garton Ash, *The Polish Revolution: Solidarity* (Cambridge, MA, 2002); Maryjane Osa, *Solidarity and Contention: Networks of Polish Opposition*

(Minneapolis, 2003); William Purdue, *Paradox of Change: The Rise and Fall of Solidarity* (New York, 1995): Robert Eringer, *Strike for Freedom! The Story of Lech Walesa and Polish Solidarity* (New York, 1982).

4. *CT*, October 22, 1981, January 2, 1983, October 6, 1983.

5. *CT*, November 19, 1989.

6. *CT*, November 20, 1989; For a more complete discussion of Wałęsa's visit and the campaign to raise funds for the Polish economy, see Helena Znaniecka Lopata, *Polish Americans* (New Brunswick, NJ, 1994), chap. 8.

7. *CT*, March 17, 20, 24, and 25, 1991.

8. Mary Patrice Erdmans, *Opposite Poles: Immigrants and Ethnics in Polish Chicago, 1976–1990* (University Park, PA, 1998), 4–9, 53, 63–65, 73–79.

9. For a comprehensive look at the Solidarity migration and its aftermath, see Dariusz Stola, *Kraj Bez Wyjścia? Migracjez Polski, 1949–1989* (Warsaw, 2010), chap. 12; Erdmans, *Opposite Poles*, chap. 2; Lopata, *Polish Americans*, 166–170. An unnamed Polish worker in Chicago told his experience as a "vacationer" to me, summer 2016.

10. Joanna Wojdon, *White and Red Umbrella: The Polish American Congress in the Cold War Era, 1944–1988* (Reno, NV, 2015), 246, 268–74; Patryk Pleskot, "The Polish Intelligence Service and the Polish Diaspora after the Imposition of Martial Law in Poland," in *Transatlantic Identities: East Central Europe in Exile*, ed. Anna Mazurkiewicz, vol. 2 (Newcastle upon Tyne, UK, 2913), 311–26.

11. Erdmans, *Opposite Poles*, chap. 3.

12. James L. Merriner, *Mr. Chairman: Power in Dan Rostenkowski's America* (Carbondale, IL, 1999), 14–18, 229.

13. *CT*, July 29, 1996, August 16, 1998; *CST*, August 12, 2010.

14. *CT*, January 31, 2002; *CST*, January 16, 2002, October 22, 2001; *Chicago Magazine*, October 15, 2010.

15. *CT*, December 21, 2001, March 12, 2002.

16. *CST*, February 15, 2002.

17. *CST*, February 27, 2002.

18. "NJDC Denounces Anti-Semitic Comments Made against Rahm Emanuel," March 7, 2002, press release, accessed May 16, 2013, http://www.njdc.org/media/entry/njdc_denounces_anti_semitic_comments_made_against_rahm_emanuel#; *CST*, March 5, 2002; *CT*, March 6, 2002.

19. Open Letter "Subject: Polish American Leadership Protest," February 17, 2000. Stanislaus A. Blejwas, the Endowed Chair of Polish and Polish American Studies at Central Connecticut State University, New Britain, Connecticut collected signatures from Polonia leaders around the country to condemn the Jankowski invitation. I was a signee of this document. See also *CST*, May 16, 1996.

20. *CT*, March 6 and 10, 2002.

21. *CST*, February 25, 2002

22. *CT*, December 12, 2001; Rob Paral, *The Polish Community in Metro Chicago: A Community Profile of Strengths and Needs*, A Census 2000 Report (Chicago, 2004), 1–3.

23. *CST*, January 23, 2002, March 16, 2002, February 28, 2002, March 3, 2002; *CT*, January 23, 2002.

24. *CST*, March 20, 2002, March 21, 2002, May 1, 2002.

25. James J. Laski, *My Fall from Grace: City Hall to Prison Walls* (Bloomington, IN, 2008); David K. Fremon, *Chicago Politics Ward by Ward* (Bloomington, IN, 1988), 231.

26. Donald E. Pienkos, "Polish Americans in Congressional Politics: Assets and Constraints," *Polish Review* 49, no. 2 (2003): 185–94.

27. *CST*, March 24, 2002; Molly Redden, "Identity Politics in Chicago Takes a Surprising Turn," *New Republic*, January 31, 2012, https://new republic.com/article/100123/chicago-polish-city-council-pogorzelski -poles.

28. *CT*, May 5, 2002, May 25, 2003, January 4, 2004; Mary Patrice Erdmans, "New Chicago Polonia: Urban and Suburban" in *The New Chicago: A Social and Cultural Analysis*, ed. John P. Koval, Larry Bennet, et al. (Philadelphia, 2006), 115–19.

29. Lopata, *Polish Americans*, 132–33.

30. *CT*, August 8, 2003, October 4, 2004, June 24, 2004, July 2, 2004, November 7, 2004, June 24, 2005; *CST*, August 21, 2002, February 5, 2003. For Polonia's argument with Nelson Algren, see Mary Wisniewski, *Algren: A Life* (Chicago, 2017), esp. chaps. 5 and 6.

31. *CT*, November 8, 2002, February 13, 2003, October 10, 2004, January 12, 2005; *CST*, March 10, 2004.

32. *CST*, April 9, 2005.

33. *CT*, August 23, 2006; *CST*, September 20, 2006; Charles Keil, Angelike Keil, and Dick Blau, *Polka Happiness* (Philadelphia, 1992), 46–60. Jeanette Kozak and her family lived in the 1950s in the same three-flat, single-story railroad tenement as my family had on South Wolcott Street in Back of the Yards. For the importance of Bob Lewandowski, see Wojciech Białasiewicz, "Pomiedzy mikrofonem a kamerą: rosmowa z Robertem Lewandowskim," in *W kręgu chicagowskiej polonii: Szkice o czasach minionych I ludziach których przeważnie już nie ma* (Chicago, 2001), 291–304.

34. *CST*, April 28, 2006, May 2, 2006.

35. *CST*, October 18, 1989, April 1, 2015. I was served jalapeño-stuffed pierogi at a Polish gathering at the Chopin Theatre on September 2, 2017.

36. Raj Chetty, David Grusky, Maximilian Hell, Nathaniel Hendren,

Robert Manduca, and Jimmy Narang, "The Fading American Dream: Trends in Absolute Income Mobility since 1940," *Science* (April 28, 2017); Carol Graham, *Happiness for All? Unequal Hopes and Lives in Pursuit of the American Dream* (Princeton, NJ, 2017); "The Origins of the Financial Crisis: Crash Course," *Economist*, September 7, 2013.

37. Ruchir Sharma, "The Next Economic Powerhouse? Poland," *New York Times*, July 5, 2017.

38. *CT*, January 13, 2013.

39. *CST*, January 18, 2010; Anna Jaroszyńska-Kirchmann, *The Exile Mission: The Polish Political Diaspora and Polish Americans, 1939–1956* (Athens, OH, 2004).

40. For continued migration to Chicago from the Polish Tatra mountain region, see Marek, Liszka, *Życie Kulturalne Polonii Orawskiej w Chicago* (Kraków, 2013).

INDEX

Page numbers in italic refer to illustrations.

Lightning Source UK Ltd.
Milton Keynes UK
UKHW011540071021
391776UK00006B/312